CONTEMPORARY WOMEN WRITERS IN ITALY

CONTEMPORARY WOMEN WRITERS IN ITALY

A Modern Renaissance

EDITED BY

Santo L. Aricò

The University of Massachusetts Press

AMHERST

Printed in the United States of America
LC 89-28436
ISBN 0-87023-710-1
Designed by Jack Harrison
Set in ITC Galliard by Keystone Typesetting, Inc.
Printed and bound by Thomson Shore, Inc.

Library of Congress Cataloging-in-Publication Data
Contemporary women writers in Italy : a modern renaissance /
edited by Santo L. Aricò.
    p.   cm.
  Includes bibliographical references.
  ISBN 0–87023–710–1 (alk. paper).
    1. Italian literature—Women authors—History and criticism.
  2. Italian literature—20th century—History and criticism.
  I. Aricò, Santo L., 1938–
  PQ4055.WSC66   1990
  850.9'9287'09045—dc20   89–28436
                                                 CIP

British Library Cataloguing in Publication data are available.

A Luisa, Marisa, Anthony
e a tutti i miei cari

Contents

Acknowledgments   ix

Introduction   3
SANTO L. ARICÒ

Elsa Morante: The Trauma of Possessive Love and Disillusionment   11
ROCCO CAPOZZI

A Lexicon for Both Sexes: Natalia Ginzburg and the Family Saga   27
CORINNA DEL GRECO LOBNER

History, Art, and Fiction in Anna Banti's *Artemisia*   45
DEBORAH HELLER

Memory and Time in Lalla Romano's Novels, *La penombra che abbiamo attraversato* and *Le parole tra noi leggere*   63
FLAVIA BRIZIO

Gina Lagorio and the Courage of Women   77
MARK F. PIETRALUNGA

Gianna Manzini's Poetics of Verbal Visualization   91
GIOVANNA MICELI-JEFFRIES

Autobiography, Art, and History in Fausta Cialente's Fiction   109
PAOLA MALPEZZI PRICE

Francesca Sanvitale's *Madre e figlia*: From Self-Reflection to Self-Invention   125
PAOLA BLELLOCH

Dacia Maraini's *Donna in guerra*: Victory or Defeat?   139
ANTHONY J. TAMBURRI

viii   Contents

Armanda Guiducci's Disposable Women   153
FIORA A. BASSANESE

Oriana Fallaci's Journalistic Novel: *Niente e così sia*   171
SANTO L. ARICÒ

Camilla Cederna: Portrayer of Italian Society   185
GIOVANNA BELLESIA

From Margins to Mainstream: Some Perspectives on Women and
Literature in Italy in the 1980s   197
CAROL M. LAZZARO-WEIS

Bibliography   219

Notes on Contributors   237

Acknowledgments

I am grateful for the opportunity to recognize those people whose interest and cooperation made this collection possible. I am indebted to Mark Pietralunga, Deborah Heller, Anna Nozzoli, and Enzo Falciani of the Libreria in Florence for their assistance in Italy; I am also obliged to the historian Lucia Chiavola Birnbaum and to the Italian critic Marco Forti for their courtesy and patience in responding to my inquiries. In University, I have always been able to count on the help and good will of the staff of the John Davis Williams Library. I thank also my colleagues at "Ole Miss"—Professors William Strickland, Jack Barbera, Jacqueline Weeks, Kolby Kullman, T. J. Ray, Carol Klein, Rebecca Morton, Michael De Landon, Melvin Arrington, Clifford Gallant, and Ben Fisher—for their support and valuable critiques of this project. Above all, I wish to acknowledge John Pilkington, Distinguished Professor Emeritus of English, whose love of the language and culture of Italy motivated his active and unqualified support of this book from its inception to its publication.

CONTEMPORARY WOMEN WRITERS IN ITALY

Introduction

SANTO L. ARICÒ

This volume seeks to illustrate the achievements of contemporary women writers in Italy—achievements that all too often have escaped public and critical notice. The essays deal with twelve women writers whose works range from fiction to biography to journalism. Some, such as Natalia Ginzburg, Elsa Morante, and the journalist Oriana Fallaci, enjoy world-wide reputations and most of their works have been translated into English. Others are less known to English readers. All the authors included in this collection, however, have made important contributions to Italian litera-ture over the past fifty years.

Until recently, critics of Italian literature have paid insufficient attention to women writers. Of the sixteen novelists chosen in 1985 by guest editor Pier Francesco Paolini, one of Italy's foremost writers and translators, for an issue of *The Literary Review* devoted to current Italian literature, all are male. In the introductory essay, "Lines of Force on Today's Italian Letters," Alfredo Giuliani, a leading poet and critic, shows how each of the sixteen writers gives new direction to the language and structure of imaginative prose.[1] Neither Paolini nor Giuliani mentions any women novelists. A reader receives the impression that serious literary communication in Italy is exclusively a male domain.

A brief survey of criticism over the past thirty years supports the view that women writers have been overlooked. In *La narrativa italiana: Tra romanzo e racconti* (The Italian Narrative: Novel and short stories), Leone Piccioni makes only brief mention of one woman—Elsa Morante: "Mor-ante and Cassola are among the new gifted writers with narrative talent, even though one is very different from the other."[2] Although Piccioni's work dates from 1959, Morante's *Menzogna e sortilegio (House of Liars)* had been published in 1948 and had already earned the Viareggio Prize,[3] but there is no mention of this important novel. Gianfranco Contini, Italy's most important contemporary philologist, projects a global and expressionistic vision of his country's literature in *Letteratura dell'Italia unita: 1861–1968* (Literature of a United Italy, 1861–1968) (1968). Nevertheless, in his analysis of one hundred writers, he studies a work by only one woman—Anna Banti's *Artemisia*.[4] In like manner, Geno Pampaloni's essay "La nuova letteratura" (The new literature) (1969) contains information on thirty-nine contemporaries but refers to only two women: Anna Maria Ortese and Natalia Ginzburg.[5] In *Letteratura italiana: I contemporanei* (Italian literature: Contemporaries) (1970), G. A. Peritore includes critical essays on Anna Banti, Natalia Ginzburg, and Elsa Morante. The essays cover, however, the works of forty-six writers and the small attention given to women reinforces the notion of their secondary status. Giovanni Getto and Gianni Solari's *Il Novecento: Cultura, letteratura, società* (The twentieth century: Culture, literature, society) (1980) surveys the writings of more than eighty-five Italian and foreign poets, novelists, and critics, and deals with only three women writers: Grazia Deledda, Elsa Morante, and Oriana Fallaci.[6] The journalist Sandra Petrignani perceptively summarizes the attitude toward women writers: "Very few critics have taken them seriously."[7]

Critics outside of Italy have also tended to overlook the contributions of women. Both Dominique Fernandez' *Roman italien et la crise de la conscience moderne* (Italian novels and the crisis of modern conscience) (1958) and J. H. Whitfield's *Short History of Italian Literature* (1960) examine in detail only the works of male writers. Except for Frank Rosengarten's brief discussion of Renata Viganò's resistance novel *L'Agnese va a morire* (Agnes goes to die), Sergio Pacifici's edited collection *From Verismo to Experimentalism: Essays on the Modern Novel* (1969) also ignores the writings of women. Ernest H. Wilkins essentially adheres to the same prejudice in *A History of Italian Literature* (1974), although he does offer a concise synthesis of the works of Grazia Deledda, who won the Nobel Prize for her novels in 1926.[8] In *Writers and Politics in Modern Italy* (1978), John Gatt-Rutter attempts a brief summary of the literary history of the postwar period and of selected writers whose works express a preoccupation with a new society. Gatt-Rutter does acknowledge that he fails to mention "Italy's many excellent women writers," but says that his choice of only males is not meant to imply an absolute supremacy.[9] In *The Modern Italian Novel from Pea to Moravia* (1979), Sergio Pacifici refers to his work as a sort of "readers' guide to the modern Italian novel: being the first to appear in almost half a century."[10] Yet the critic makes no significant mention of women: he deals with the internationally famous Alberto Moravia, Giuseppe Tomasi di Lampedusa, and Carlo Levi; he also treats lesser-known writers who deserve greater recognition: Carlo Gadda, Cesare Pavese, Elio Vittorini; finally, he considers authors who are appreciated mainly in Italy: Enrico Pea, Bruno Cicognani, Aldo Palazzeschi, Corrado Alvaro, Vittorio Brancati, and Dino Buzzati. With his selections Pacifici gives the impression that only Italian men are competent writers of contemporary prose. Michael Caesar and Peter Hainsworth's *Writers and Society in Contemporary Italy* (1984) examines Italian authors who capture the economic, social, political, and cultural transformations in Italy since 1956. With the exception of Elsa Morante their subjects are all male.[11]

In *Le donne e la letteratura* (Women and literature), (1984), Elisabetta Rasy regards such exclusion as an unmistakable sign of linguistic repression but suggests that quiescent acceptance of this unacknowledged condition was the only possible response by women writers to their second-class status.[12] This thesis receives reinforcement in the ten interviews with contemporary women novelists in Sandra Petrignani's *Signore della scrittura* (The grande dames of writing) (1984). According to many of these colloquies, each subject faces negative reactions in varying degrees that are attributable to sex rather than to artistic talent. They all experience feelings of isolation as professionals. Petrignani's contention is that scholars systematically ignore them and that bibliographies of critical works hardly ever acknowledge their existence. "In books dealing with literary history, women writers who do receive credits are barely mentioned in the footnotes." This neglect constitutes a grave injustice, since many already have a large reading audience. "Amongst them there are some writers who are not only highly important but who also have written best-sellers in Italy."[13]

Even those women whose literary talent is recognized speak of a reserved acceptance by critics. Anna Banti explains: "I am quoted in encyclopedias; I am present in anthologies. But in any case, a woman writer, even if successful, is marginalized. They will say that she is great among women writers but they will not equate her to male writers. It is a widespread practice."[14] Lalla Romano reinforces Banti's point: "Being a woman still weighs heavily in the literary milieu of our country. The critics treat you with a sort of condescension and concession."[15] The contemporary critic Anna Nozzoli states that numerous studies deal with the historical, political, sociological, psychoanalytic, and anthropological aspects of women's studies. She also speaks of the meager presence of critical contributions dedicated to the relationship between the condition of women and literature and attributes this scarcity to philosophic bias. "Ideological types of prejudice . . . lead to holding back the anthologizing of women writers—an incorrect and dangerous procedure, capable of becoming itself a potential vehicle for new sex discrimination."[16]

Some developments in Italy, however, indicate a change in attitude. Among the first to break the pattern of critical neglect was Emilio Cecchi. His "Prosatori e narratori" (Prose and narrative writers) (1969) not only includes a significant essay on Grazia Deledda but also reports on the accomplishments of Anna Banti, Gianna Manzini, and Elsa Morante.[17] After 1976, the feminist journals *Donnawomanfemme*, *Effe* (F), *Quotidiano donna* (Woman daily), *Noi donne* (We women), *Memoria* (Memory), and *Orsa minore* (Ursa Minor) were started.[18] Although these periodicals often represent the views of political activists, their orientation is cultural as well. The 1977 issue of *Donnawomanfemme* deals completely with the subject of women and literature; a more recent edition critically analyzes the image of women in sixteenth-century literary texts.[19] A major step in the process of rectifying historical neglect occurred in 1978 with the appearance of Anna Nozzoli's penetrating study, *Tabù e coscienza: La condizione femminile nella letteratura italiana del Novecento* (Taboo and awareness: The condition of women in twentieth-century Italian literature). The critic's insight into the years of this century, the presence of women in the futurist movement, and the formal feminist novels of the 1970s, as well as an analysis of the works of Gianna Manzini, Anna Banti, Fausta Cialente, and Elsa Morante project a clear picture of what has taken place in this century.

In 1984, Marco Forti's *Prosatori e narratori nel Novecento italiano* (Prose and narrative writers in twentieth-century Italy) presented detailed essays on exemplary writers of prose. Significantly, Forti assigned important positions to seven women novelists: Anna Banti, Lalla Romano, Gianna Manzini, Maria Bellonci, Natalia Ginzburg, Elsa Morante, and Fausta Cialente.[20] Sandra Petrignani's *Firmato donna: Una donna un secolo* (Signed woman: A woman a century) (1986) analyses the relationship between Italian women and problems in the twentieth century. In addition, a section deals with past epochs as seen by authors living in previous centuries: Gaspara Stampa in the sixteenth; Angelica Tarabotti in the seventeenth; Elisabetta Caminer in the eighteenth; and Caterina Percoti in the nineteenth. Paola Blelloch's *Quel mondo dei guanti e delle stoffe* (That world of gloves and of fabrics) (1987) defines the various themes that characterize the writings of contemporary women writers in Italy. A recent issue of *Italica* (1988) is entitled "Women's Voices" and contains three articles: on feminist literature of the 1970s; on Elsa Morante, and on Gina Lagorio.[21]

The present volume represents a continuing effort to break down the wall of silence by analyzing the creative prose of a dozen distinctive Italian women writers, although the list is hardly comprehensive. Renata Viganò, Paola Masino, Alba de Cèspedes, Laudomia Bonanni, Anna Maria Ortese, Livia De Stefani, and others are not included, but they certainly need extensive attention. Maria Bellonci especially deserves recognition as the founder of Strega, the most prestigious literary prize in Italy, and as the author of historical fiction.[22] Limitations of space and purpose required that choices be made, although they may appear arbitrary. This book makes no claim to completeness. Nor are its structural dimensions those of a comprehensive catalog, like Mario Gastaldi and Carmen Scano's *il Dizionario delle scrittrici contemporanee* (Dictionary of contemporary women writers).[23] Instead, it offers selective commentaries on a group of authors—some of whom are feminist in orientation, some of whom are not—whose work reflects the variety, dynamism, and creativity of women writers in modern Italy. If at the same time it encourages fresh interpretations and additional translations into English of these and other Italian women, so much the better.

NOTES

1. Pier Francesco Paolini, ed., "Italian Writing Today," *The Literary Review* 28, no. 2 (1985): 181–328.

2. Leone Piccioni, *La narrativa italiana: Tra romanzo e racconti* (Milan: Mondadori, 1959), p. 130. Titles of Italian works cited in the essays are generally translated into English only the first time they appear. Works that have actually been translated and published in English are so indicated in the bibliography. All quotations in the Introduction are my translations.

3. Premio Viareggio is an Italian literary prize; other awards include the Premio Bancarella, the Premio Strega, and the Presidente.

4. Gianfranco Contini, *Letteratura dell'Italia unita: 1861–1968* (Florence: Sansoni, 1968). Other examples of books that neglect the writing of women include: Giuseppe De Robertis, *Scrittori del Novecento* (Writers of the twentieth century) (Florence: Le Monnier, 1958); Claudio Marabini, *Gli anni sessanta: Narrativo e storia (The Sixties: Narrative and history)* (Milan: Rizzoli, 1969); Gianni Grana, ed., *Novecento: Gli scrittori e la cultura letteraria nella societa italiana* (The twentieth century: Writers and literary culture in Italian society) (Milan: Marzorati, 1982), vol. 2.

5. Geno Pampaloni, "La nuova letteratura," in *Storia della letteratura italiana: Il Novecento* (History of Italian literature: The twentieth century), ed. Emilio Cecchi and Natalino Sapegno, 9 vols. (Milan: Garzanti, 1969), 9: 749–879.

6. G. A. Peritore, ed., *Letteratura italiana: I contemporanei* (Milan: Marzorati, 1970), vol. 3; Giovanni Getto and Gianni Solari, *Il Novecento: Cultura, letteratura, società* (Milan: Minerva Italica, 1980).

7. Sandra Petrignani, *Le signore della scrittura* (Milan: La Tartaruga, 1984), p. 7.

8. Dominique Fernandez, *Le roman italien et la crise de la conscience moderne* (Paris: Bernard

Grasset, 1958); J. H. Whitfield, *A Short History of Italian Literature* (Baltimore: Penguin Books, 1960); Sergio Pacifici, *From Verismo to Experimentalism: Essays on the Modern Novel* (Bloomington: Indiana University Press, 1969); see, however, Frank Rosengarten's essay, "The Italian Resistance Novel (1945–1962)," pp. 226–27; Ernest Hatch Wilkins, *A History of Italian Literature* (Cambridge: Harvard University Press, 1974).

9. John Gatt-Rutter, *Writers and Politics in Modern Italy* (New York: Holmes and Meier, 1978), p. 16.

10. Sergio Pacifici, *The Modern Italian Novel from Pea to Moravia* (Carbondale: Southern Illinois University Press, 1979), p. x. In his earlier two works on Italian fiction, Pacifici does mention women writers in greater detail. *The Modern Italian Novel from Manzoni to Svevo* (1967) includes a chapter on Matilde Serao (pp. 129–37); *The Modern Italian Novel from Capuana to Tozzi* (1973) has a chapter on Anna Neera and Sibilla Aleramo (pp. 49–67) and devotes half of another chapter to Grazia Deledda (pp. 86–97). The women writers included in these two works, however, composed their novels during the earlier part of the century.

11. Michael Caesar and Peter Hainsworth, eds., *Writers and Society in Contemporary Italy* (Warwickshire: Berg, 1986).

12. Elisabetta Rasy, *Le donne e la letteratura* (Rome: Editori Riuniti, 1984), pp. 15–17.

13. Petrignani, *Le signore della scrittura*, p. 8.

14. Ibid., p. 106.

15. Ibid., p. 17.

16. Anna Nozzoli, "Premessa," *Tabù e coscienza: La condizione femminile nella letteratura italiana del Novecento* (Florence: La Nuova Italia, 1978), p. vii.

17. Emilio Cecchi, "Prosatori e narratori," in *Storia della letteratura italiana: Il Novecento*, ed. Emilio Cecchi and Natalino Sapegno, 9 vols. (Milan: Garzanti, 1969), 9: 533–727.

18. Lucia Chiavola Birnbaum, *Liberazione della Donna: Feminism in Italy* (Middletown: Wesleyan University Press, 1986), p. 7. Birnbaum's historical treatment of Italian women in relation to Catholicism and communism also highlights the literature of the feminist cultural revolution.

19. "Donne e letteratura," *Donnawomanfemme*, no. 5 (October–December 1977): 3–152; "Sulla scrittura: Percorsi critici su testi letterari del XVI secolo," ibid., no. 25–26 (1985): 5–104.

20. Marco Forti, *Prosatori e narratori nel Novecento italiano* (Milan: Mursia, 1984).

21. Sandra Petrignani, *Firmato donna: Una donna un secolo* (Rome: Il Ventaglio, 1986); Paola Blelloch, *Quel mondo dei quanti e delle stoffe* (Verona: Essedue edizioni, 1987); "Women's Voices," *Italica* 65, no. 4 (1988). A significant international symposium, "Women in Italian Studies," took place at York University in Ontario from February 28 to March 1, 1987. The proceedings have recently been published: Ada Testaferri, ed., *Donna: Women in Italian Culture*, University of Toronto Italian Studies 7 (Ottawa: Dovehouse, 1989).

22. Maria Bellonci is the author of *Lucrezia Borgia* (1939), *Segreti dei Gonzaga* (A Prince of Mantua: The life and times of Vincent Gonzaga) (1947), *Marco Polo* (1984), and *Rinascimento perduto* (Private renaissance) (1985).

23. Mario Gastaldi and Carmen Scano, eds., *Scrittrici italiane—Sec. XX—Dizionari* (Milan: Gastaldi, 1957). The dictionary gives short biographical notes on over twenty-six hundred women writers from the twentieth century.

ELSA MORANTE

Elsa Morante was born in Rome in 1912. After high school, she enrolled at the University of Rome but she did not graduate. She began her career by writing children's fables for *Il corriere dei piccoli*. In 1941 she completed *Il gioco segreto* and *Le bellissime avventure di Caterì*. Her most famous works followed: *Menzogna e sortilegio* (1948), *L'isola di Arturo* (1957), *Lo scialle andaluso* (1958), *La storia* (1974), and *Aracoeli* (1982). In addition to her narrative prose, Morante edited a collection of poems entitled *Alibi* (1959) and attempted a stylistic blend of prose, poetry, and experimental graphics in *Il mondo salvato dai ragazzini* (1968).

In 1941 she married Alberto Moravia and, twenty-one years later, separated from him without obtaining a divorce. Morante consistently refused interviews and meetings with journalists, invitations to appear on television programs dealing with the arts, and requests to adapt her books to cinema. In April 1983 she attempted suicide after a two-year struggle with hydrocephalus; her death in 1985 deprives Italy of one of its most prestigious authors.

Elsa Morante: The Trauma of Possessive Love and Disillusionment

ROCCO CAPOZZI

In Gianni Venturi's *Elsa Morante,* instead of the usual interview that precedes a monographic study, the reader finds quotations from Morante's essays and Venturi's explanation that the writer had once again refused any oral communication, maintaining that her books contain the pertinent biographical information about her.[1] Elsa Morante, considered a solitary and even peevish personality, secluded herself almost entirely in the early 1960s after her separation from the famous novelist Alberto Moravia and thereafter rarely allowed interviews.[2]

Morante was born in Rome in 1912 of a Sicilian father and a mother from Emilia. She began to write at an early age, left home in her teens, and received shelter from a rich aunt; she was self-educated and possessed a love for books, music, and cats. She considered Achilles, Don Quixote, and Hamlet the literary archetypes, admired such important poets as Leopardi, Rimbaud, Saba, Penna, and Pasolini, particularly appreciated the masters of "well-made novels" of the nineteenth century, and had little patience with *letterati* who made literature a business.[3] Except for these few facts, however, critics repeat that little information exists about the author. Nevertheless, a close examination of her work reveals a good deal of the implied author and, indirectly, of the real Elsa Morante who has consistently used alibis to narrate important personal experiences that have conditioned her life and writing.

"Alibi" is the title of a poem and is also the name of a collection of Morante's poetry. She deliberately used this word in her well-known essay-reply to "nine questions on the novel." Critics often refer to this essay when they define her position on art and the role of writers in presenting "incorruptible poetic truths." Not one, however, has focused on the definition of *alibi* in relation to her own poems and narrative. Morante stated:

> Instead of invoking the muses, the modern novelist is led to arouse a *reciting-I* (protagonist and interpreter) that can serve as an *alibi*. Almost as if to say, in his own defense: "Of course that which I represent is not *the* reality but *a* reality

relative to the I of myself, or to another I, different in appearance from myself, which in substance, however, belongs to me, and in which I now impersonate myself entirely."[4]

This statement is most revealing, especially for its use of such terms as *alibi* and *reciting-I,* which, while referring in general to narrative voices in novels, can and should also apply to Morante's own writings. The term *alibi* includes such major Morante figures as Andrea and her narrator-protagonists Elisa, Arturo, and Manuele; whether male or female, they all function in various degrees as the author's dramatis personae. In brief, they are all modifications and complements of the same autobiographical, narrating subject. Andrea from *Lo scialle andaluso* (The Andalusian shawl), Arturo from *L'isola di Arturo (Arturo's Island),* and Manuele from *Aracoeli* represent Morante's most important male alibis. They both hide and reveal the author's intimate desires, fears, delusions, and personal experiences related to love and rejection; through them, the writer accentuates the drama of addiction to expressive love and the anxieties of emotional exclusion.

Narcissism is a central motif in Morante's work, and the critic Carlo Sgorlon emphatically alludes to the author's flirtation with her own biography. Although Sgorlon's observations are based on *Menzogna e sortilegio (House of Liars)* and *L'isola di Arturo,* they also apply to other writings as well.[5] However, the critic's suggestion that this interest in the self is a form of narcissistic coquetry seems inaccurate,[6] since the amount of suffering her alibis experience makes it difficult to view them in terms of their coquetry. Her alibis are all projections of an autobiographical narrator who, like a modern Sheherazade, seeks cathartic relief, self-therapy, and hope through her narration. Referring to narcissism, Cesare Garboli terms Arturo's malady *narcissistic neurosis,*[7] which is an appropriate diagnosis for all of Morante's narrator-protagonists. In fact, Manuele, the main character of Morante's last novel, *Aracoeli,* confesses that he is afflicted by "neuroses" and that as a child he was "Narcissus-like."[8] Furthermore, most of Morante's alibis crave affection; they are obsessively and overly concerned with feeling unattractive; they often manifest low self-esteem. In addition, they are drawn to so-called beautiful individuals who seem both blessed and cursed by their own physical assets, as in the case of the prototype character Edoardo of *Menzogna e sortilegio.* On a different note of narcissism, throughout her work Morante gives innumerable signs that her narration represents a highly self-conscious act of writing—for the most part about personal memories. From the early days of *Le bellissime avventure di Caterì dalla trecciolina* (The beautiful adventures of Caterì)[9] to *Aracoeli,* Morante constantly affirms her presence in her books through various forms of intrusions and stylistic devices.

Almost a year before her death, Elsa Morante granted a rare and most revealing interview to Jean-Noël Schifano, the translator of her novels in France. In this exchange, the writer reasserts: "The complete me can be found in my books"; she also adds: "Arturo *c'est moi*." She speaks freely of her attempted suicide, of her desire to be a mother, and of her love for love, children, cats, real women, and real mothers, sounding in this like the character Nunziatella in *L'isola di Arturo*. She also expresses her desire that people enjoy themselves at her funeral listening to the music of Mozart, Bach, and Bob Dylan. The author mentions her possible Spanish roots; she confesses that, when she was two and a half, she fell in love with a nine-year-old boy and that love for her, ever since, has been first "heaven" and then "hell."[10] Morante's metaphoric presentations of this metamorphosis from paradise to inferno in her own life are pertinent to a discussion of the ever-present theme of blinding and possessive love that she portrays as a passion and obsession leading to despair and destruction.

In addition to the alibis used in her novels, the collection of poems entitled *Alibi* (1958)[11] provides excellent material for the analysis of Elsa Morante's dramatis personae. The sixteen poems that appear in *Alibi* were written between 1941 and the publication of *L'isola di Arturo* in 1957. In *Alibi,* the author explains that these poems are an echo, a chorus of her prose,[12] or, to some extent, a musical form of enjoyment. As Morante suggests in her preface, this poetry is important and should not be taken lightly.[13] In fact, she seems to desire compliments for her so-called hobby of writing poems—a hobby that actually demonstrates great artistic talent in *Il mondo salvato dai ragazzini* (The world saved by little children) (1968). Although *Alibi* has received little attention from critics, a close reading of the collection reveals distinct signs of a familiar voice that repeatedly and with few variations unveils the personal drama of a highly sensitive person;[14] like Manuele in *Aracoeli,* the narrator appears destined from early childhood to suffer from rejected love and solitude: "A difficili amori io nacqui" (To difficult loves I was born).[15] Morante remembers, relives, and narrates this drama of anguish with great vividness in each of her writings.

The poetic voice in *Alibi* is the same one found in Morante's novels where the author-narrator-protagonist sees herself as a Sheherazade who is destined to be "fantastica"[16] and who must narrate, hoping that the stories will bring others pleasure and give her hope. Throughout these poems, the writer speaks of herself and also of cats, fables, allegory, Hamlet, childhood

friends, and invented characters. In the title poem "Alibi," Morante specifically addresses her alibis; however, these narrating voices hide their real
identity. Moreover, in addition to the familiar Morantean theme of the
importance of love, these introductory verses also expose the beautiful
metaphor of a *"gatta-fanciulla"* (the catlike girl) who stands as a self-
portrait of the author. In "Alla favola," written in 1947 and published in
Menzogna e sortilegio in 1948, Morante refers to herself as a *"fenice"* (a
phoenix), clearly alluding to her role as a narrator who returns in every
writing:

> O illusion, I draw about me
> your concealing garment
> and adorn it with the golden plumage
> that was mine in the great lost season
> before I grew all fire
> and rose as a radiant phoenix.[17]

In her candid interview with Schifano, the author stated that Arturo
represents her and that one of her lifetime wishes had always been "to be a
boy."[18] A more encompassing confession would have been: "Andrea, Arturo, and Manuele, as well as Elisa, are all *moi.*" Through her alibis, as well
as through her characters, Morante discloses her feelings, views, and neuroses and is thus quite justified in refusing interviews about her personal
life, since, indeed, she can be found in her books. The writer's *opera omnia*
shows that her imagination capitalizes on mythical, fabulistic, lyrical, and
psychological elements. *Il mondo salvato dai ragazzini* and *La storia (History:
A Novel)* demonstrate that she rarely favors ideological points of view; in
both works, she treats history, as well as governmental institutions, as a
scandal and a joke. Rather than follow literary trends, Morante has consistently followed her heart and her whims.[19]

Although her contribution to literary psychoanalysis is beyond the scope
of this essay, Morante appears to use the act of writing as a possible
therapeutic instrument, especially with Elisa of *Menzogna e sortilegio* who
employs her lies as fiction to arrive at her own truth and that of others.[20] In
addition, the author often empathizes with childhood illusions and emotional alienation that result from rejection by loved ones. In *Aracoeli,*
Morante speaks explicitly through Manuele of her writing as an instrument
of therapy and as a last attempt to heal the self in this final journey through
memories: "I ask myself whether, also with this journey, on the mad pretext
of finding Aracoeli again, I am not actually attempting a last, absurd
therapy to be cured of her" (20). Eradicating childhood and family experi-

ences unfortunately proves futile and absurd not only for Manuele but for all of Morante's alibis.

Children often play a central role in Morante's work. They are portrayed as great custodians of fables, myths, idols, and heroes; they are hurt by love, confused about death, and thirsty for attention. In addition, they are blessed with fantasy and the ability to communicate with nature and animals—essential qualities lost in adulthood. Pier Paolo Pasolini, in fact, wrote an exceptional review of *Il mondo salvato dai ragazzini* in free verse, the same form used by Morante in what is undoubtedly her most unusual work; in it, the critic calls the author a *"nonna-bambina"* (a grandmother child) who says unheard things about society and who is able to scandalize not only the bourgeois but all levels of class structure.[21] In the expression *"nonna-bambina,"* Pasolini has captured the essence of Morante's soul, her personality, her conscious childishness, and her passion for children and for adults who remain like them.

Critics have viewed *L'isola di Arturo*—winner of the prestigious Premio Strega in 1957—as a novel of initiation to adulthood. Most of Morante's novels deal primarily with this theme of maturation, consistently accentuating bitter and alienating experiences in the process of growing up. Useppe, in *La storia*,[22] is Morante's only protagonist to die when still a child; Pazzariello is a young man who remains youthful, happy, and childlike from beginning to end in *Il mondo salvato dai ragazzini*. On the other hand, most of Morante's major figures, especially Elisa, Arturo, and Manuele, are disillusioned adults whose remarkable memory of childhood events facilitates a retrospective narration of those incidents that have led to their present unhappy condition.

The overwhelming success of Morante's first novel, *Menzogna e sortilegio*, has stimulated various studies of its characters, themes, and techniques. In this monumental work—which in a number of ways is Morante's macrotext and, for many, her masterpiece—the reader easily recognizes allusions to the author Elsa in the omniscient narrator Elisa;[23] she is the first fully developed prototype of Morante's narrator-protagonists who have grown to adulthood with little parental attention, who love reading books, especially fables and adventure novels, and, most important, who write about their childhood and adolescent experiences through flashbacks and hindsight. Other characters such as Anna, Cesira, Concetta, Teodoro, Francesco, and Edoardo receive a sketchy existence in previously written short stories and emerge in the later novels with minor differences; they reveal various forms of love-hate, attraction-repulsion, and master-slave relationships. Furthermore, Teodoro and Francesco prefigure such other male characters as Michele in "Qualcuno bussa alla porta," Davide Segre in *La storia,* and Manuele and Eugenio in *Aracoeli;* they all become human wreckage, drowning their sorrows and destroying themselves in drugs or alcohol.

Critics have searched through Morante's early short stories for indications of magic, fablelike settings, oneiric descriptions, themes, motifs, and characters who become prominent in later novels.[24] In 1980, Eugenio Ragni analyzed what is perhaps Morante's earliest short story "Qualcuno bussa alla porta" (Someone is knocking at the door), published between 1935 and 1936 in the journal *I Diritti della Scuola.*[25] The importance of this relatively long short story, which has gone unnoticed for many years, lies primarily in the abundance of familiar themes encountered in Morante's later works. She gives special attention to a semimagical ambience, to such visual contrasts as blue and dark eyes, blond hair and darker shades, light skin and darker complexions, to children abandoned by parents, to adults with childlike characteristics, to the contrast of social classes, to secluded places surrounded by gardens, to the solitude of old people, and, of course, to possessive and tyrannical love.

The main male character in "Qualcuno bussa alla porta" is Michele Waug, a handsome, tall, fair-skinned, and middle-aged man who has nightmares about his young wife, a beautiful woman of dark complexion, whom he killed out of jealousy shortly after their marriage. The principal female protagonist is Lucia, a little girl adopted by Michele who grows up respecting her wealthy benefactor but not loving him.[26] She first falls in love with Jack, a young and rich American tourist, and shortly afterward leaves him for Francesco Abbate, a poor, solitary man who has been raised by his grandmother and who plays music so well that he wins Lucia's heart. This rare Morantean story with some *lieto fine* comes to an end as the author zooms in on the square of the island's tiny village, where a middle-aged gypsy woman dances and sings.[27] The reader has no difficulty recognizing Lucia's mother as the gypsy; she is Mirtilla, the young woman who became enamored at the beginning of the story with a mysterious, beautiful stranger who abandoned her after seducing and impregnating her. Furthermore, Michele Waug significantly illustrates Morante's first treatment of jealous, possessive, and destructive love.[28]

The other pertinent short story is "Lo scialle andaluso," written in 1951 during the composition of *L'isola di Arturo.* This story explains the relationship between young Andrea Campese and his mother Giuditta—a relationship that will echo in *L'isola di Arturo* and *Aracoeli*. After her husband's death, Giuditta, who loves dancing and the theater, is left with two children, Laura and Andrea. What distinguishes Andrea from his twin sister is his slow growth, his beautiful blue eyes, his pleasure in writing poems, and, above all, a strong attachment to his mother and an equally strong dislike for her dancing, which keeps her away from him. Whenever Giuditta goes to work, Andrea feels like a little "unhappy kitten" abandoned in a basket by its mother.[29] Andrea consequently grows older, hating both the theater and Giuditta. At the end of the story, however, Andrea leaves the seminary he has entered and rejoins his mother, believing at first that she has deserted her profession in order to be close to him once again. He soon realizes that it was Giuditta's old age and lack of talent that forced her to leave the theater. Andrea will cherish like a talisman the "Andalusian shawl" that Giuditta wrapped around him on the night when the two were reunited,[30] but more important he will harbor a great disillusionment—the realization that love was not his mother's motive for reunion. Andrea's awareness of Giuditta's metamorphosis from a loving mother to a selfish woman previews Wilhelm's change in Arturo's mind, as well as Manuele's view of Aracoeli's transformation. In addition, Giuditta's accentuated and dark Spanish complexion is yet another distinguishable sign of a future condition in *Aracoeli*.

In *L'isola di Arturo,* Arturo Gerace spends his youth like a mythological character in the idyllic setting of the island of Procida.[31] His mother died giving birth to him and thus the little dark-haired boy, fed goat milk by the house servant Silvestro, grows up mostly alone and free to roam around the island partially unclothed. Arturo has no formal schooling and yet, like many of Morante's narrator-protagonists, has developed a great passion for books, especially adventure stories. Arturo's father, Wilhelm Gerace, half German and half Italian, with blue eyes and blond hair, spends very little time on the island but in the eyes of Arturo is a hero who travels to exotic places for great adventures. This setting constitutes the environment of the first fourteen years of Arturo's life.

The young boy's problems begin when Nunziatella, a sixteen-year-old Neapolitan girl, is introduced as his new mother and is thus brought into the Gerace home—the notorious Casa dei Guaglioni (literally "The House of Boys"), a large run-down former monastery, which the former owner, Romeo l'Amalfitano, had never allowed a woman to enter. In this novel about adolescence, the protagonist discovers love and sex but for the most part obtains knowledge about himself and those close to him. The boy

Arturo, who considered women ugly, who hated his stepmother, and who was jealous of the attention paid to his baby brother's blue eyes and blond hair, becomes the victim of an oedipal drama.[32] In fact, Arturo's hate for Nunziatella soon turns to love, as he watches her kiss, caress, and love her baby. Arturo has never received a mother's affection and becomes obsessed as he dreams and fantasizes about Nunziatella's kisses. After an intended fake suicide that almost proves to be fatal, Arturo forces a kiss from Nunziatella, and from then on his life changes drastically. He can no longer face his stepmother and has frequent encounters with his initiator, Assunta. Shortly afterward, he discovers that his idolized father is no hero, so between Arturo's fourteenth and sixteenth birthday, the island and his life change rapidly into a prison from which he must try to flee.

The most traumatic experience for Arturo is naturally the disillusionment with his childhood idol, Wilhelm Gerace. His father, far from being an adventurous hero, proves to be a wretched individual who abandons his family for an exconvict; the former criminal in turn rejects Wilhelm's homosexual attentions and openly ridicules him. In like manner, Wilhelm had earlier refused the affection of his friend Romeo. Thus, as World War II explodes, Arturo leaves his sheltered existence with the bitter realization that "outside of limbo there is no Elysium."[33]

Another salient feature of this novel is the underlying theme of misogyny, first introduced by Romeo l'Amalfitano and then more acrimoniously expressed by Wilhelm, who had suffered from inordinate motherly love in his childhood and from Romeo's equally despotic affection in later years. Given the environment, Arturo's distrustful attitude toward women is not surprising. Wilhelm often lectures and warns his son of the dangers of mothers: "But who's to save you from your mother? Sanctity's her vice . . . and as long as she's alive she won't let you live, with that old *love* of hers. . . . Oh, what hell it is to be loved by someone who doesn't love happiness, or life, or herself, but just you!" (124).

These strong words bring to mind the tyrannical and tragic love between a mother and her son described in the short story "La nonna" (1937) and also announce Manuele's feelings toward his mother, Aracoeli, in the novel of that name. Wilhelm and Manuele are both children of mixed marriages, the offspring of German and Italian or of Spanish and northern Italian parents; in addition, they are representatives of a more general combination that includes opposites from north and south and, more specifically, persons of dark and fair complexions. The attraction and repulsion of these opposites appear so frequently in Morante's writings that the reader cannot help thinking of the author's own family situation, where dark and fair, north and south, both attracted and repelled.

In *Aracoeli,* various idols are toppled, but the most important example is Manuele's mother, Aracoeli, a beautiful, childlike, Spanish woman who was so chaste before marriage that she believed that one conceived by kissing.[34] Even her name is symbolic. Aracoeli is like the great "Altar of Heaven" and the famous Aracoeli Church of Rome; her name also suggests a more notorious Roman institution, the prison of "Regina Coeli." This character, in fact, is first described as a saint but later becomes the source of Manuele's hell. In this novel, much more poignantly than in previous works, Morante's alibis unleash the author's feelings toward parents and especially toward what a mother can be and what she may become—a giver of life and a tyrant, an idol and a monster, a source of love and hell, a caring individual and a witch.[35] Fathers, on the other hand, frequently depicted as weak persons, are embodied in Eugenio; he is the man for whom Manuele feels no pity, only "rancor and dislike" (285). Eugenio is extremely sensitive but equally weak and, because of his military career, is almost always away from his family. Furthermore, as the war comes to an end he feels abandoned by his own idols—his wife, Aracoeli, and his king, Victor Emanuel—and becomes a drunken and unrecognizable individual in a semi-destroyed apartment overlooking the Verano Cemetery, where Aracoeli had been buried.

Manuele initially idolizes his mother, who does the same with him. He begins to think of himself as unattractive the day he starts wearing glasses. He comes to see himself as his mother's discarded toy when she withdraws all signs of affection from him. After the death of her obsessively desired baby girl, Aracoeli evolves from an overly loving person to a hysteric nymphomaniac who eventually dies of a brain tumor. The child who initially experienced much affection and reassurance from Aracoeli turns to hating her. After two unsuccessful attempts at making love to women—emotionally disastrous experiences with prostitutes—Manuele focuses his attention on male companions; however, he also fails as a homosexual. To make matters worse, the character Mariuccio refuses and even ridicules Manuele's affection in the same fashion that the exconvict had rejected Wilhelm Gerace: "I have no need of your LOVE" (44).

Never before had Elsa Morante been so graphic in her description of sex,[36] so critical of God's role,[37] so skeptical and adamant of bourgeois society,[38] so concerned with death, so obsessed with the narrator's self-image and his unusual memory, and so strong in her invectives against mothers as she was in *Aracoeli*. Manuele, in fact, dwells at great length upon the causes of his anger toward Aracoeli, blaming her for his anguish and even wishing that she had never given him life:

> It would have been better if you had aborted me . . . instead of nourishing and raising me with your treacherous love, like a little animal being raised for the slaughterhouse. . . . The enchanted potion that you worked day and night into my flesh was actually this: your false, excessive love, to which you addicted me, as if to an incurable vice. (94)

Manuele resembles Arturo in that they both leave their "Garden of Eden," an obvious symbol of innocence and early childhood, and discover only loneliness and despair.[39] Manuele realizes that his destiny is to be unattractive and without love, as a gypsy and his horoscope had predicted when he was a young child: *"Your constant and definitive destiny will be to live without love"* (270; author's italics). Morante's protagonist believes, however, that love should constitute an integral part of everyone's life: "Isn't love a natural element of living matter? Free? Distributed everywhere, and necessary? Isn't it, along with death, promised from birth to all animals, including ugly ones?" (270). For Manuele, just as for Andrea and Arturo, the worst aspects of human destiny become manifest if maternal love, the first and most important of affectionate attachments, is withheld: "Your first love will never be violated."[40] In *Menzogna e sortilegio,* however, Elisa recognizes motherly attraction as excessive tenderness and also as the source of personal hell: "My mother was the first and most serious of my unhappy loves. Thanks to her, I knew from early childhood the bitterest agonies of the unaccepted lover" (19).

Elsa Morante's alibis and their traumatic love stories focus specifically on the formative years of childhood and adolescence; they propose that during this particularly sensitive age many people suffer permanently damaging traumas from sibling rivalries, jealousies, lack of attention, and possessive or neglectful love. As Donatella Ravanello also suggests, Morante's work places a primary responsibility for alienation of individuals on the family.[41] Her alibis illustrate that a person may experience psychic injury in the immediate family even before societal forces exploit, neglect, and destroy the same human being. Andrea, Anna, Elisa, Arturo, Wilhelm, and Manuele all exemplify this conclusion as they emerge from their early life scarred by disorders clearly originating from a lack of emotional well-being. Furthermore, Morante's alibis often contain a sentimental idea of love that finds its source in fables, romances, and literature in general; they frequently appear to be in love with love. While Arturo believes himself to be in love "with this or that person," he really has no affection for anyone and confesses: "I was too much in love with love; this has always been my real passion" (315–16).

This "real passion" for love that Morante repeatedly embodies in her alibis proves a truth at the core of the writer's thinking. When tender inclinations assume despotic, egotistical, irrational, narcissistic, or idolatrous dimensions, they become destructive. Morante's alibis desire and despise intensely; their relationships, as Sgorlon suggests, are barbaric and morbid;[42] they are either heaven or hell with nothing in between. Love occasionally transforms itself into pity;[43] at other times, it turns into hate. It consumes and continues, however, even after the object of desire disappears or dies. In Morante's narrative, emotional attachment is rarely joyful, peaceful, or reciprocal. As a result, this type of rapport causes a misanthropy. Morante voices her own childhood drama when Elisa openly confesses this tendency: "Per troppo amore io diventai misantropa" (For excessive love I became misanthropic).[44]

On the final page of *Aracoeli*, Manuele tries to explain why he wept the day he last saw his father in the squalid apartment overlooking the Verano Cemetery. He walks into the street with tears in his eyes and realizes for the first time that he cries because he loves his father. Almost a year later, when he hears the news of his father's death, as if stung by an insect, he once again feels the urge to shed tears and then states: "Certain individuals are more inclined to weep for love than for death" (311). These words are Manuele's last phrases and also the conclusion of Morante's published work. This sentence intimately reveals an author whose final two years of life contained misery and torment. Her sickness, solitude, myopia, and detested old age tormented her daily existence.[45] She jokingly referred to her failed attempt at suicide as her unsatisfactory self-euthanasia. Ironically Arturo and Manuele also fare poorly in their minisuicides; fearing that his effort will become a subject of ridicule, Manuele reveals: "My mini-suicides (all failures) had been, actually, tragicomedies" (68). Nonetheless, Schifano's interview with Morante reveals that during the last days of her life she was still in love with love and her memories. Perhaps she looked at death as an end to her mental and physical anguish, or better yet, as an end to her personal hell, rather than as something to be dreaded.

The intensive and overwhelming emotions expressed by Manuele in his desperate search for his mother's roots and for a return to the womb are in direct proportion to the emotional drain suffered by the author as she expressed herself through an alibi for the last time.[46] Manuele's allegorical and visionary journey, like all Morante's voyages into memory, represents a painful, self-revealing, and self-conscious experience rather than a glorious adventure. In *Aracoeli,* a Morante-Sheherazade exists who can no longer continue narrating; she has no more strength to postpone her death with the power of words. In fact, the writer explained to Schifano that a resumption of writing would have certainly meant a return to life, but she admitted that she was also quite sure that writing again would have been extremely difficult. In addition, she admitted having two fathers in life and having no intention of speaking about either one.[47] This information is another reason for seeking a biography in her books, where through her alibis she exposes her fathers, family dramas, and "amori difficili" (difficult loves).

Analyses of Morante's alibis in her poetry and prose give no sure familiarity with the real author. Nevertheless, they facilitate a highly valuable exposure of a writer who has consistently focused on the traumatic experiences of love, rejection, and solitude. In these alibis, the implied author— or better, the autobiographical narrating subject—grows increasingly neurotic and obsessed with feeling unattractive, abandoned, and unloved. Cesare Garboli states that in reading Morante's narrative he easily juxtaposes and confuses the author who emerges from the work with the real-life person whom he knows. According to Garboli, the actual Elsa Morante remains like a beautiful mystery that is hard to define.[48] Morante's alibis are certainly approachable and relatively easy to analyze, but their real author remains a mysterious and fascinating Sheherazade who preferred to reveal herself through her stories, myths, and fables.[49] Elsa Morante has in fact chosen to remain wrapped in a veil of fiction and narrative lies that intend simultaneously to reveal and hide universal and poetic truths.

NOTES

This article is a revision of my " 'Sheherazade' and Other 'Alibis': Elsa Morante's Victims of Love," which will appear in *Rivista di Studi Italiani* 5–6 (forthcoming).

1. Gianni Venturi, *Elsa Morante* (Florence: La Nuova Italia, 1977).

2. See Carlo Sgorlon's psychologically perceptive monographic study: *Invito alla lettura di Elsa Morante* (Milan: Mursia, 1972), p. 15.

3. See Morante's reply to "Pro o contro la bomba atomica," *L'Europa Letteraria* 4 (1965): 31–42. She speaks at great length about writers and *letterati.*

4. Morante, "Nove domande sul romanzo," *Nuovi Argomenti* 38–39 (1959): 17–38 (material cited is from pp. 24–25; author's italics and my translation).

5. Morante, *House of Liars* (New York: Harcourt, Brace and Co., 1951), trans. Adrienne Foulke, and *Arturo's Island* (London: Collins, 1962), trans. Isabelle Quigly. Parenthetical references to these texts come from these editions.

6. See Sgorlon, *Invito*, p. 18.

7. Cesare Garboli, *La stanza separata* (Milan: Mondadori, 1969), p. 63.

8. "The child Manuele—supertalented and subnormal, precocious and retarded, ugly and Narcissus-like . . ." (Morante, *Aracoeli*, trans. William Weaver [New York: Random House, 1984], p. 276). Parenthetical references to this text come from this edition.

9. Morante, *Le bellissime avventure di Caterì dalla trecciolina*, written when the author was about thirteen, has not been translated into English.

10. Jean-Noel Schifano: "Parla Elsa Morante. Barbara e divina," *L'Espresso*, 2 Dec. 1984, pp. 122–33; quotations are from p. 125.

11. Morante, *Alibi* (Milan: Longanesi, 1958). All parenthetical page references to this text come from this edition and are my translation.

12. Some of the poems were, in fact, written specifically for two of her novels. "Alla favola," "Ai personaggi," and "Canto per il gatto Alvaro" appear in *Menzogna e sortilegio;* "L'isola di Arturo" was, naturally, written for *L'isola di Arturo.*

13. See Morante's preface to *Alibi*, p. 9.

14. Morante's work illustrates very well the point that some authors—through the process of "repetition and difference"—basically write the same story over and over again. Moreover, as she does on the dust jacket of *Lo scialle andaluso* (Turin: Einaudi, 1963), the author speaks explicitly of how autobiography is often at the center of writing (her writing?): "As much as he may think that he is inventing, every narrator, even in the maximum objectivity, is always merely writing his autobiography" (my translation).

15. From the poem "Avventura," *Alibi*, p. 51.

16. The poem "Sheherazade" states: "It is not my merit, but the heaven's/that made me fantastic." This verse clearly means that it is a matter of fate that she is so fanciful.

17. The poem appears in translation in *House of Liars*. The original poem in *Alibi*, however, specifically uses the word "*finzione*," which means *fiction* and not *illusion*. The image of the phoenix reappears in "Avventura," where the poet states: "Lungo e incerto il viaggio fino al nido/di questa *civetta-fenice*" (long and uncertain the journey to the nest/of this *coquettish-phoenix*) (*Alibi*, p. 52; my italics).

18. This comment also sheds light on the author's choice of the opening epithet for *Arturo's Island*, which is a line from Umberto Saba: "If in him I see myself, I am content." In the interview, Morante significantly says that she wished to be a boy and not a man. Her novels certainly attest to this wish.

19. Her anarchism is clearly manifested in *Il mondo salvato dai ragazzini* (Turin: Einaudi, 1968), especially through the carefree character Pazzariello. Just as *La storia* should not be seen as an anachronistic neorealistic work, *Il mondo* should not be considered Morante's contribution to the experimental literary wave of the late 1960s. For a stimulating account of *Il mondo salvato dai ragazzini*, see Venturi's *Elsa Morante*, pp. 87–105.

According to Sgorlon, Elsa Morante's very nature precludes her from writing a sociopolitically involved literature: "Morante is a very subjective and narcissist writer who is too instinctively bound to her own story to be classified amongst writers who are motivated primarily by the need to underscore the basic structures of a civilization" (Sgorlon, *Invito*, p. 26; my translation). Moreover, in *Aracoeli*, Morante clearly reiterates this notion through Manuele's statement: "My nature rejects politics and history" (134).

20. Referring specifically to *Menzogna e sortilegio*, Michael Caesar states: "The act of narration itself is posited as a liberation from the ghosts and traumas of childhood, a passage into adulthood, achieved by seeing the other adults' actions and fates in their true perspective . . . and refusing the childhood consolation of fantasies" (*Writers and Society in Contemporary Italy* [Warwickshire: Berg, 1986], p. 218).

21. Pasolini's review appears in two parts in *Paragone*, (Oct. 1968, pp. 120–26 and April 1969,

136–42). The expression "*nonna-bambina*" is repeated three times as Pasolini, a close friend of the author, also makes interesting biographical references to Morante's myopic blue eyes, to her anarchist views, and to her self-confinement in her apartment in Via dell'Oca.

22. Morante, *History: A Novel,* trans. William Weaver (New York: Avon Bard Books, 1979).

23. Morante perhaps gives readers the first self-revealing portrait of herself in the description of Elisa: "This awkward creature called Elisa can seem an old maid one moment and an immature child the next, but everything about her person suggests timidity, loneliness and proud chastity" (*House of Liars,* p. 4).

24. Sgorlon feels that Bontempelli's "magic realism" is at the foundation of Morante's magiclike ambience. See *Invito,* p. 19.

25. I am grateful to Eugenio Ragni for providing a copy of this short story, which is not easily available. See his excellent monographic article "Elsa Morante," in *Il Novecento* (Milan: Lucarini, 1980), pp. 767–81.

26. This type of relationship is a central (autobiographical?) Morantean motif that re-emerges throughout her work in variations of daughter and father or son and mother.

27. The author's cinematographic techniques and extensive use of flashbacks can be noticed in most of her narratives and especially in *Aracoeli.* In her early works, Morante used camera techniques by focusing in and out of characters and places, while switching back and forth between present and past. In his analysis of *Menzogna e sortilegio,* Angelo Pupino was among the first critics to mention this Morantean art of treating time; see his *Struttura e stile della narrativa di Elsa Morante* (Ravenna: Longo, 1968).

28. The story "La nonna," which focuses on tyrannical and possessive motherly love, was published shortly after in 1937.

29. Animal imagery, especially of cats, birds, and dogs, are numerous and frequent in Morante's work, and they provide abundant material for a separate study. Special attention should be given to imagery in which children and small animals are combined—as is the case in *La storia.*

30. Talismans and personal mementos, given to narrator-protagonists by fallen idols, are common in Morante's novels: in *Menzogna e sortilegio,* Edoardo gives a golden ring to Elisa; in *L'isola di Arturo,* Nunziatella gives Arturo her broken earring; and in *Aracoeli,* Manuele receives from his mother a Spanish talisman to cast off evil spells.

31. In his illuminating article on *L'isola di Arturo,* Giacomo De Benedetti has suggested some interesting interpretations of mythical allusions that other critics have in turn echoed. See "L'isola di Arturo," in *Saggi (1922–1966),* ed. Franco Contorbia (Milan: Mondadori, 1982), pp. 379–96.

32. The suspicion that these familiar themes in Morante's work may indeed derive directly from her personal life is confirmed by the author's brother, Marcello Morante, who provides readers with a biographical account of the writer in *Maledetta benedetta* (Milan: Garzanti, 1986). Critical readers will find it much more satisfying to interpret Elsa Morante's alibis in her work, however, than to read the cursory remarks made by Marcello Morante about Elsa, her mother, and her two fathers. The text, which literally violates the secrecy that Morante kept for so many years about her private life, can be helpful, however, in confirming that a great deal of autobiography lies beneath the alibis, especially detected in Cesira, Anna, Elisa, Teodoro, and Francesco in *Menzogna e sortilegio.*

33. See the closing verses of the poem "To Remo N." that appears as the preface and epigraph to the novel. The term *limbo* can be interpreted to mean both Procida and Arturo's childhood, that is, both a place and time in Arturo's life.

34. As in *Menzogna e sortilegio,* in this final novel there is also a series of idolizing relationships. Aracoeli idolizes her brother, Manuelito, her husband, Eugenio, and her baby girl, Incarnation; Eugenio's idols are Aracoeli and King Victor Emanuel; Aunt Ramona idolizes

Mussolini; Manuele idolizes Aracoeli and Manuelito; and the maid Zaira (a prejudiced social climber) has her idols: Eugenio and the crown prince.

35. In a most allegorical and fablelike fashion, the first of these transformations occurs in "La nonna" where, as Sgorlon has rightly noticed, a mother who had a morbid love for her son is transformed in appearance and characteristics into a witch who commits suicide and causes the death of her two grandchildren.

36. Morante does not verge toward pornography or toward a Moravia type of eroticism. According to the author, sex and eroticism are natural elements of life and, when necessary, should be certainly expressed. See: "Otto domande sull'erotismo in letteratura," *Nuovi Argomenti* 51–52 (1961): 46–49. Davide Segre's words in *La storia*, however, are an interesting commentary: he expresses his disillusionment with literature and admits that he may begin to write pornography.

37. Manuele claims that God created a lager (concentration camp) on the sixth day and then abandoned it to the people: "Grow and multiply in your beloved Lager, he said . . . as a farewell. And since then he has retired to rest, no longer bothering about his construction" (*Aracoeli*, p. 160). Needless to say, Morante has little admiration for fathers who abandon their families, and the irony of having Manuelito speaks of his father "as a deity" is understandable (173).

38. In his condemnation of the bourgeoisie, Manuele clearly echoes Davide Segre of *La storia*.

39. According to Arturo, the "Garden of Eden" consisted of the whole island and not just of the unkept garden in the courtyard of the Casa dei Guaglioni; Manuele's point of reference is the garden that he recalls at his childhood home in Monte Sacro and, in a metaphoric sense, also the period of his infant years.

40. A verse from the opening poem of *Aracoeli*.

41. Donatella Ravanello, *Scrittura e follia nei romanzi di Elsa Morante* (Venice: Marsilio, 1980), p. 44. Also see Luigina De Stefani, "Elsa Morante," *Belfagor* 26 (1971): 296.

42. Sgorlon, *Invito*,, p. 36.

43. Beginning with Edoardo's feelings toward his cousin Anna (*Menzogna e sortilegio*) and ending with circumstances in *Aracoeli*, Morante furnishes numerous examples of love and pity being confused.

44. See the original in *Menzogna e sortilegio* (Turin: Einaudi, 1982), p. 20. The published translation reads: "I became unloving through too much love" (*House of Liars*, p. 10).

45. It is easy to understand why an author who relived her childhood, adolescence, and youth over and over again through her writings, that is, who relived an age associated with dreams, beauty, and illusions, would consider old age—especially one accompanied by infirmity—as the real hell, where all illusions, fables, romance, and any other means of escaping reality come to an end. In her last two years, Morante must have felt that she had become much too similar to the image of her *nonna* (the familiar grandmother) often depicted in a chair, alone, silent, and immobile.

46. Manuele's most explicit reference to his wish to return to his mother's womb can be seen in his desperate cry: "Mamita, help me. As mother cats do with their ill-born kittens, eat me again. Receive my deformity in your pitying abyss" (102).

47. This detail is confirmed by Marcello Morante in *Maledetta benedetta*. In all Morante's works, fathers are hardly ever around to love their children; when they do not abandon their families entirely, they make brief and/or occasional appearances at home.

48. Garboli, *La stanza separata*, p. 71.

49. Ravanello states that "Morante prefers to express everything through her work in which each individual can trace that which is of most interest" (*Scrittura*, p. 26). This way of reading further explains the lack of enthusiasm for Marcello Morante's *Maledetta benedetta*.

NATALIA GINZBURG

Natalia Levi Ginzburg was born in Palermo in 1916 but grew up in Northern Italy where her father taught at the University of Turin. At the age of seventeen, she published her first short stories in the journal *Solaria*. During World War II, Ginzburg became involved in anti-Fascist activities with such gifted intellectuals as Cesare Pavese, Carlo Levi, and Leone Ginzburg, whom she married in 1938. When she and her family were sent to a little village of the Abruzzi as political exiles, Ginzburg wrote a short essay, "Mio marito" (1941), and then completed her first work of fiction, *La strada che va in città* (1942). During this period, she also translated Proust's *Du côté de chez Swann,* a work that exerted a strong influence on her aesthetics. Because of her family's Jewish ethnicity, her husband was arrested in 1943. After much torture, he died in prison.

The publication of Natalia Ginzburg's first postwar novel, *Tutti i nostri ieri* (1952) initiated a long series of narrative prose works: *Valentino* (1951), *Sagittario* (1957), *Le voci della sera* (1961), *Le piccole virtù* (1962), and *Lessico famigliare* (1963). More recent novels include: *Caro Michele* (1973), *Famiglia* (1977), *La famiglia Manzoni* (1983), and *La città e la casa* (1985). Ginzburg has also earned a reputation as a successful playwright. Her comedy, *L'inserzione,* was awarded the Premio Internazionale Marzotto in 1967.

A Lexicon for Both Sexes: Natalia Ginzburg and the Family Saga

CORINNA DEL GRECO LOBNER

Natalia Levi Ginzburg is a writer who demands absolute honesty. Her rejection of literary commonplaces and her refusal to subordinate the reality of life to fictional truth compel the reader to take a serious look at daily rituals conceived and enacted in the name of family unity. Ginzburg's outlook hides a deep disenchantment with contemporary mores that affect the family and other human institutions. Her narrative and stylistic evolution reflects this attitude of disillusionment. Her position, especially noticeable in such recent fiction as *Caro Michele* and *Famiglia,* offers little hope for the future of the family. What saves members of this traditional institution from total destruction is a refreshing honesty that forbids useless hypocrisy. People must face their nakedness daily to remind themselves that "cover-ups" are more obscene than their bodies stripped of all illusions.

Ginzburg neither advocates new trends nor claims to represent feminist voices in literature. Her goal is simple enough: she wants authenticity at all costs and proposes to show young and old, white- and blue-collar workers, revolutionaries and reactionaries, "that men and women . . . are neither good nor bad, but comical and pitiable at the same time."[1] Ginzburg pointedly places herself outside current fads; she is a writer only doing her job. She makes this point in her essay, "Il mio mestiere" ("My Vocation"), where she states that writing is mainly a trade perfected through hard work and the appropriate use of language. She refers to Pascoli, Gozzano, D'Annunzio, Hugo, and Proust as examples of this literary discipline.[2]

The outstanding characteristic of her vast production, which ranges from short stories to novels, comedies, and essays, is the consistency of her candid self-appraisal. She sees herself as a writer fully conscious of her limitations rather than as a great artist. What really matters is her individuality: "I prefer to think that no one has ever been like me, as small as I may be, as much as I may be as a writer, a flea, or a mosquito. The important thing is to be convinced that writing is truly a vocation, a profession." The only risk is "the danger to cheat with words that do not exist within us, that we have fished outside us by chance, and that we shrewdly put together. . . . The danger is to become clever and cheat" (89). Ginzburg does not deceive; she remains devoid of artifice. Her choice of insects, a flea and a mosquito, points to the importance she attaches to words as individual trademarks. Under the big top where lions and tigers compete for attention, mosquitoes and fleas are modest performers; their persistence, however, keeps them around long after lions and tigers are back in their cages. According to Ginzburg, there are no *scrittori* (writers, masculine) or *scrittrici* (writers, feminine), but only individuals who work hard at their trade. By insisting on honesty, she eliminates gender as a distinctive feature in the craft of fiction. This choice represents no denial of her femininity, since she reaches this conclusion by scanning her own creative process with great care.

In "Il mio mestiere," she explains how she originally felt compelled to write like a man and how she consequently created characters who displayed physical deformities. "They had broken arms hanging from their necks in a black bandage, or they had sties in their eyes, or they stuttered, or scratched their rears while talking, or limped a little. It was always necessary for me to characterize them in some fashion" (82). She admits that her basic lack of creative resources prompted this grotesque portrayal of men. She simply failed to understand the function of language in shaping characters, as earlier in her career she had misinterpreted the use of words in poetry, a form she abandoned as soon as she exhausted her repertoire of rhymes.

At the age of seventeen, Ginzburg attempted to write short stories, convinced that caricature would add to the virility of her cardboard heroes. "Irony and malevolence . . . seemed to help me write like a man, because then I desired terribly to write like a man. I was horrified at the thought that people would discover I was a woman from the things I was writing. I made most of my characters male" (82). Eventually, however, Ginzburg realized that male and female were interwoven in the fabric of life so that neither could nor should command stylistic preferences. In "La condizione femminile" ("The Female Condition"), she explains that she no longer cared to write like a man and that individuals could only express themselves the way they were. "Starting from our personal feminine or masculine experiences, we should reach a type of writing that is not influenced by the sex of the author, a type of writing where it is possible to recognize, not men or women, but people." She indicates that good thinking is genderless but also clarifies that individual sexuality influences everything. "If we are women, the feminine mark of our temperament imprints itself in our actions and words." Nevertheless, the writer's final aim "is to reach a space where men and women can be indifferently recognized within us, and our personal physiognomy is forgotten."[3]

Ginzburg's refusal to empathize with either feminine or masculine roles becomes increasingly evident in her mature narrative, where women find no preferential treatment, and men are not purposely romanticized as a source of joy or sorrow to the opposite sex. Both are merely actors in an existential drama determined by their family ties, shared memories, self-ishnesses, and culpable stupidities—the last failures that Ginzburg exorcises with unfailing comic spirit, thereby avoiding melodramatic pitfalls. In "La condizione femminile," Ginzburg insists that feminism is born from "an inferiority complex." She rejects what she sees as the movement's philosophy that women "even if humiliated, are better than men." According to the writer, "women in reality are neither better nor worse than men. They are qualitatively equal" (22).

This equality between the sexes is expressed by an unpretentious, democratic language written for the most part as an intimate indirect discourse that allows male-female views to merge into a palimpsest of human foibles, ineptitude, apathy, quiet desperation, compassion, and humor. The complex stratification of the discourse leads her characters into meanders where they discover and quietly reject the passing of an institution that their ancestors defended with the same tenacity they reserved for the Bible: the family. The erosion of this institution moves Ginzburg to record nostalgically and ironically its structure, function, and imperiled survival. The disruption of the family becomes symptomatic of a mobile, consumer society, always looking for something that no longer exists. Ginzburg's low-key language, described by Italo Calvino as "always below the exigencies" of the emotional impact it conveys, reveals an earnest longing for simpler modes of diction.[4] Only a democratic language free from clichés will successfully portray the moral void of our times and infuse new life into linguistic structures cleansed, at last, from excessive rhetorical embellishment.[5]

Like most Italian writers who emerged from World War II, Ginzburg found neorealism to be a literary current that satisfied her personal sensitivity. Her texts consequently exclude scientific expressions, technical terms, psychoanalytical references, and elaborate literary allusions. She achieves "a monotonous cadence of the real" by freeing language from erudite connotations worn out by excessive use.[6] Once demystified and freed from stereotypes, words will again acquire their pristine innocence and gradually recuperate their meanings.

Ripetizione signica, the repetition of signs, becomes Ginzburg's distinctive device for gaining textual correspondences. This method enables her to achieve a rhythmic balance between the narrative, slowed by repetition, and the minimal evolution of characters. She confesses a distinct dislike for pronouns that distinguish male from female; if she uses them, she makes a conscious choice, such as the one she makes in her essay "Lui e Io" ("He and I"), where the *lui* in question represents her second husband, Gabriele Baldini.[7] Here *lui* stands in constant contrast with *io* and establishes a base for dissension and humor. "He is always warm, I am always cold. . . . He knows how to speak some languages well, I don't even speak one well. . . . He has a tremendous sense of direction, I have none. . . . He loves the theater, painting, and music. . . . I know nothing about music."[8]

Although women are only present by implication in Ginzburg's early fiction, "Mio marito" (My husband), a short story written in 1941, introduces a woman narrator who relates her physician husband's passion for Mariuccia, a peasant girl who dies in childbirth. This unexpected death precipitates the doctor's suicide. The narrator, an outsider who has remained extraneous to local culture, summons enough objectivity to tell the story with both detachment and compassion. "Mio marito" develops a characteristic that becomes central in Ginzburg's later fiction: the need for truth at all costs in personal relationships. The doctor honestly tells his wife why he was attracted to Mariuccia; she was different from all the women he had known before. She had been hungry, beaten, and forced to work in the hot sun; in short, she was everything his wife was not. In a moment of brutal sincerity, he adds: "Why should I care about you? . . . You resemble your mother, and the mother of my mother, and all the women who have lived in this house."[9] What emerges here is Ginzburg's interest in the role of social stratifications in tragedies. The implication is clear. Had the doctor married Mariuccia and refused to succumb to social pressures, he could have averted the tragedy.

In 1942, Ginzburg published her first novel, *La strada che va in città (The Road That Goes to the City)*. She used the pseudonym Alessandra Torninparte to avoid racial reprisals. The situation in this work is a reversal of "Mio marito." Delia, the provincial narrator, marries her seducer, a medical student from a well-to-do family. Delia then realizes that she is in love with Ninì, a factory worker who used to live in her parents' home. This discovery, however, occurs too late, since Ninì soon dies. Delia overcomes her grief and continues to live with fatalistic resignation. Her sister Azalea, who is married, unhappy, and adulterous, tries to console her and expresses a philosophical tenet shared by several of Ginzburg's characters: "Ninì or another is the same. What counts is to have someone because life for a woman, if she is alone, is too sad.[10]

Characters in this first novel are dissatisfied, restless, and far from likeable. Even Ninì, who reads books to Delia and takes time to explain their meaning, ends his existence "half rotten with *grappa*" (78). Delia proves to be a far from perfect mother. She finds her baby quite ugly and spends afternoons with Azalea flirting at the local café. "While walking, I looked around with an impertinent smile, like Azalea always did" (79). Delia's husband, Giulio, had tried to bribe her at one time to avoid marrying her but behaves as a model of tolerance after the wedding. He even defends his wife's daily sorties against the verbal assaults of his tyrannical mother. A subtle exchange of roles is already in progress. Giulio's agreeable disposition and Delia's growing indifference generate a peripety that offers irony and poetic justice the chance to exert a subtle influence on characters and situations, giving the novel a lifelike dimension. Ginzburg will eventually refine her narrative skills and allow characters to exchange emotional responses, modes of thinking, and even sexual attitudes in an incredible process of reciprocal behavior modification.

Tutti i nostri ieri (All Our Yesterdays), hailed by major critics as one of Italy's finest contributions to resistance literature, benefits from Ginzburg's historical perspective and distancing irony—qualities often missing in this type of genre. The novel opens with a close-up of a portrait of a mother, which hangs on the wall of a dining room—Italy's shrine of family nourishment and quarrels. A rapid succession of births—Ippolito, Concettina, Giustino, and Anna—causes a heart problem that eventually brings about the mother's death. The father, a fiercely antifascist Jewish lawyer, charges his wife's former companion, Signora Maria, with the care of the family. This surrogate parent finds solace in her new duties by remembering vacations spent in luxury hotels and leisurely rides in open carriages. Her memories enable her to endure her demotion from *dama di compagnia* to substitute mother in a household where work increases as revenues decrease. The blame for the deteriorating family fortune is largely ascribed to the father, who has renounced his lucrative profession to dedicate his time to writing a book.

Tutti i nostri ieri gives equal weight to the sexes in its twofold structure: the first part is narrated mainly from the daughter Anna's point of view, while the second is seen largely through the eyes of her husband, Cenzo Rena. His voice ultimately gives way to the murmur of survivors fading in the distance, as if foretelling the end of an era. The intricate relationships exposed in the novel are greatly enriched by Ginzburg's use of indirect discourse, a stylistic device that often enables her to satirize bourgeois attempts to camouflage social taboos with euphemisms. Looking for the neighbors' dog, Anna remembers that it "was not at home because they had sent him with some friends to get married."[11] She had obviously received this explanation from an adult eager to keep her innocence intact.

Anna's romance with Giuma, a neighbor boy, parallels the movement of the narrative rhythm. Ginzburg allows objects to build an effective contrast between Anna's naive admiration for him and his complacent nonchalance. "He took her to the movies. . . . Or they wandered in the city; they entered bookstores and looked over magazines and art books. Giuma went wild over reproductions of painting where there were only triangles and tiny circles." Their excursions to the city usually took them to a park bench where they shared roasted chestnuts and read poems by Montale. Anna eventually became accustomed to Giuma's unusual tastes and would sit "quietly with her hands folded, with chestnut peels trapped in the wool of her coat" (98). Tiny circles in paintings, Montale's poems, and chestnut peels are the *ripetizione signica* that will lead to Anna's mental reconstruction of her short-lived happiness. The garden bench, however, will also be associated with Anna's brother Ippolito, who commits suicide in the park as a hopeless gesture of rebellion against the dictatorship.

With unflinching realism, Ginzburg stresses the impartiality of war that plays no favorites among men, women, and children. Signora Maria dies during an American raid while trying to save the sheets and towels that she had religiously packed in a suitcase. Anna, a widow, returns to her hometown, where she is reunited with her family and her friends across the street. Life resumes where it left off, but monotony and dissatisfaction inevitably set in. Giustino, who was known as the notorious "Balestra" during his partisan days, longs to go back to the mountains to fight the Germans and blow up trains; but "there were no more trains to blow up, and he had to finish his university studies and find a job to make ends meet" (317). Even Anna longs for the excitement of days gone by. Giuma, the father of Anna's child, feels guilty for having spent the war in Switzerland, but a psychiatrist assures him that not all Italians were meant to be partisans and risk their lives. "He was supposed to wait quietly to go back to Italy after the war and turn the soap factory into something exceptional" (319). Giuma's American wife takes the suggestion seriously and sets out to transform the soap factory into a model day-care center, planning to make southern Italy the next target for her social reforms. Among broken dreams, quietly nourished regrets, and Marxist reformers succumbing to bourgeois ambitions, the only remaining source of hope is the friendship that makes Anna and Giustino glad to be together "to think of those who were dead, and about the long war, and the sorrow and the noise and the long difficult life that was facing them now, full of all things they did not know how to do" (321).

The somber, ironic tone of *Tutti i nostri ieri* reappears in *Le voci della sera* (Voices in the Evening), the story of Elsa, another introspective narrator, who observes with voyeuristic resignation the demise of traditional family values. The uneventful plot relates the protagonist's love affair with Tommasino De Francisci whose family owns the local textile mill; each week they have a rendezvous in a nearby town. This disregard for bourgeois sexual conventions seems to give Tommasino a sense of freedom; he realizes, however, Elsa's unexpressed desire for a more stable relationship. Thus, he conforms to the expected code of behavior and asks for her hand. When the engagement becomes official, the young girl's mother sweeps them into a shopping extravaganza, and the couple loses the intimacy they had known during their secret encounters. Elsa understands the futility of ratifying a union that no longer has meaning, breaks the engagement, and quietly returns to her lonely existence.

Elsa's love affair evokes an uninterrupted flow of memories that parallels and enriches the narrative with the unhappy experiences of Tommasino's brothers and sisters, their futile search for happiness, and their emotional isolation. The incongruous union between socialism and capitalism that had emerged in *Tutti i nostri ieri* again occurs when Purillo, a Fascist protégé of the old socialist De Francisci, increases the productivity of the textile mill and makes it a model in the postwar *miracolo economico*. The irony becomes more eivdent when Purillo marries De Francisci's daughter, Rafaella, who had been a dedicated partisan during the Resistance. Ginzburg does not use the incident as a symbol of political reconciliation but rather as an additional example of euphoric ideological commitments that often conceal unfulfilled romantic desires. Even here, masculine and feminine desires hardly differ. While accusing Elsa of helpless romanticism, Tommasino reveals his own emotional inclinations by admitting that their liaison would have prospered under different skies. "I wish I had found you in Montreal or somewhere else; if we could only have met and got married! We would have felt so free, so light, without these houses, these hills, these mountains! I would have been as free as a bird!"[12]

The seasonal pattern of *Le voci della sera* marks the passing of time and determines a Proustian cycle of reminiscences. Ginzburg's mastery of speech enables her to employ techniques where proper names are abjured in favor of dramatis personae. She often introduces her characters with the verb *dire* (to say) and varies the tenses to allow for timeless recollections. *Dice* (he or she says), *disse* (he or she said), and *diceva* (he or she was saying) are followed by dashes as if to force the attention of the reader toward voices suspended into a typographical time sequence and recaptured through the magic of print. Ginzburg uses gaps in communication to allow a simultaneous choral-crossing of narrative space, thus disrupting chronology and all expectations of logical sequence. The result of this unruly melee is real, paradoxical, and often hilarious. Caught by the wiles of Babel, Ginzburg's characters, who are usually concerned with the feelings of others, invariably clash with the people whom they try to please. Italo Calvino comments that many hues can be detected in Ginzburg's multifarious expressions and in the way she writes plain, elementary sentences that are nevertheless capable of sustaining "a rapport of affection, surprise, irony, the sense of her own and others' limitations, the reiteration of gestures, hours, the flow of life, happiness possible at any moment, gone forever the next."[13]

The critical and popular success of *Le voci della sera* may have encouraged Ginzburg, who had already professed "a sacred horror of self-revelation," to publish *Lessico famigliare (Family Sayings),* a biographical novel so explicit that not even names have changed. In the preface to *Cinque romanzi brevi* (Five short novels), the writer explains that *Lessico famigliare* may not be her best book but that it is the only one written with a feeling of absolute freedom. For the first time in her writing career, she has dismissed the presence of chance—a condition that has always influenced her creative efforts. "Chance has left me completely. Thus I arrived at pure memory: I arrived there stealthily, like a wolf taking side roads, telling myself that the springs of memory were those from which I should never drink, the only place in the world where I should refuse to go." In the same introduction, Ginzburg clarifies her use of *per caso* (by chance) and *non per caso* (not by chance). She indicates that while the former consists of communication based exclusively on observation and invention, the latter implies writing that expresses pure love for what one knows and feels. "Memory is loving and never casual. It plants its roots in our lives, and, therefore, its choice is . . . always passionate and commanding."[14]

Lessico famigliare functions as a stylistic catalyst between the two modes of *per caso* and *non per caso*. It deals with "passionate and commanding" family memories, cleverly arranged into linguistic patterns structured to produce the desired effect. Ginzburg conveys voices from the family group through codes that isolate the family lexicon from conventional speech and evoke with delicious immediacy past memories awaiting rediscovery. In her apologia of evocation, the writer highlights her criterion.

> We are five children. We live in different cities. Some of us live in foreign lands, and we don't correspond very often. When we meet again, we can be indifferent and absent-minded with each other. All we need, however, is a word, a phrase, one of those very old phrases heard and repeated endless times, in . . . our . . . childhood. . . . One of those phrases . . . would have us know each other . . . in the darkness of a cave or among millions of people.[15]

Ginzburg proceeds to compare the jargon of her family to a foreign language, a "dictionary of our days gone by," sufficient in itself to recall memories and to preserve them untainted from the "corrosion of time" (33). This radical upgrading of the family's lexicon plays a fundamental role in exorcising and democratizing language. Nonsensical quotations greeted with jubilant approval by family members substitute "in" family sayings for standard literary formulas.

The Levi family (Ginzburg's birth name) was especially susceptible to linguistic mix-ups. Ginzburg's father was a native of Trieste, a city where Italian steeps in a caldron spiced with German, French, Slavic, Venetian, Friulian, and dialects unknown even to glottologists. Although the problem is peripheral to Professor Levi, who was not a literary man, Natalia kept the playful Triestine habit of making fun of this linguistic hodgepodge. Her ears, attuned to her father's dialectical peculiarities—*sbrodighezze* for *porcherie* (refusals), *potacci* for *pasticci* (mess), *babe* for *chiaccherone* (gossips), and so on—retained the habit of using unusual speech patterns to shape repetitive structures. Eventually, these quintessential bits of family locution become familiar enough to the reader to invite an immediate recognition of individuals and situations. The network of recalls includes the reminiscences of Lidia, Natalia's mother, who regaled the family with musical extravaganzas presented with great success in the prep school she attended in her youth. An opera she composed was inspired by the romantic yearnings of a Spanish gentleman, Don Carlos Tadrid, whose name had the good fortune of rhyming with Madrid.

These illustrious precedents could not go unheeded. Natalia soon responded with "Palermino, Palermino / Sei più bello di Torino" (Little Palermo, Little Palermo / You are more beautiful than Torino); she quickly followed with a homage to an Alpine peak: "Viva la Grivola / Se mai si scivola" (To Grivola long life / Be careful or you slide). Although Natalia's talent was awarded with family accolades, it was not considered as out-standing as that of Alberto, her ten-year-old brother, who wrote poems considered "pure fruit of poetic invention."

La vecchia zitella
Senza mammella
Ha fatto un bambino
Tanto carino (51)

(The spinster whose chest
is missing one breast
Has mothered a child
So very nice)

Since Ginzburg's lexicon is a code used by all members of the family, it becomes a genderless indicator of collective experiences distinguished by semantic association. Words deeply rooted in family tradition, however, demand constant revision; once becoming infused with unusual meanings, they no longer respond to usual connotations. *Il Demente* (The Insane), for instance, was the name given to a family relative, a brilliant psychiatrist who owned a mental clinic near Florence. Although a quick disassociation between signified and signifiers cancels the meaning imposed by the switch (doctor-mental hospital-patient), a lengthy exposure to such a method of thinking can become a *forma mentis* and forcibly trains attention on the specific meaning of words or, more exactly, on their questionable efficacy to express meaning in the context of rapidly evolving connotations. The drama of words acting as signs in a void coincides with the drama of the family, an institution increasingly functioning in a vacuum, and of sexual roles equally losing distinctive characteristics in a changing society. What emerges is the need for a chronicler who records memories of what the family nucleus used to be in a past still close enough to remember. Thus, toward the conclusion of *Lessico famigliare,* Ginzburg understands that a narrator must meet certain requirements in order to keep the vocation honest. "It was necessary to choose the words again, to scrutinize them to see if they were false or true, if they had or had not roots within us, or if they had only the ephemeral roots of common illusion" (200). To practice their calling with seriousness and dedication, writers must forget the "general intoxication" of the war and commit themselves to discipline and hard work.

Caro Michele (No Way) unites men and women in a hopeless pilgrimage where life's ultimate goal becomes the avoidance of suffering. Apathy and resignation have struck full force, destroying illusions and voiding potential acts of redemption. Mara, an unwed mother in the story, summarizes this scrupulous honesty and stoicism in her note to Michele, a mediocre painter and part-time revolutionary: "The important thing is to keep walking and to distance ourselves from the things that make us cry."[16] There is plenty to cry about. Mara's unhappy existence takes her from apartments loaned by acquaintances whom she hardly knows to the penthouse of her lover, a wealthy editor she calls "The Pelican"; living this peripatetic life, she always drags along a yellow plastic suitcase where her baby sleeps. Mara and the child are often mentioned in the intense epistolary exchange that links Michele, who is in England for possible political reasons, to family and friends. Michele remains unsure of his political allegiance. "I keep not being Communist, I keep on being nothing. It seems impossible that I left for political reasons. . . . I would not find it easy to say why I left" (102). Nor, for that matter, would characters in the novel find it easy to say why they do anything they do. Men and women in the novel are actually too amoral to be judgmental. A strong awareness of their limitations sustains their loneliness as they watch their dreams disintegrate bit by bit without their experiencing any hope of ever being happy.

Caro Michele alternates direct conversation, indirect discourse—the technique effectively fashioned in *Tutti i nostri ieri*—and an extensive exchange of correspondence. With the exception of Adriana, whose residential stability symbolizes a farewell to the family home, characters move from place to place in a subconscious quest for values that the older generation tries to preserve and the younger simply does not know. Grammar, however, serves as a clue to the attentive vigilance behind the scenes. Tenses focus on the time element and forecast chilling prophecies of death. Speaking of her previous meetings with her now deceased husband at a Roman café, Adriana writes: "You, the children, knew that we used to meet there in the afternoons but did not know that his damnable cousin advised us to do so. I notice that I used the past descriptive but in truth I think your father is very ill and that we will never meet again at the Caffè Canova the first Thursday of each month" (6). Tenses monitor life. It is rare for Ginzburg to use the future but she does so here in a negative sense. Past tenses better express the gentle inertia of people who drift along and who remain unwilling or unable to find a way out of their present stalemate.

In *Caro Michele,* Ginzburg emphasizes repetition in speech patterns along with comical quid pro quos that tie personal memories to unrelated data. Mara's peculiar system of associations causes the title of a book written by Adriana's sister-in-law Matilde to undergo unexpected protean changes. She first transforms the original *Polenta e veleno* (Cornmush and poison) into *Polenta e vino (Polenta and wine)* and then into *Polenta e castagne* (Polenta and chestnuts).[17]

Repetitive patterns effectively blur the narrative and give readers a sense of déjà vu. The conversation about Mara between Ada and her former husband, Osvaldo, illustrates this structure.

> —She seems completely stupid—said Ada.
> —Not completely—said Osvaldo.
> —Yes. Completely—said Ada.
> —She is not stupid. She is dumb—said Osvaldo.
> —I don't grasp the difference—said Ada. (63)

Osvaldo and Mara later discuss Ada.

> —I find her immensely stupid—said Mara.
> —You are wrong—said Osvaldo.
> —Immensely—said Mara.
> —She has rare moments of acumen and insight. She is limited, that is true. However, she is my wife, and I beg you to stop calling her stupid. (79)

This circular mode of reciprocal evaluation generates a leveling influence on the characters' social position, sexual roles, financial circumstances, and family status. Ada is wealthy, socially prominent, and hyperactive; Mara is poor, fatalistic, and a transient. Linguistic impartiality, however, links them in an ironic rapprochement of which they are completely unaware.

Objects contribute a telling counterpoint to the narrative and become essential to the evolution of the story. The telephone, for instance, the only means of communication that would have allowed Adriana to hear Michele's voice in the privacy of her home, is installed only after Michele's death. This perfect scheduling suggests the rejection of fictional time in favor of an organic sequence that develops life rather than imitates it and stops when it comes to an end. Animal imagery also intercepts human metaphors in a gradual reversal of Aristotelian categories. Lower forms of life slowly replace things in the lives of humans or people themselves, once considered reasonable creatures but no longer worthy of such distinction; these zoological connections produce surrealistic effects. Angelica's daughter is "a green lizard, five years old with a blue shirt and red tights" (37); Mara, whose last name, Castorelli, is a diminutive for the word *castoro* (beaver), keeps building damns to shelter herself and the child she drags along in a plastic suitcase. Traveling bags serve all purposes: they transport babies, dirty clothes, crumbled cookies, and terrorist guns. Once a symbol of elegant travel and plush hotels, as they were for Signora Maria in *Tutti i nostri ieri,* they have now become the plastic cradle of new generations.

As the family disintegrates, so does its inner sanctum, the home. Michele only paints crumbling houses with owls watching over the ruins. Shortly before Michele dies, his father buys an ancient tower on the Tyrrhenian sea, planning to refurbish it and give it to his son. However, it is "The Pelican" who eventually buys the tower and never sees it; he also becomes ill and retires to his country villa. Although Ginzburg denies Freudian themes, the crumbling tower symbolizes emasculation and reinforces a notable switch in conventional male-female roles. Women become the key to bourgeois affluence. Adriana generously bestows money and gifts on her children; although her artist husband lives well enough, an indefinite undercurrent identifies his decline in health with his decreasing fortunes. Ada separates from Osvaldo, becomes active in social programs, and acquires a voice in the editorial decisions of "The Pelican." Although Osvaldo's preference for homosexual relationships remains a whisper throughout the novel, it receives its confirmation at the end. Ginzburg portrays this character's inclinations as the fragile manifestation of gentle, feminine qualities rather than as the manifestation of Ada's overpowering presence.[18] Confusion in sexual roles affects adult choices. Michele, who always wanted to be a woman in his childhood games, does housework while his wife works outside the house. His domesticity keeps them together until her alcoholism destroys the marriage. As Cesare Garboli writes in his introduction, *Caro Michele* is an orphaned novel in every sense: "Life resembles the continuous bleeding and irreparable loss of the joy of living. At the same time, the novel is a requiem to virility. . . . It is a novel without men, or where men are too immature, or too exhausted to survive" (ix).

In her more recent fiction, Ginzburg takes an old Italian proverb—*dimmi con chi vai e ti dirò chi sei* (Tell me who your friends are, and I'll tell you who you are)—and amends it to read: "Tell me what things you live with, and I'll tell you who you are." This transposition is especially true in *Famiglia,* where objects underscore the futile existence of both sexes and pronounce a silent indictment of contemporary mores. This novel tells the story of Carmine, a mediocre architect of humble origin but considerable income; he marries the lovely and insipid Ninetta, who is gifted with a smile "offered like a precious jewel."[19] They have a little boy Dodò, whose suppers of farina, milk, and ice cream make him a candidate for obesity. Before marrying Ninetta, Carmine almost marries Ivana, mother of a baby who dies right after birth. The couple soon tire of each other, and Ivana leaves for England to study architecture. There she meets a student by whom she becomes pregnant, "although not in love" (11), because she wants a child. The young man is unaware of the child's conception or birth.

The story, entirely narrated in indirect discourse, starts on a Sunday afternoon when Carmine and Ivana take their children, Dodò and Angelica, to the movies. They see the movie *Baratro* (Abyss), an ironical prophecy of the cancer about to strike Carmine. The novel, however, is not as concerned with the protagonist's illness as with relationships between the two sexes and the growing threat posed by selfish indifference. Carmine next meets the unhappy and restless Olga, who becomes one more of the ubiquitous unwed mothers who populate Ginzburg's fiction. Tired of Carmine's moralistic tirades about the child she does not want to keep, Olga leaves Carmine to his inevitable end.

Carmine's infidelity chronologically follows Ninetta's. Since both characters are equally adulterous, they also remain immune to reciprocal hostility and they fear to upset their unhappy but stable status quo. Ninetta makes arrangements for Carmine to vacate the bedroom for her greater comfort rather than as a personal reprisal. All along, Ninetta's mother speaks of an urgent need "to reconstruct the marriage" (44), a reductionist expression totally unsuited to the complex ramifications of human emotions.

Impassive and ubiquitous objects rule the household with increasing power. Ninetta and Carmine's favorite color red appears lavishly splashed on tapestries, tablecloths, and even on the butler's jacket. The first time Ivana confronts the turgid display, she mentally connects it with the last scene of *Rosemary's Baby* "when nothing is left that is not the color of blood" (16). Furniture covered with shrouds during Ninetta's frequent absences appears throughout the house without specific order; in like manner, the black credenza full of dishes remains in the room where Carmine dies, a funeral stele to the worthy tradition of family dining. Decorative objects include a lamp "of opaque white paper, extremely long" hanging from the ceiling of the dining room and dubbed "contraceptive" by Ivana, the story's caustic commentator. This item stirs the curiosity of Matteo Tramonti who confirms Ivana's impressions in his *r*-less jargon. "E pvopvio un pvesevativo" (It really is a contraceptive) (46).

Even more unsettling is Ginzburg's surrealistic framing of Carmine's somber, old-fashioned parents seated at "the large crystal dining room table under the contraceptive swinging back and forth, placing small bits of bread in their mouths, quietly embarrassed" (52–53). Their emotional discomfort obviously stems not from the lamp—contraceptives are out of their frame of reference—but from their being helpless witnesses to a marriage that quickly deteriorates before their uncomprehending, peasant eyes. Objects eventually become the only link to a given moment in time. Thus, Carmine associates the end of his affair with Olga to a sweater tied over her shoulders. The incident survives in his memory as "the moment of the sweater," when his relationship seemed to become a "a marginal circumstance of a frivolous nature, a useless, irrelevant detail" (49).

In *Famiglia,* objects eventually become mute witnesses to human insensitivity. Words become a dead end, suspended on a canvas where retroactive associations stop cold at the sight of sweaters, lamps, farina, red chairs, or dishes solidly gloved in their semantic reality. While dying, Carmine remembers himself as a child in his mother's arms at the railroad station; under the evening's torrential rain, people carry umbrellas and mud rushes between the flooded rails. His stubbornly selective memory retains "by chance, a small heap of minimal impressions, touching but slight . . . the mud, umbrellas, people, the night" (69). These "minimal impressions," as well as the black fringe of Ninetta's hair pressed against the window, function as *ripetizione signica* that accompany Carmine into eternity. Ninetta hardly hears the dying man's explanation: "Separations should be soft spoken, tranquil, free from rancor" (68). Both characters know too well that emotional reactions are no longer in order. The family, stripped of its traditional role and disbanded by the apathy of its members, has lost all credibility. What remains is a feeling of honesty and the willingness to tolerate reciprocal weakness.

In her essay "I rapporti umani" ("Human Relationships"), Ginzburg summarizes the need for a new evaluation of interaction between people. "Human relationships must be rediscovered and invented anew each day. We must always remember that every encounter with each other is a human action and as such is either good or evil, truth or lie, charity or sin."[20] Faithful to her commitment to expose false pretenses in human behavior, Ginzburg proceeds to strip superfluous frills from language and, in so doing, gives it an authenticity that transcends traditional patterns of expression and makes her lexicon a voice for both sexes. At last, man and woman have reached the point where they are, in Ginzburg's own words, "qualitatively equal."

NOTES

1. Natalia Ginzburg, "Il mio mestiere," in her *Le piccole virtù* (1962; reprint, Turin: Einaudi, 1982), p. 88. Subsequent quotations from this edition will be indicated in the text by page numbers within parentheses. Although most texts by Ginzburg are available in English, I used

my own translation to highlight, whenever possible, the unique idiomatic flavor of Ginzburg's lexicon.

2. In 1942, Ginzburg translated Proust's *Swann's Way* from French into Italian for the Casa Editrice Einaudi.

3. Natalia Ginzburg, "La condizione femminile," in Luciana Marchionne Picchione, *Natalia Ginzburg* (1967; reprint, Florence: Il Castoro, La Nuova Italia, 1978), p. 22. Subsequent quotations from this essay will be indicated in the text by page numbers within parentheses.

4. Italo Calvino, "Natalia Ginzburg e la possibilità del romanzo borghese," *L'Europa Letteraria* 31 (June–Aug. 1961): 13.

5. Ginzburg's vision, in a sense, represents Strindberg's technique of fragmentation, as he explains it in his 1888 Preface to *Miss Julie:* "My characters are conglomerations of past and present stages of humanity, rags and tatters of fine clothing, patched together as is the human soul" (see Malcolm Bradbury and James McFarlane, eds., *Modernism* [New York: Penguin, 1987], p. 100.

6. In *Natalia Ginzburg,* Picchione remarks: "The scarce variety of punctuation used by Ginzburg does not reveal the prosodic intonation of the discourse; such a method underscores the monotonous cadence of the real" (40).

7. Goffredo Parise writes: "Ginzburg discovers that she dislikes not only tenses in verbs, but also personal pronouns. . . . Each word brings out in her . . . a sensation of enmity and makes clouds of dust rise. To lie still in that dust—she finds—is the only alternative left to humanity." Parise is quoted by Picchione in *Natalia Ginzburg,* p. 9.

8. Ginzburg, "Lui e Io," in *Le piccole virtù,* p. 53.

9. Ginzburg's "Mio marito," as quoted in Picchione, *Natalia Ginzburg,* p. 27.

10. Natalia Ginzburg, *La strada che va in città* (1942; reprint, Turin: Einaudi, 1982), p. 78. Subsequent quotations from this edition will be indicated by page numbers within parentheses.

11. Natalia Ginzburg, *Tutti i nostri ieri* (1952; reprint, Turin: Einaudi, 1975), p. 29. Subsequent quotations from this edition will be indicated by page numbers within parentheses.

12. Natalia Ginzburg, *Le voci della sera* (1961; reprint, Turin: Einaudi, 1984), p. 121.

13. Calvino, "Natalia Ginzburg," p. 13.

14. Natalia Ginzburg, introduction to *Cinque romanzi brevi,* quoted in Picchione, *Natalia Ginzburg,* pp. 65, 66.

15. Natalia Ginzburg, *Lessico famigliare* (1963; reprint, Turin: Einaudi, 1972), p. 33. Subsequent quotations from this edition will be indicated by page numbers within parentheses.

16. Natalia Ginzburg, *Caro Michele* (1973; reprint, Turin: Einaudi, 1985), p. 163. Subsequent quotations from this edition will be indicated by page numbers within parentheses.

17. *Polenta e vino* (Cornmush and wine) is a jesting reference to Ignazio Silone's anti-Fascist novel, *Vino e pane (Wine and Bread),* published in 1955.

18. Ginzburg had already confronted homosexuality in her previous novel, *Valentino,* where she uses the inversion of male-female roles as proof of weakening boundaries between the sexes. Commenting on the character Valentino, Picchione writes: "Valentino, physically attractive, . . . kept by his wife and not eager to work, incorporates attributes traditionally associated with the female stereotype, the stereotype of beauty absorbed in an empty and narcissistic contemplation of self" (*Natalia Ginzburg,* p. 37).

19. Natalia Ginzburg, *Famiglia* (Turin: Einaudi, 1977), p. 8. Subsequent quotations from this edition will be indicated by page numbers in parentheses.

20. Ginzburg, "I rapporti umani," in *Le piccole virtù,* p. 120.

ANNA BANTI

Anna Banti (the pseudonym of Lucia Lopresti) was born in Florence of a southern Italian family in 1895. After majoring in art history at the University of Rome, she married her teacher Roberto Longhi, who was already well known in Italy as an art critic. She began her literary career with *Itinerario di Paolina* (1937) and followed with *Il coraggio delle donne* (1940), *Settelune* (1941), and *Le monache cantano* (1942). Her most famous novel, *Artemisia,* was published in 1947. Her prodigious activity continued throughout the 1950s with the publication of *Le donne muoiono* (1951), *Il bastardo* (1953), *Allarme sul lago* (1954), and *La monaca di Shangai* (1957). She continued her work into the 1960s and 1970s, writing *Corte Savella* (1960), *La casa piccola* (1961), *Le mosche d'oro* (1962), *Campi Elisi* (1963), *Noi credevamo* (1967), *Due storie* (1969), *Je vous écris d'un pays lointain* (1971), *La camicia bruciata* (1973), and *Da un paese vicino* (1975). The autobiographical *Un grido lacerante* appeared in 1981 and won the Antonio Feltrinelli prize from the Academy of the Lincei. In addition to her reputation as a prolific novelist, she is recognized as a critic of literature, cinema, and art. After her husband's death in 1970, she took over his directorship of the art review *Paragone*. She died in September 1985.

History, Art, and Fiction in
Anna Banti's *Artemisia*

DEBORAH HELLER

When Anna Banti died in Ronchi di Massa at the age of ninety on 2 September 1985, she was remembered and honored above all as the author of *Artemisia*. "Addio, Artemisia" ran the headline in *La Nazione,* the daily paper of Banti's native Florence. To be sure, Anna Banti—the literary pseudonym of Lucia Longhi Lopresti—had written other novels, as well as short stories, art criticism, and drama. The recipient of various prestigious literary awards, she was also for many years the editor of *Paragone,* the review founded by her husband, the art historian Roberto Longhi, and was president of the Foundation for the Study of Art History "Roberto Longhi" (Fondazione di Studi di Storia dell'Arte "Roberto Longhi"). It was Banti's fictionalized biography of the real seventeenth-century painter Artemisia Gentileschi, however, that established her literary reputation and remained her most enduring achievement. In *Artemisia,* Anna Banti brought to life and celebrated this "woman painter of excellent abilities, one of the few whom history remembers." Artemisia Gentileschi was, moreover, as Banti tells us in her introduction, "one of the first women to uphold through words and achievement the right to fulfilling work and spiritual equality between the two sexes."[1]

Banti's construction of the painter's life and character is interwoven with her account of the novel's genesis. The work begins with the author-narrator in the Boboli Gardens, seeking refuge from the exploding mines and machine-gun fire accompanying the German retreat from Florence in August 1944. In the midst of the disasters of war, her imagination conjures up Artemisia as a living presence who is eager both to console and to be consoled. "Don't cry"—the first words of the novel, spoken by the halluci-nated protagonist to the author-narrator, set the tone for the narrative that is to follow, which is marked, structurally, by a dynamic interchange be-tween protagonist and author-narrator and, thematically, by the rejection of despair.

In the opening scene, the author-narrator's grief at the violent destruction of her city is subsumed within the deeper pain of a more immediate, personal loss: that of an almost completed manuscript, entitled "Artemisia," destroyed, as Banti states in her preface, by the events of a war "which, unfortunately, are not at all exceptional" (3). "Beneath the rubble of my house," she laments, "I have lost Artemisia, my companion of three centuries ago" (6). However, the author-narrator's anguish quickly merges with that of her suddenly hallucinated companion, who now becomes more real to her than the historically reconstructed figure buried with her manuscript. Together, they begin to create anew the life whose retelling becomes a shared, almost compulsive, need. From the outset, then, the narrative presents itself as something other than a simple documentary reconstruction, something at once more personal, more imaginative, and more arbitrary. In various instances, Banti will deliberately alter known facts about the life of the historical Artemisia Gentileschi. Moreover, throughout the narrative she invents what no historian can ever know—a complex, consistent, and rich inner life for her protagonist—thereby conferring a sense of reality on Artemisia's imagined moment-to-moment thoughts, motives, and actions as she interacts with her world.

This, of course, is the very stuff of fiction. But while Banti invents the psychology and many details of her character's private experiences, she also incorporates certain salient public facts of the real Artemisia Gentileschi's life into the narrative, thereby unmistakably tying the protagonist to her origins in the world of history. The writer follows historical records that chronicle Artemisia's birth and childhood in Rome, her rape at an early age, the all-too-public rape trial at which she was tortured as her virtue was publicly placed under attack, her marriage to Antonio Stiattesi, her subsequent separation from her husband, an interval of work as a painter in Florence, her role in running an academy of painting in Naples, and her trip alone to join her father, the painter Orazio Gentileschi, at the English court in 1638 or 1639. Above all, Banti calls attention to the most important historical data about Artemisia Gentileschi, that is, her paintings. Detailed accounts of two paintings, in fact, constitute the dramatic high points of Banti's narrative and frame much of the protagonist's psychological development in the course of the novel.

The narrative's status, then, while not easily defined, may nonetheless be illuminated by locating its antecedents in realistic psychological fiction on the one hand and, on the other but to a far lesser extent, art history and criticism. At the same time, any account of the novel's idiosyncratic status must also consider the crucial interaction between author-narrator and protagonist, which self-consciously violates the more "traditional" narrative convention of self-sustaining illusion. To be sure, from the very beginnings of the modern realistic novel in the eighteenth century, such brilliant works as Sterne's *Tristram Shandy* or Diderot's *Jacques le fataliste* deliberately undercut the illusion of the fictional world's autonomy. While it is, therefore, historically inaccurate to view as a recent development the emergence of narrative that calls attention to the arbitrariness of its own construction, reminding the reader that its design depends on the writer's act of will and could just as easily have been different, this type of fiction is nevertheless often seen as distinctively "modern." Banti's novel belongs to this "modern"—if not new—tradition.

In the interactions between author-narrator and protagonist, moreover, we naturally recognize that we are dealing with not one but two fictional constructions, for the persona and experiences of the author-narrator are themselves, necessarily, part of the fiction, whatever their original basis is in fact. Within this frame of Banti's fictionalized autobiography, then, the protagonist's story unfolds, told variously—by Artemisia in her own voice, by the narrator to Artemisia in the second person, by the narrator who assumes the first person in passages where her identification with the heroine becomes almost complete, and, finally, by the narrator in the more conventional mode of the third person, which becomes the dominant voice after the first fifth of the novel. During the initial several days that mark the German retreat and the Allied liberation of Florence, however, the tone of the exchange between Artemisia and the narrator is fluid and volatile, shifting erratically from playfulness, even mischievous teasing, to urgency and relentless compulsion. As the narrator moves from the Boboli Gardens, to the lawn in front of Fort Belvedere, and to the indoor refuge of the Palatine Gallery in the Palazzo Pitti, by turns she finds Artemisia, loses her, and then meets with her again. The thread of their mutual construction of Artemisia's history is picked up, dropped, and taken up again. Past and present interweave, mirroring the chaos and disorder around them. Artemisia herself passes through a series of rapid changes, her age oscillating backward and forward, as she is kaleidoscopically envisioned in different phases of her development. At times, the narrator is frankly arbitrary and fanciful, inventing aspects of Artemisia's history. The protagonist listens, occasionally docile and attentive, seeking to reassure the narrator of her credulity; at other moments, she impatiently demands that the narrator retell a particular episode; at still others, she corrects the narrator and interrupts to take over the narration herself. Then the situation is reversed and it is Artemisia who requires an assurance of belief, and the narrator who variously gives the desired encouragement or else corrects the protagonist's faulty memory. While the dynamic interplay between narrator and protagonist becomes less prominent as the novel gradually focuses more sharply on Artemisia's own story, the relationship between the two women continues to resonate, even when not directly in view. The narrator's involvement with her protagonist's story is crucial not only to the way in which Banti presents her material but also to the reader's final understanding of the narrative's wider signification.

What broader vision, then, do these structural pyrotechnics help to establish? This basic question is closely related to another: What is the nature of the bond between the narrator and Artemisia? While answers to both questions evolve gradually over the course of the novel and receive clarification only near the end, from its opening a variety of impulses immediately becomes apparent. Artemisia appears in the first lines of the novel to offer her creator/resuscitator words of comfort for both her individual and her more general loss. She will help the narrator to reconstruct and even improve the story contained in her lost manuscript. At the same time, Artemisia's emergence from the ruins of war suggests the reemergence of the writer's enduring cultural heritage, as an Italian and a woman, in the face of the present destruction of her homeland following two decades of Fascist rule that have led to this debacle. In turning to Artemisia as "an elder in Death that is all around us" (8), the narrator is seeking both a distraction from the surrounding destruction and a means of transcending it through her identification with that positive past in which she can take pride and find sustenance. Artemisia is one who has suffered and died yet who triumphs and lives. Although the full scope and meaning of the narrator's purpose become clear only late in the novel, through her resuscitation of Artemisia she will ultimately come into possession of the inheritance for which there is, tellingly, no adequate word in English or Italian: her rightful *female* patrimony. (It is perhaps interesting to reflect how far beside the point "matrimony" is in this context.)

The relationship between narrator and protagonist, moreover, is reciprocal. While the narrator depends on Artemisia for a complex of motives—to give her comfort, pride, purpose, inspiration, distraction, and transcendence—Artemisia depends no less on her creator—also to console and offer sympathy, to bring her to life, to tell her story, to justify her, and to allow her to exonerate herself in the eyes of history. "And what else did

Artemisia do if not justify herself, from the age of fourteen onward?" (18). The mutual dependence of narrator and protagonist implies, in turn, an ideal of female friendship—the giving and receiving of reciprocal aid and support.

In the early part of the novel, as the narrative approaches the experiences responsible for Artemisia Gentileschi's historical notoriety—her rape and the subsequent trial—the bond between the two women appears overwhelmingly as one of suffering and mutual support in the face of enormous upheaval and loss. It is, moreover, a bond forged on the basis of a distinctively female vulnerability.

> Our own meager freedom is linked to the humble freedom of a virgin in 1611 who has nothing if not that of her own intact body and who can never ever accept the fact that she has lost it. For her entire life she strove to substitute another, higher and stronger kind of freedom, but her regret over that single loss remained. With the pages I had written it seemed to me that I had soothed that regret. (23)

Locating a source of her early identification with Artemisia in their shared female vulnerability, the narrator suggests as well a motive both for her current retelling of the story and for Artemisia Gentileschi's historic achievement as a painter.

Artemisia is developed through a series of vignettes, moving from her childhood friendship with a wealthy paralytic in Rome at the age of ten to the initial stages of her return from England, where she had gone at the age of forty to join her father. From the opening pages of the book Banti establishes a firm footing for Artemisia's life in the fictional universe, where the author's imaginative constructions assume the status of reality: "I had given her a friend" (8). Reflecting on her wholly arbitrary creation of a childhood companion for Artemisia in her lost manuscript, the author-narrator now brings the invented character back to life as a demonstrated proof both of her sympathetic friendship toward her subject and of the power of her autonomous imagination. Through this invented girlhood episode, moreover, Banti lays the foundation for Artemisia's personality as it will emerge in the course of the novel—her bold impetuousness, her vivid imagination that makes itself felt in boastful exaggerations and inventions, her stubbornness and pride, and her tenacious concern for her own dignity and sense of worth. The fabricated childhood is also important in making palpably vivid the innocence that will be violated by the historically documented rape.

In her presentation of this brutal act of force and the resulting trial, Banti uses the actual legal records. In 1612 Orazio Gentileschi petitioned the pope, complaining that his daughter had been raped by Agostino Tassi, a friend and fellow painter whom he had engaged to teach her perspective. At the trial, Orazio gave Artemisia's age as fifteen, on the basis of which historians established her date of birth as 1597.[2] Banti appears to have allowed herself a minor novelistic liberty here, in the interest, it would seem, of greater pathos. In her preface, she gives Artemisia's date of birth as 1598, and hence in her novel, which leaves the date of the historical trial unchanged, Artemisia is able to reiterate plaintively, "I was fourteen years old" (20). Ward Bissell's more recent chronology, which establishes Artemisia's birth date as 8 July 1593, suggests that Orazio deliberately understated his daughter's age by four years in order to make her "conveniently younger than what appears to have been the seventeenth-century age of majority."[3] This correction, however, postdates Banti's novel.

At the time of the rape, Artemisia testified that she attempted to defend herself, wounding Tassi with a knife, but to no avail. Afterward, Tassi promised to marry her. Orazio Gentileschi's petition stated that the sexual offense had been repeated "many successive times," a fact that has led most male historians to sneer at the charge of rape.[4] However, Banti (who has been joined by recent feminist art historians) finds no inconsistency in this account. Her narrative convincingly shows how Tassi's original rape and subsequent promises of marriage combined to make Artemisia feel bound to him as a wife, even against her inclination.[5] Presumably, Orazio initiated proceedings when it became clear that Tassi was not going to keep his repeated promises. Banti quotes Artemisia's flash of grim wit from trial records when, under cross-examination, she was tortured with thumb-screws: "This is the ring you [Tassi] give me, these are the promises!" (21). Banti also follows the historical account in showing Tassi first imprisoned and then released, his defense resting chiefly on his contention that he was not the first, nor the only one.

After closely following the historical sources that document the trial, Banti reverts to her own sympathetic imagination to re-create the emotional texture of Artemisia's response to her public humiliation: "Today she feels guilty, as guilty as anyone could want her to be. . . . If they treat her like this, they must be right" (32). As Artemisia prepares to seek lonely comfort in "the girlish and somewhat boastful pride of her nature," promising herself that "they will see who Artemisia is" (33), Banti is no longer undertaking to portray her known, public life but rather, once again, the private, invisible one of moment-to-moment experience. Artemisia, "a figure . . . of illustrious fame . . . whose biography is clear, year by year," is also a character "whom it is worth resuscitating, hour by hour, precisely in the days about which her history is silent" (33–34). Agostino Tassi's acquittal, Orazio's withdrawal of love and esteem, and "Artemisia reduced from an ephemeral, scandalous celebrity to an intractable and menaced solitude—these are facts that are as important to me—and I don't know if I should blush at this—as a second Punic War" (34). Might there be here an echo of Virginia Woolf (whom Banti had translated), who had earlier challenged the prevailing "masculine values" that held wars more important than the private creative experiences of women? Woolf had referred to the historical moment when "middle-class women began to write" as "a change . . . which, if I were rewriting history, I should describe more fully and think of greater importance than the Crusades or the Wars of the Roses."[6] And here is Banti, beginning to imagine the formation of Artemisia as an artist, following her loss of social respectability and her consequent self-imposed isolation behind closed, shuttered windows: "One can easily conjecture what the African elephants ate in Italy; one can easily imagine Artemisia's evenings in the summer of 1615" (34).

So compelling, in fact, is the imagined experience which follows that it is a jolt to learn how sharply it diverges from historical fact. Bissell's chronology tells us that in November 1612, one month after the end of the trial, Artemisia was married in Rome to Pietro Antonio di Vincenzo Stiattesi, a Florentine. Bissell adds, "Stiattesi may have taken Artemisia to Florence almost immediately" as "they are documented there in November 1614."[7] Banti may well have worked with a less-accurate chronology; at any rate, the Artemisia she creates remains in her father's home for almost three years of painstaking, solitary apprentice work after the rape trial, as she hides from the world and grows as a painter, partially compensated for the love and recognition her father withholds by the devoted admiration of her younger brother, Francesco. In Banti's account, Artemisia's marriage takes place at the end of this period, a marriage at first in name only, hastily arranged by Orazio so that he can take his newly respectable daughter with him to Florence, leaving the husband behind.

In Florence, where her much adored father abandons her almost at once, heading off for Pisa, Artemisia paints what Banti presents as her first great painting, "Judith Beheading Holofernes" (now in the Uffizi). One among several treatments of Judith painted by Artemisia Gentileschi—the subject was common enough among paintings of the era—this version, which presents the murder itself, is striking for its gory violence. Assisted by a maid servant who helps pinion the naked Holofernes to a bed, Judith grasps the helpless general's hair with one hand while the other plunges a sword into his neck as jets of blood spurt forth in many directions. The French critic Roland Barthes observed that to modern viewers of Gentileschi's paintings the scene—whose traditional signification was religious and patriotic—now appears to embody the ideology of "la revendication féminine."[8] He saw the painter's "first stroke of genius" in

> having put two women on the canvas rather than a single one, whereas in the biblical version the servant waits outside: two women, associates in the same work, arms interlaced, combining their muscular efforts on the same object— subduing an enormous mass whose weight exceeds the strength of one woman: might one say, two women workers in the act of slitting a pig's throat?

Barthes' remarks gain a particular poignancy in view of the fact that the other women present at the time of Artemisia's rape—according to both the court records and Banti's narrative—was her nurse Tutia (or Tuzia), who, far from assisting the motherless girl as might have been expected, was implicated instead as an accomplice of Tassi. The prominence of Judith's maid servant in Artemisia Gentileschi's painting may well reflect the painter's wish for the unrealized female solidarity that could have prevented Tassi's act of violence.

Banti's treatment of this painting, however, ignores the role of the maid servant (a figure who is equally important in Artemisia Gentileschi's other, more serene versions of Judith). The author concentrates, instead, on Artemisia's identification with the biblical heroine, hypothesizing that the painter has modeled Judith's features on her own. The novelist thus goes one step beyond the widely accepted view that "Judith's decapitation of Holofernes appears to provide a pictorial equivalent for the punishment of Agostino Tassi."[9] More intriguing and original than this hypothesis, however, is the atmosphere Banti constructs surrounding the composition of Judith. In Florence, Artemisia is befriended by a handful of court ladies who come to watch her as she paints, taking a voyeuristic interest in her independence, her professional competence, and, above all, her confident command over her powerful male model. Their feelings toward her are a mixture of social superiority, envy, and uneasy fascination. Also prurient is their fixation on "all that blood" (57) in the painting that takes shape before their eyes. Though distrustful of one another, they are nonetheless unwittingly drawn into sharing dark confidences, as their conversation obsessively reverts to men—those they live with, those they know—revealing attitudes of which they are unaware: contempt, resentment, fear, hatred. These are impulses that Artemisia recognizes all too well, but, through her mastery of her art and the sense of self-esteem this painting earns her, she is able to overcome and reject them. Whatever the original motives behind the composition, the process of painting itself is envisioned as a "working through" and, hence, a purgation of her rage and shame. The achievement of the finished work liberates Artemisia from anger and self-denigration, freeing her energies so that she may become the great painter she became. "The vendetta was consummated, the protracted humiliation of Rome expiated. Men once more became men. . . . It seemed to her that, all hatred spent, she was extending her hand toward repented violence, she was strong and unarmed" (61, 63).

After this crucial point in Artemisia's development, she returns to Rome to join her husband when her father Orazio leaves for England. A wholly invented, unexpected love idyll then follows between the heroine and her husband, a whimsical peddler. But when the exigencies of her career lead the couple to relocate in more fashionable surroundings, the husband suddenly looks awkward and out of place, and Artemisia, despite her love for him, cannot keep herself from driving him away. Her unfading memory of this lost love, however, persists throughout the novel, contributing to the continuity of the protagonist's consciousness and giving unity to the episodic structure. From Rome, Artemisia moves to Naples, where she runs an academy of painting, bears a daughter, and becomes famous. Accompanying her mounting achievements in those years, Banti imagines, is an unassuageable uneasiness at the indeterminacy of her social position. Artemisia must grope toward the creation of her own complex identity without the help of any known precedents or "role models," reflecting that

> a mother without a husband is not the mother of a family. Precisely what her status might be, no confessor had been able to explain to her, no matter how much she had insisted; as, moreover, however much she pondered it, she had not yet succeeded in recognizing herself and finding self-definition in any exemplary and approved figure of her century. . . . This is a woman who in her every gesture would like to find inspiration in a model—decent and noble—of her own sex and era; and she does not find it. (125)

During these years in Naples, Artemisia's intense love for her only daughter emerges as yet another source of pain. In the course of her convent education, the fictional daughter refuses to learn drawing, even from the nuns; she emerges from the convent with a deep respect for propriety and order, strongly rejecting her mother's unconventional way of life. The historical Artemisia's experience was far different. She had two or three daughters, at least two of whom were painters, suggesting a possible mother-daughter camaraderie that Banti denies to her fictional heroine.[10]

In her account of this period, Banti paraphrases comments from Artemisia's letters of a decade or so later, revealing her keen sensitivity to the importance of her gender in the eyes of her patrons. Her correspondence complains that they are skeptical about her abilities or want to pay lower prices for her canvases because she is a woman; at the same time, in addition, it contains defensive affirmations of her ability to prove herself—though Banti somewhat softens the most memorable line from the letters, "you will find the heart of Caesar in the soul of a woman"[11] to "I carry the heart of Caesar in my breast" (134). Banti also cites almost verbatim the closing lines of a letter of 1637 to a patron: "May it please your lordship to give me news of the life or death of my husband" (122).[12]

In 1638–39 Artemisia leaves Naples to join her father in England, moving up the Italian coast and across France in a beautifully imagined odyssey in which the painter's consciousness registers a shifting variety of experiences and visual impressions. While the historical Artemisia reported in 1635 that she had received an invitation to England from King Charles I, the cause of Banti's heroine's decision to leave for England is simply the painful news that her husband has a new woman and now wants a legal divorce.

Banti's inventions and distortions of the historical record all seem designed to emphasize Artemisia's solitude and the pain and vulnerability she will have to overcome, while sometimes suggesting as well sources of future strengths. As we have seen, the author creates an Artemisia who is a year younger at the time of her rape and trial than even Orazio had claimed; she postpones her heroine's (in fact, hasty) marriage after the trial, thereby giving her three years in which to hide from the world and study painting in isolation. Moreover, Banti postpones the protagonist's cohabitation with her husband until after her Florentine period and her painting of Judith, through which she overcomes her hatred and distrust of men. The writer also provides Artemisia with a husband she comes to love and then, uncontrollably, drives away. In contrast to the historical record, she gives her character only one daughter, who rejects her mother's way of life, thus supplying her with cause for an additional sense of maternal loss. Finally, Banti chooses to have the familiar motives of pride and hurt feelings determine Artemisia's trip to England rather than her fame as an artist or a desire to be with her ailing father. Even during the years of Artemisia's growing fame in Naples, Banti dwells on her social blunders and personal humiliations, which are often portrayed as the accompaniment of her successes and while the historical Artemisia appears to have collaborated with her father both at the beginning of her career and during her brief stay in England, Banti's protagonist always paints alone. Yet, in the end, the solitude, loss, vulnerability, and pain, so tangibly felt throughout the book, will be seen as a necessary preparation for Artemisia's affirmation and sense of achievement.

Although the historical Artemisia's stay in England was actually brief—she probably left to return to Italy shortly after Orazio's death in 1639 (and she lived until at least 1651)—it is in England that Banti brings the novel to a satisfying climax. The heroine at last gains the long-desired recognition of her father, and the two are able to relate as equals: "Two spirits, not a man and a woman, not a father or a daughter. . . . It doesn't matter, having been a woman, many times discouraged, twice betrayed. There is no longer any doubt, a painter has earned a name: Artemisia Gentileschi" (231–32). This reconciliation and affirmation free her to think of her husband without bitterness, of her daughter with renewed maternal love, and of her devoted brother with fresh appreciation. The most important consequence of this sense of self, however, is the work many consider her greatest, that of a woman painter (hanging today in Hampton Court). Seen in three-quarter view, her left hand holding a palette and her right one, at the end of a foreshortened arm, reaching a brush toward a canvas undiscernible to the viewer, the artist appears wholly absorbed in the act of painting; a medallion hangs casually over the front of her dress and a few straggling locks of hair escape from a bun tied at the nape of her neck, falling loosely over her forehead and cheek. The painting was posthumously entitled "Self-Portrait" and, alternatively, "La pittura." A recent study has confirmed the appropriateness of both titles, and feminist studies in particular have pointed to the work's ingenuity in reconciling hitherto conflicting female roles.[13] The painter's muse, as well as the abstract personification of the art or allegory of painting, was historically represented as a woman. On the other hand, since most artists were men, the artist's realistic self-portraits were most frequently male.[14] As a woman, Artemisia Gentileschi's figure is able to integrate the symbolic embodiment of muse and personification with the realistic representation of a female painter seriously engaged in practicing her craft.

Whether as an inspirational muse, allegory of painting, or simply as a model, the female figure was typically viewed as the object of a male painter's creativity, rather than as a possible creator in her own right. Gentileschi's portrait of a woman artist confutes and subverts this expectation within the medium of painting itself. Banti's novel echoes this challenge to conventional stereotypes through the medium of fiction, while setting up some further reverberations with traditional associations between women and painting in literature. Of course, Banti's choice of a great woman painter as fictional protagonist distinguishes her narrative from the tradition of the realistic (above all, nineteenth-century) novel on several grounds, the most obvious of which, as previously noted, is the documented authenticity of Artemisia Gentileschi. Conventions of the realistic novel required that its protagonist be a fictional creation, unknown to history. Where actual historical figures appear in the nineteenth-century novel (as, for example, in Manzoni or Stendhal), they play, as Lukács long ago pointed out, minor rather than major roles. Moreover, traditional novelistic heroes may be exemplary only to the extent that they remain typical, or at least broadly representative. However much greatness of spirit they may possess, they are invariably limited by constraints of custom and opportunity—time and place—and, usually, by flaws of their own characters as well: hence another of the realistic novel's underlying conventions, that even potential greatness can never result in great achievement.

Banti's Artemisia, then, triumphing against overwhelming odds and not forgotten by history, belongs only in part to the tradition of the realistic novel, diverging from her literary predecessors as much because of her substantial artistic achievement as because of her historical prototype. Still, Banti's fictionalized historical heroine may be more fully appreciated if we pause to reflect on the familiar limitations of the traditional relation between women and painting in literature, from which Banti's character so conspicuously departs. Certainly, in the novel, as in the history of painting, women have frequently served as models, muses, or the symbolic embodiment of an art form itself, for the male artist. Additionally, women in nineteenth-century novels are often presented as pursuing drawing and painting as dilettantes, as if the skill were one item in a package of feminine "accomplishments" that were supposed to distinguish the properly educated young lady. Even more serious fictional treatments of women's creativity tend to focus on the meaning of their artistic efforts as a key to the psychological depths and complexity of their souls or as a reflection of a certain inner liberation, rather than on their work as substantial objective achievement, as independent, self-justifying artifacts.[15]

Probably the most notable break from the dominance of this fictional tradition (which in turn reflects a broader cultural one) comes with the creation of Lily Briscoe in *To the Lighthouse* by Virginia Woolf, an author admired by Banti. Though Lily will never achieve fame, she nonetheless takes her work seriously, as does her creator (unlike other characters in the book, one of whom repeatedly maintains, "women can't paint, can't write").[16] In fact, Woolf, the novelist, quite transparently shares her fictional painter's concern with art as objective achievement and even shares Lily's articulated view of its desired nature: the transformation of the moment into something permanent, of chaos and fluidity into enduring form. The woman novelist, mirroring her artistic aspirations in those of a painter-protagonist, who similarly upholds art as a serious vocation for a woman practitioner—here, some two decades before *Artemisia*—we find an earlier and kindred treatment of a woman painter, which also evokes and subverts older, more entrenched expectations. Lily's canvases, however, exist chiefly as verbal suggestion, in terms of a professed theoretical goal; they are not described in great detail. On the other hand, the extraliterary existence of Artemisia Gentileschi's paintings adds a new kind of dimension to Anna Banti's narrative. At the same time, reverberations of earlier literary treatments of women and painting help enrich the significance of her climactic discussion of Artemisia's boldly innovative portrait of a woman painter.

In addition, Banti takes a radically innovative step in choosing to present this painting—so repeatedly designated as self-portrait and the art of painting—instead as a portrait, from memory, of another woman, one Annella de Rosa. In the novel, Annella is a gifted younger artist whom Artemisia meets in Naples, a battered wife whose early death will prevent her from fulfilling her promise. In a briefly sketched episode that becomes significant only retrospectively, Annella rejects Artemisia's overture of friendship, causing her to speculate at the time on the impossibility of friendships between women in a world created by men for their use and convenience. Yet Artemisia's later painting of the younger artist emerges as a triumphant affirmation of female solidarity. Earlier, during her painting of Judith, Artemisia had refused the female intimacy based on shared fears and hatreds that the court ladies offered her. Here, at last, as an accomplished artist, she realizes the ideal of female friendship through a painting that celebrates the creative spirit in another woman. "That a woman achieves honor, honors her as well" (248).

As the author's Artemisia, in celebrating Annella and giving her life, finds that another woman's honor also becomes her source of pride, so too Anna Banti, in celebrating and resuscitating Artemisia, finds honor for herself in another woman's creative achievement. Thus, the novelist-narrator commemorates Artemisia Gentileschi, the woman painter whom history remembers, by imagining her as commemorating Annella de Rosa, the woman painter whom history has forgotten. This vision returns us to the initial mirroring of narrator and protagonist, so crucial to the novel's structure. The fundamental truth of this reciprocal relationship remains, even if Banti's fanciful redesignation of the painting as a portrait of Annella is fiction: "Portrait or not, a woman who paints in 1640 constitutes an act of courage; this applies to Annella and to at least a hundred others, down to today. 'It applies to you, too,' concludes a brusque, dry sound, by candlelight, in a room darkened by war. A book is closed, abruptly" (251–52). Contemplating the painting, the narrator decodes a vital message for herself. Through her undying work of art, Artemisia reaches out from her century to ours, to teach and inspire Banti—and through her, her readers—by her enduring, shared affirmation of female courage and achievement.

NOTES

An earlier, briefer version of this chapter appeared as "Remembering *Artemisia:* Anna Banti and Artemisia Gentileschi," in *Donna: Women in Italian Culture,* ed. Ada Testaferri, © 1989 by Dove House, and is reprinted with the permission of Dove House, Inc.

1. Anna Banti, *Artemisia* (1947; reprint, Milan: Mondadori, 1974), pp. 3–4. All citations of the novel will be from the Italian edition and subsequent references will be included in the text. The translations are mine. Various art historians also testify to Artemisia Gentileschi's importance, and Gentileschi has recently received particular attention from British and American feminist art historians. For example, Ann Sutherland Harris and Linda Nochlin write, "Artemisia Gentileschi is the first woman in the history of Western art to make a significant and undeniably important contribution to the art of her time" (see *Women Artists: 1550–1950* [New York: Knopf, 1981], p. 118). Mary D. Garrard asserts: "Artemisia Gentileschi is today widely regarded as the most creative and most significant woman artist of the premodern era" (see "Artemisia Gentileschi," in *The Female Autograph,* ed. Domna C. Stanton and Jeanine Parisier Plottel, p. 91 [New York: New York Literary Forum, 1984]). In Germaine Greer, *The Obstacle Race* (London: Picador, 1981), Gentileschi is the only woman painter to receive a full chapter to herself ("The Magnificent Exception," pp. 189–208). After the completion of this chapter, Mary D. Garrard published a major, full-length study, *Artemisia Gentileschi: The Image of the Female Hero in Italian Baroque Art* (Princeton: Princeton University Press, 1989), which has received considerable attention in the United States and Britain.

2. See Roberto Longhi, "Gentileschi padre e figlia," *L'Arte* 19 (1916), collected in *Scritti Giovanili: 1912–1922* (Florence: Sansoni, 1961), 1: 253; and Ward Bissell, "Artemisia Gentileschi—A New Documented Chronology," *Art Bulletin* 50, no. 2 (1968): 153.

3. Bissell, "Artemisia Gentileschi," p. 156.

4. Bissell, in fact, puts the word "rape" in sneer quotes (ibid., p. 153). Something of this attitude is evident even in Longhi who, writing of Artemisia, seems quite ready to accept Tassi's self-serving countercharges: "She must have been very precocious in everything—one should consult, in this regard, the record of Tassi's trial—and thus too in painting, if, around 1612, at the age of fifteen, when Tassi was teaching her, among other things, perspective, she was painting the portrait of a child" (*Scritti Giovanili,* p. 254; my translation). Less cere-

moniously, Rudolf and Margot Wittkower, largely on the basis of Tassi's own defense, blithely refer to Artemisia as "a lascivious and precocious girl," while at the same time they write: "The list of Tassi's 'escapades' is impressive: it includes rape, incest, sodomy, lechery, and possibly homicide" (*Born under Saturn* [London: Weidenfeld and Nicholson, 1963], pp. 163, 164). An account of treatments of Artemisia Gentileschi by predominantly English male historians and scholars over several centuries can be found in M. Garrard, "Artemisia and Susannah," in *Feminism and Art History,* ed. Norma Broude and Mary D. Garrard, p. 164 (New York: Harper and Row, 1982).

5. See Garrard, "Artemisia and Susannah," pp. 163–64. See also Greer, "The Magnificent Exception," p. 192, where Greer speaks specifically of the *nozze di riparazione,* pointing out that marriages of reparation are still considered an acceptable sequel to rape in southern Italy. Garrard says the same of Sicily.

6. Virginia Woolf, *A Room of One's Own* (1928; reprint, Harmondsworth: Penguin Books, 1972), pp. 66, 74.

7. Bissell, "Artemisia Gentileschi," p. 154.

8. Roland Barthes, *Le Texte et l'image* (Paris: Edition Paris Musées, 1986), p. 95. Barthes's phrase, which loses in translation, might be rendered as "redress of female grievance." The subsequent citation is of the same page and the translation is mine.

9. Garrard, "Artemisia and Susannah," p. 165.

10. Artemisia refers to works by a daughter in two letters, separated by some thirteen and a half years: for the first, of 11 October 1635, see A.M. Crinò, "More Letters from Orazio and Artemisia Gentileschi," *Burlington Magazine* 102 (1960): 264, and for the second, of 13 March 1649, see *Bollettino d'arte* (1916), p. 49. Bissell argues persuasively that these must be two different daughters ("Artemisia Gentileschi," p. 158). Greer interprets Bissell's additional data in a way that would suggest Artemisia had at least three daughters ("The Magnificent Exception," p. 195).

11. *Bollettino d'arte* (1916), p. 51. Artemisia's original Italian contains a nice play on *animo* (heart, courage) and *anima* (soul).

12. Giovanni Gaetano Bottari and Stefan Ticozzi, *Raccolta di lettere sulla pittura, scultura ed architettura scritta da' più celebri personaggi dai secoli XV, XVI, XVII* (1822; reprint, Hildesheim/New York: Georg Olms Verlag, 1976), 1: 349–55.

13. Michael Levey, "Notes on the Royal Collection—II: Artemisia Gentileschi's 'Self-Portrait' at Hampton Court," *Burlington Magazine* 104 (1962): 79–80; Mary D. Garrard, "Artemisia Gentileschi's Self-Portrait as the Allegory of Painting," *Art Bulletin* 62, no. 1 (1980): 97–112; Rozsika Parker and Griselda Pollock, *Old Mistresses* (London: Routledge and Kegan Paul, 1981), pp. 25–26; and Greer, "The Magnificent Exception," p. 201.

14. Notable exceptions to this pattern are the many self-portraits by Sofonisba Anguissola (1532/35–1625); see Ann Sutherland Harris and Linda Nochlin, *Women Artists: 1550–1950* (New York: Knopf, 1981), pp. 27–28, 106–8, and Parker and Pollock, *Old Mistresses,* pp. 18, 84–86. Parker and Pollock also suggest as a "precedent for . . . [the] image of a woman artist dishevelled and absorbed in work" an anonymous portrait medallion (though it is not a *self-*portrait) of the Bolognese painter, Lavinia Fontana; at the same time, they contrast this view of a woman artist "seized by some strange form of lunacy and ecstasy" with "Gentileschi's quiet, serious and dignified realism" (p. 25). Some delightful early self-portraits of women artists are included in *The Medieval Woman: Illuminated Book of Days,* ed. Sally Fox (Toronto: Key Porter Books, 1985; Boston: Little, Brown and Co., 1985), see 19–24 March, 19–24 May, 13–18 November.

15. For example, during her "honeymoon" with Vronsky in Italy, Tolstoy's Anna Karenina sits for portraits by both her lover and a resident Russian artist. And she is considerably more successful in her role of model than she will be later in the novel when she turns to creative

endeavors in her own right; her work on a children's book in the increasingly strained final period of her liaison with Vronsky is presented as a kind of desperate busywork, tending chiefly to emphasize her tragic alienation from society and, ironically, her inadequacies as a mother to both her legitimate son and her illegitimate daughter. In George Eliot's *Middlemarch,* Dorothea Brooke Casaubon, also on a honeymoon in Italy, serves as inspirational model for a portrait by a German artist friend of Will Ladislaw. With the exception of her early plans for tenant cottages, however, Dorothea never turns to creative work herself; when she later speculates on the possibility of Will's becoming a poet, asserting that she herself could never produce a poem, Will counters, "you are a poem." Both Jane Austen's Emma Woodhouse and Flaubert's Emma Bovary have learned to dabble at sketching as part of their proper education, and the reader of both novels gets amusing glimpses of their scarcely impressive work. As a governess, Brontë's Jane Eyre both teaches and practices drawing and painting; but, although she is more truly accomplished than either the French or the English Emma, even her haunting water-color paintings, which are described in some detail, are important only for what they tell us about her sensibility and imagination. Fontane's Effi Briest and Kate Chopin's Edna Pontellier (*The Awakening*) both turn to sketching and painting with relative earnestness in the interval between their estrangement from their husbands and the death that inevitably seals the fate of adulterous heroines in nineteenth-century fiction. But both women are presented as having the wisdom and good grace not to take their artistic activity too seriously, and neither novelist bothers to say much about the content of either heroine's work.

16. Virginia Woolf, *To the Lighthouse* (1927; reprint, New York: Harcourt, Brace and World, 1955), p. 238.

LALLA ROMANO

Lalla Romano was born in 1906 in the city of Demonte, Cuneo. She studied poetry and art at the University of Turin. After graduation, she began to paint and studied at the school of Felice Casorati. She contributed many of her paintings to exhibits and, by the beginning of World War II, had become a fairly well-known artist. In 1941 she published a collection of poems entitled *Fiore* that was favorably greeted by critics; she also received major acclaim ten years later for her first novel, *Le metamorfosi*. Her hectic activity as a writer of prose fiction has produced a long string of bestsellers: *Maria* (1953), *Tetto murato* (1957), *L'uomo che parlava solo* (1961), *La penombra che abbiamo attraversato* (1964), *Le parole tra noi leggere* (1969), *L'ospite* (1973), *Giovane è il tempo* (poetry; 1974), *La villeggiante* (1975), *Una giovinezza inventata* (1979), *Inseparabile* (1981), *Nei mari estremi* (1987), and *Un sogno del nord* (1989). In addition to fiction and poetry, Romano has published three books of photography: *Lettura di un'immagine* (1975), *Romanzo di figure* (1986), and *La Treccia di Tatiana* (1986). She has also translated Gustave Flaubert's *Trois contes* (1944; 1980) and *L'education sentimentale* (1984), as well as Eugene Delacroix's *Journal (1822–1863)* (1945) and Béatrix Beck's *Léon Morin, prêtre* (1954).

Memory and Time in Lalla Romano's Novels, *La penombra che abbiamo attraversato* and *Le parole tra noi leggere*

FLAVIA BRIZIO

According to Georges Poulet, the great discovery of the eighteenth century was the phenomenon of memory—a faculty that enables humans to escape the purely momentary and the nothingness that lies in wait between moments of existence. "To exist, then, is to be one's present and also to be one's past and one's recollections."[1] The French philosopher also attributes the increasing contemporary concern for one's past to the inability to capture the present. "Whatever is new eludes the grasp of conscience, and when seized by it becomes transformed into a thing of the past."[2] Time and memory still intrigue numerous writers who handle these issues differently, often subverting traditional temporal categories. Lalla Romano problematizes time extensively in her narrative fiction and exhibits a constant concern with the interplay between past and present, seeing both elements as equally important and necessary for the creation of the artistic object. A structural examination of two of Romano's main works, *La penombra che abbiamo attraversato* (The shade that we crossed) and *Le parole tra noi leggere* (Flighty words between us), illustrates the writer's sensitivity to recollection. An analysis of these novels not only reveals their inherent complexity but also highlights the rapport between what occurs at the actual moment of an individual's life and what has come before.

La penombra che abbiamo attraversato is divided into two parts, each twelve chapters long, broken into lyrical sections defined as *lasse*.[3] These brief textual divisions and their refined language impart a poetic atmosphere to the novel. The multilayered narration has a spatial dimension. The narrator visits the house in which she was born and the village where she spent her childhood. The story can be viewed as a horizontal surface constantly intersected by different temporal levels, metaphorically imaginable as perpendiculars cutting the spatial plane. There are four alternating temporal phases: the time before the narrator was born ("the time of before"), which is fabulous, almost "mythic" because it is perceived only in fragments, from things her parents have said; the time of her childhood; a more recent past during which she visits Ponte Stura, staying at the Hotel Giglio (the first page in the text, the "now" in which the story begins); and some moments of illumination in which she dives into the nontime of consciousness, where everything "is." Careful attention to the first chapter of the book reveals how the author gives artistic unity to such a structure.

The first *lassa* opens with the narrator sitting in her hotel room in Ponte Stura, letting her mind wander:

> The room was as small as a cell and its color was a ferocious yellow. The enormous bed was made of iron. . . . I had lain on the bed and tried to think about innocuous things. . . . As a child I had heard hotels criticized. I was told that there were fleas. It seemed to me a sort of privilege. Everybody got alarmed if a flea was found at home. . . . My poor classmates had many red spots on the surface of their necks, which were flea bites. It resulted from their sleeping with no sheets. Even Muro had fleas sometimes; but dog fleas did not attach themselves to people. Dad had found lice in a hotel. . . . Dad had lifted the pillow: black flat lice ran about on the sheet. Dad recounted it all slowly with fabulous precision. I pictured the lice as the distant image of an army in miniature. . . . But perhaps it had not happened in a hotel. Maybe it had been the Sanctuary of Saint Anne of Vinadio, where Dad was a revered guest. . . . He would bring scapulars from the sanctuary to us children.[4]

The tense utilized ("its color was," "was made of iron") denotes an indefinite time in the past; "as a child" marks the sudden shift of memory into a more distant past, and what follows is what the narrator heard and thought about hotels when she was little. Her memory progresses through associations: hotel, fleas, schoolmates, dog; then she remembers that her father had found lice in a hotel; the child imagines them crawling like an army, while the adult is not sure whether the event happened in a hotel or in a monastery.

In the second *lassa*, the adult woman who poses questions about her past coexists with her younger self and probes this earlier existence. She acknowledges never having stayed in a hotel in Ponte and even recalls that her parents had always been invited to stay in private homes. She remembers that her father designed the luxurious Hotel Giglio in Piazza Nuova but she now experiences disappointment at the current state of its commonplace condition: "I had read in the guide book that all hotels in Ponte Stura are fourth class. It hurt me. Was this village where Dad had been admired and loved, where "they" had been happy, and where we had been rich, so miserable? I felt it as a step down, as a humiliation for them" (5). The protagonist's scrutiny leads her to discover truth; what the child believed is challenged by the rationality of the adult, who realizes that the village and the hotel are no longer, and maybe never were, as she perceived them.

The third *lassa* opens with the narrator remembering that the family left Ponte at the end of World War I and moved to a city. At the same time, she did not know the reason for moving but recalls that it was autumn: "Mom was giving away all sort of objects. . . . I do not remember anything else. I only know that there was the war—it was the autumn of Caporetto—and there was a feeling of defeat" (6). Years later the mother reveals to the daughter that the father's failure to receive a raise necessitated their move. The departure from Ponte marks the end of an "era" in the protagonist's life, and the half-forgotten event carries more importance in the story than it first seems. The years spent at Ponte are a "golden age"; the proof of this utopia lies in the narrator's emotional disarrangement when she realizes that her family's "rich," "happy," and "admired" condition never really existed, except in her imagination.[5]

In the fourth *lassa*, the narrator explains why she has returned to her childhood home: "As girls, we realized that Mom preferred not to speak about Ponte. . . . But in one of her last days—during a brief respite from her illness—she unexpectedly spoke about it: 'How happy we were!' " (7). Her mother's death, as well as her own association of happiness with life in Ponte, arouses Romano's desire to return to her roots and learn more about her parents and thus about herself. Hers is a trip into consciousness that goes as far back as memory reaches. As a child, the narrator experienced happiness only in flashes. Nevertheless, this period of contentment resembles a stream that nourished the very beginning of her existence. Although conflicts, doubts, and fears battered the young girl, she tried to understand the reality around her. "As soon as I was capable of reflecting I began to distinguish between present and past; in the past I recognized two phases: one that included my early childhood and my parents' life . . . and a vaguer one that dealt with episodes of my parents' childhood and their youth," (8); (fifth *lassa*). She often felt that she had arrived too late, after the most important events had already occurred. As she explains in the sixth *lassa* this marvelous period was "the time of before" (8). As a result, exclusion from that magical era of her parents' life frustrated and disappointed her: "I tried to imagine certain holidays belonging to the time of before" (8). Her mother's manner of talking about places and people created an atmosphere of charm. She pronounced names with such ecstatic feeling that they appeared intangible and mysterious. The town of Festiona assumes a surrealistic dimension simply because of the way her mother relates that she and her husband had gone sleigh riding there.

The narrator's parents, their adolescence, the first years of their marriage, and their love story compose the thematic core of the first chapter. The opening of the second chapter indicates that revisiting the past represents a way to grow closer to her parents and to comprehend their puzzling relationship with each other. "I went out into the street . . . and I breathed the air. . . . It is my air. . . . My need for this air is never depleted. I think of this air from afar and it nourishes me. It torments me too as something unreachable, but also fatal. For me it is the past. . . . It is 'them.' . . . Understanding them and myself was never a separate process in those days, it is even less today" (14). The narrator's desire to acquire a clearer knowledge of herself and of those she loves motivates her passionate research into the components of an earlier existence; understanding ancestry becomes equivalent to a genuine comprehension of her own being.

The effort to grasp the meaning of origins relates initially to any attempt made to become more comfortable with oneself and with the complexity of one's choices and personality. Digging into the past involves not only the use of memory as a tool to retrace what the child has perceived but also to reinterpret the "screen-memories" found. An awareness of their contents, at first seemingly insignificant, gains subsequent importance in the light of later events. This process occurs in the novel, now that "everything has already happened" and her parents are both dead. Her quest starts when she explores relationships with her parents. The journey begins in the house where she was born. Each room evokes different memories: in the living room she remembers family friends; in the guest room the people who slept there: uncles, aunts, and beautiful cousins; in the kitchen, Ciota, the maid. The narrator's mother, father, and little sister prevail in importance over the other characters and remain the nucleus of her emotional life. In the corridor she remembers her mother looking at herself in a mirror: "I am in Rinette's [a family servant's] arms and I am looking at my mother's image in the mirror. Mom sticks a hat pin in her big, feathered hat. Her eyes shine brightly in the shadow. I remember them sad, even though her face was smiling. Her entire self lies in this mystery. . . . Later I explained it, I denied it, but I always found it again" (40). Her mother was tender but introverted and perceived as a "mystery" by the narrator when she was a child and later, as an adult daughter. Although the narrator never manages to comprehend her fully, she still strives to clarify her mother's enigmatic personality.

The twelve chapters of the first part re-create the whole world of the narrator's early childhood: neighbors, relatives, her father's interest in music, painting, and photography, his jealousy of his beautiful wife, and his hunting expeditions. The narration flows in a simple, precise prose: "I leaned against the railing of the little balcony. The old, furrowed wood had become like cork. The varnish (the same old one!) had penetrated the wood—washed and rewashed, dried and redried" (42). Details are crucial since they stand for the proof of a prior existence; they represent remnants of the past. The railing of the balcony is the same one along which the narrator used to play as a young girl; this object is part of her life. The old wood, observed closely as a rarity or an antique, is the nugget she has sought and remains as evidence of an existence that time has managed to erase. Objects and environment must become familiar to a child; they are part of the security that parents embody on a fuller scale. Later, adults tend to invest the same object with feelings, so that they become signs of an epoch that ebbs and flows in the beginning of consciousness.

Part 2 opens with the narrator's statement: "Around my home was the world into which I had to venture alone" (102). All the following chapters deal with her life outside the family. In the first part of the novel, the setting of the house framed the narrator's recollection; in the second, her wandering around Ponte unifies the flow of events. Strolling from the house toward the center of the village (Piazza Nuova), she remembers the shopkeepers, their sons and daughters who became her playmates (chapter 4), and the garden of Tota where they used to play (chapter 5). Entering the old school (chapter 6), she evokes her schoolmates and teachers and then proceeds from the school building to the square and finally to the cemetery. At this point, the reader realizes that the majority of the characters encountered so far are dead: teachers, school friends, parents' friends, and almost everybody previously mentioned is buried in the Ponte cemetery. Time takes revenge on life; death, perceived by the narrator when young as decay and associated with a fear of being abandoned (chapter 8, *lassa* 5), is now accepted as an inevitable consequence of living. Her visit to the cemetery closes the circle; the evocation of Ponte Stura's world ends; everything falls back into place; the past is as dead as the people who lived in it.

The emotional climax of the novel, however, occurs when the narrator visits the town hall. She ascends the main staircase to her father's former office and views with surprise the modesty of the environment: "It was as though I had almost realized for the first time how humble Dad's work was and how magnificent his life had appeared to me as a child" (173–74). His life continues to appear beautiful to her but in a way that she could never have understood as a child. The maturity of her perceptions brings small comfort to the earlier disillusionment. "My present certitude is not even a comfort for my former lack of understanding" (174).

After having recollected the years of her childhood, the adult woman reconstructs the past in a clearer perspective. Now that she has experienced great grief she can understand her parents and give meaning to their lives. During childhood, her mother seemed to be light hearted and even naive while her father appeared more interesting and reserved. The narrator's judgment changed, however, with the passing of time: "We girls began to perceive a seriousness in Mom's silence, something intense and mysterious in her beauty" (199). The children never doubted their parents' well-being: "We accepted naturally and almost indifferently that they were good and almost condescendingly that they were happy" (199). Only the loss of these loved ones initiates a cruel thrust into the world of full emotional and intellectual development. "When Father got sick, we did not realize that she was still young; we only knew that he was old. But when she died, we experienced that loss with cruel lucidity, like an operation with no anesthesia" (199–200). Maturity takes place after overcoming both the indifference that usually characterizes adolescence and the grief brought by death, especially her mother's, which has severed the last link with the narrator's touchable past. The death of her mother enables the writer, now "alone in the world," to understand her parents. This final acceptance of a living condition of solitude, common to any human being entering maturity, marks the concluding note of *La penombra che abbiamo attraversato*. The narrator remains standing at the same spot where, long ago, she and her mother had taken lunch to her father, who frequently worked in the woods. Suddenly an affectionate image of her father flashes through her mind, and she realizes that "the valley, as well as the house, is inhabited forever by 'them'" (204). Ponte Stura and her parents live in the nontime of the narrator's mind. The present has no meaning for her; the village, the valley, and the people of her childhood are forever alive in her emotional consciousness.

From the beginning of the book, the narrator hints at the eternal existence of the world of Ponte: "Piazza Nuova is basically the same. . . . It bears a partisan's name; but as far as I am concerned, history—that which happens afterward—does not exist in Ponte. I believe Ponte to be unchanging. Its 'real' existence lies in its immutability, and mine too" (20). Ponte, the place of her origins, partakes of the quality of myth; it is timeless. Romano herself points out this aspect.

In an interview I was asked if I considered the world of Ponte lost. I answered: "The book contains no nostalgia, because that world is not lost. It is true that it belongs to the past, but I perceive its value in the present, I understand it, I love it now and therefore I possess it. As Faulkner says, 'happiness is not is but was.'" (209)

The clearer vision of that shadowy area (*penombra*) called childhood, acquired by revisiting it, enables Romano to possess this world. Faulkner's epigraph used by Romano in her book—"Happiness is not is but was"—represents the discovery of an emotional richness that has passed but that remains present in consciousness.

The poetic quality of the novel emerges through the use of a language that allows the sensitivity, thoughtfulness, and naïveté of the child to surface and that at the same time permits the narrator as an adult to be sincere and to correct the child's perceptions with a mature but sympathetic outlook on life. Romano also explains in her "Note" why she chooses a sentence from Proust's *Combray* as a title for the novel: "But even if the title contains a homage to Proust . . . it was chosen only for its mysterious and highly allusive meaning" (208). The *penombra* is the shadowy, uncertain, hazy area that every human being must cross in order to reach maturity and that must be revisited by each adult in order to become a source of happiness and enlightenment.

In 1969 Romano published *Le parole tra noi leggere*.[6] As the author herself explains, uniting the many motifs of the novel required an exhausting effort. "I had worked on this book for four years under great tension in order not to betray the main idea and the essential theme of the story."[7] The writer's anxiety derives from the fact that the plot deals directly with her own son: "I started writing about my son in order to reconstruct and to be able to read (as in 'to read a book') him as a hermetic and emblematic character" (vi). Romano, quoting a passage taken directly from the novel, emphasizes the biographical link between her and the narrator of the story. From a critical point of view in this essay, however, no identity will be assumed between the narrative persona and the author; the characters receive recognition only as fictional creations.

Dealing with the intimacy of a mother-son relationship, the writer runs the risk of slipping into the "exceedingly human," as she defines the excess of pathos. Nevertheless, her literary skill and experience overcome the challenge of finding a style that suits the theme and captures her rapport with a difficult and unscrupulous young person. "I had to eliminate the elegiac component and stress the ironic one. This search went on for several months. Then I finally realized I had solved the problem. Language is everything: it is the key" (vi). From the first page of the text the poetic, evocative language of such earlier works as Romano's *Maria* and *La penombra che abbiamo attraversato* is here completely displaced by a terse and biting language that approaches the brevity and conciseness of footnotes. Despite a few similarities with the writer's previous novels, *Le parole tra noi leggere* marks a new development in her production from both a stylistic and thematic point of view.

Although the story is told in the first person by the narrator, the mother of P., ambiguity arises as to whether the protagonist of the book is the mother-narrator or the son. A close reading of the text reveals however, that the son is the main character, and that the mother stands as the antagonist. P.'s mother recalls their relationship from her son's earliest years to the first years of his marriage, covering a span that extends from his birth in 1933 to the year 1966. Time seems to progress chronologically through the six parts of the book: part one, beginning during the Fascist regime and ending with the onset of World War II, deals with P.'s childhood and his first school difficulties; part two, in the postwar period, describes P. attending junior high school in Turin and the family's subsequent move to Milan; part three deals with his school years, his numerous motorcycle trips, and his love for Marlene; part four highlights his love story and various unsuccessful career decisions; parts five and six focus on his banking job and marriage.

The temporal dimension is not as linear as it may appear; the chronological order is challenged by continuous shifts between "now" and "then" as the first *lassa* of the book demonstrates. In the present, P.'s mother rarely confronts her son directly, but she admits: "Formerly, however, I assaulted him. But even now, although more rarely, I have an outburst of anger with him. . . . My present anger must be a residue of the old battles, when I reacted as though he were a part of me that betrayed itself and thus betrayed me" (20). Present efforts to establish a relation based on comradery and respect receive cool, annoyed, and unpleasant reactions. In spite of continued frustration and failure, P.'s mother tenaciously strives for meaningful dialogue: "I know that asking questions is the mistaken approach; but I keep asking. He is seated in front of me, engrossed in a book. . . . I try to begin a conversation. . . . Without raising his head he responds: 'I don't know'" (20).

The narrator's relationship with her son changes little over the years. They continue to fight, although less violently at the present time. The mother's visceral bond with her son remains the cause of both her past and present aggressive behavior. Her passionate offer of love, however, is not returned, arousing in her feelings of rejection, frustration, and, ultimately, betrayal. "He reacts with coolness, annoyance, and even a distracted courtesy" (20). Their "war" has essentially known only temporary truces, since the mother-narrator cannot desist from her efforts to know her son, whose life has been a constant effort to be himself and to ignore society's expectations and requirements. She must thus impose order upon the emotional magma of their love-hate story in an attempt to control maternal feelings.

Although an ironic tone imbues Romano's account and avoids the pathos ordinarily associated with the expression of passion and feelings, the novel's basic structure provides the distance needed for emotional detachment from the events. A series of "documents" permeate and appear throughout the narration. The son's comments, his drawings, objects he has built, letters, excerpts from conversations, poems, dreams, and school compositions characterize him and facilitate an understanding of his personality. Ultimately, anything P. has made, said, or written, whether or not the original appears in the text, qualifies as a "document." The narrator's memory is the source of recollection, but the documented material, either inserted into the novel (poems, letters, themes, diary notes) or only described (drawings, paintings, sculptures, handicraft objects, dreams), stimulates the act of remembering.

Episodes having no documentary basis are few. P.'s mother uses the "documents" as a narrating tool, linking them logically and chronologically with her own comments. Sometimes "documents" speak for themselves. One *lassa* contains a letter written from P., and the following one includes the mother's answer to him. Another is simply a letter sent from the mother to C., her husband, commenting on their son. The interaction needs no external explanation. The "documents" are not extraliterary elements but they constitute the spine of the narration; without them the book would be a one-sided maternal chronicle, running the risk of becoming a story marred by an excess of love. The "documents" represent tangible entities of P.'s actions to the narrator, who fails to comprehend the personality of her son and to acquire an acceptable relationship with him. The only way of obtaining knowledge about him, especially since he has no desire to be known, is an examination of the objects he has made, the letters he has written, the things he has drawn, or what he has said. The dramatic core of the novel results from the narrator's struggle, since the "documents" often prove her thoughts or past beliefs to be wrong.

By constructing the whole narration on "documents," Romano follows a clearly defined pattern. In one instance, she objectively reports her son's past statements, since he "was capable of memorable sentences" (20). In this sense, what the young man says becomes a "document." She reveals his personal reaction to the concept that the Almighty is the Lord of Hosts. "I do not like God, He reminds me of Mussolini" (20). She relates his biting sarcasm toward the Assumption of the Virgin Mary: "Who knows how badly she feels in Paradise, she, the only one with a body!?!" (20). His comment to his religion teacher about lions in the ideal Eden places additional emphasis on his ironic bent. "What good are lions' claws in the earthly paradise. In holy pictures, lions fraternize with gazelles" (20). As a young child, he would often sit in front of his food with no desire to eat. On one such occasion, he expressed an unexpected philosophical outlook. "Better not to be than to be" (22).

After reporting facts and details, the narrator frequently derives logical conclusions or affiliated associations from the information. Her son's use of logic to question the Bible reminds her of her famous Uncle Peano. "Was he his heir? I doubted it. . . . As a child he looked like his uncle a lot. . . . He still does" (22). Her emotional side hopes for a resemblance between the two, since her uncle was a famous mathematician, but rationally she recognizes this to be impossible. If a similarity once existed, it is now confined to the realm of personal rather than intellectual. P.'s initial remarks about religion lay the groundwork for his mother's observation about his mental process. "Even now logic rules his agnosticism and dictates his quick, sharp statements" (21). Following P.'s comments on being and nonbeing, the narrator's desire to see her son excel in life surfaces as a simply human and justifiable reaction. "I realized that the sentence was only partially philosophical. However, it floored me. His aptitude for logic could have facilitated his becoming a philosopher one day" (22). Nevertheless, the narrator's rational restraint controls any excess of maternal pride. "The sentence can be explained. . . . It must have been motivated by the meal" (22).

The mother's careful consideration of all the consequences of her son's statements and behavior is even more apparent in the conclusions that she draws. In *lassa* 23, P.'s refusal of food is seen as a sign of the dissatisfaction and unhappiness that have characterized his attitude toward active life since early childhood. She recognizes his refusal to accept the meal as the first sign of his future *oblomovismo,* which other documents such as school compositions or letters from P.'s adolescence further indicate and which eventually develops into indifference toward success in life. "His abstract thinking was an unfortunate sign of his inherent and organic pessimism"

(22). The word "unfortunate" betrays the narrator's suffering for her son, whom she considers a lifelong pessimist doomed to unhappiness. At the time of the incident, the narrator experienced a comic reaction. "I am afraid I laughed; on the other hand, he never paid any attention to me" (22). Her present fear reflects severe self-criticism and regret at having felt amusement toward something that first seemed enjoyable but later assumed dramatic proportions. The second part of the sentence that concludes *lassa* 23 reveals—only thinly disguised by the statement's brevity—the grief caused by P.'s continual indifference.

The insertion of "documents" follows an iterative pattern: documents-deductions-conclusions; documents-deductions-conclusions. Romano presents the "facts," comments on them, and then brings them to an outcome; such a succession repeating itself ultimately has the effect of characterization. P. is portrayed by what he says and does in the "documents," while his mother's judgments reveal her own individuality. The narrator's portrait of her son mirrors her own self; trying to define one soul she discloses two. Using the "documents" achieves an original thematic and stylistic result: a double effect of character portrayal, although a distinction highlights the general pattern. While most of the "documents" reconstruct the past, the dialogical excerpts clarify the present and always occur between the narrator and the adult P. in the narrative "now."

> He is now saying that he has read somewhere the characteristics of the asocial type and they are (correction: they were) his: anorexia, pyromania. . . .—Pyromania?—He reminds me of that time when he started a fire in the kitchen. . . . My forgetfulness is due . . . to the fear of a criminal drive in him. I knew his passion for fire, strolling around the city he always hoped to see a fire. . . . I know that the (aesthetic) passion for fire is not a symptom of pyromany: pyromany is caused by solitude. . . . The (painful) core of his existence is what it is; but the pathological definition is his. (88–89)

This *lassa* can be divided into two parts. The dialogue is first rendered in all its directness; the reader has the impression of actually listening to the conversation, since the writer has suppressed the "I said" or "he answered." The narrator's thoughts are confined to the second part of the *lassa*. Since her participation in the conversation is minimal, P. receives the opportunity to express himself fully in one of his rare talkative moments. By avoiding the use of words normally employed in reported speech, the narrator achieves the concise, direct immediacy of spoken language. This *lassa* appears in the text between others that recall the so-called criminal deeds P. has committed during adolescence; the cause of these adventures still remains unclear to the mother who asks for explanations from her adult son. The dialogical documentation verifies past impressions and enables her to change her point of view in the light of what P. says in the present.

By the end of the novel, the narrator has made minimal progress in acquiring knowledge of P. She is still circling her son and incapable of comprehending him. The reader, retaining the privilege of a broader understanding of both characters, views the story as the interplay of two passionate, gifted, special, and kindred souls who cannot help being both attracted and repulsed by each other. Mother and son share the same creativity, independence, and exclusivity of love; hence their personalities clash endlessly. The mother's disappointment and the son's autonomy posit a no-win or no-surrender situation. The narrator astutely observes that "one cannot become what one is not" (48).

La penombra che abbiamo attraversato and *Le parole tra noi leggere* both acquire their nonlinear structure from the narrators' recollections of the past. In the former, physical environment stimulates the narrator's memory and revives the past; in the latter, "documents" constitute the loose thread that leads the mind. The temporal scheme of the two novels projects a double movement from present to past and then back to present. Such a complex temporal itinerary, as well as opposition between past and present, serves a definite purpose. Romano has stated in various interviews that "we are the past"; she agrees with Poulet who writes: "The present is something that has not yet become past."[8] According to Romano, earlier phases of human existence enlighten the present. Human experiences constitute a temporal process that transpires in time. The lessons of the past enable an understanding of the present and form a unified entity. In both novels, remembrances force the narrators' minds to confront their present selves with their former ones. In this sense, Romano's narratives are more than merely simple recollections of the past; they are enriching revisitations of it. Timelessness—a third temporal dimension—characterizes these novels. In the affective memory of the narrator, everything is; Ponte Stura remains as it appears in the present and as it used to be long ago. P. is unhappy both as a young man and as a child. By placing the past in direct contrast to the present and narrating the simple events of everyday life, Romano depicts the growth of a conscience and thereby represents the fascinating process of living that is always difficult and complex.

NOTES

A mio padre e a mia madre (in memoria).

1. Georges Poulet, *Studies in Human Time* (Baltimore: Johns Hopkins University Press, 1956), pp. 23–24.

2. Ibid, p. 26.

3. *Lassa*: singular; *lasse*: plural. English: *laisse,* a stanzaic or verse structure in epics (see J. A. Cuddon, *Dictionary of Literary Terms* [New York: Penguin Books, 1982], p. 354).

4. Lalla Romano, *La penombra che abbiamo attraversato* (Turin: Einaudi, 1964), pp. 5–6. Subsequent references from this edition will be indicated in the text by the page number in parentheses. The translations are mine.

5. What seems true to the child usually appears in the text in quotation marks.

6. The title is derived from a verse of Eugenio Montale's "La Bufera."

7. Lalla Romano, *Le parole tra noi leggere* (Turin: Einaudi, 1969), p. v. Subsequent quotations from this edition will be indicated in the text by the page number in parentheses. Translations are mine.

8. Poulet, *Studies in Human Time,* p. 35.

GINA LAGORIO

Gina Lagorio was born in Bra, a small town in the Langhe area of Piedmont, where her paternal grandparents owned property in its rich countryside. After World War II, she moved with her family to the city of Savona on the Italian Riviera but, she often returns on vacations to the Langhe, the land that inspired her passion for literature. She pursued her literary interests at the University of Turin, where she earned a degree in literature, with a concentration in English. Lagorio now lives in Milan, where she works as a consultant for the Garzanti Publishing Company. She is also a member of the Italian Parliament. Her books include two children's works, *Le novelle di Simonetta* (1960) and *Attila re degli Unni* (1964), a collection of short stories, *Il polline* (1966), and the novels *Un ciclone chiamato Titti* (1969), *Approssimato per difetto* (1971), the best-seller *Fuori scena* (1979), *Tosca dei gatti* (1983), and another best-seller *Golfo del paradiso* (1987). Among her critical works are a monograph on Beppe Fenoglio, a biography of Camillo Sbarbaro, and an essay on the poet Angelo Barile. She has also published critical editions of the writers Mario Tobino, Pearl Buck, Cesare Pavese, and Beppe Fenoglio for the Italian school system.

Gina Lagorio and the Courage of Women

MARK F. PIETRALUNGA

Since the publication of *Il polline* (Pollen) in 1966, Gina Lagorio has focused on the theme of women's moral superiority as a central factor in social history. Inspired by what she has seen of the political world, she writes that women possess a "courage for truth," which their male counterparts have lost in the struggle for power. She points out that such an affirmation would have evoked irony and pity a few years ago, when female characters in literature were customarily treated as objects of weakness and ambiguity. In rebellion against this bias, Lagorio has chosen to adopt the theme of feminine indomitability as the central tenet of her oeuvre. As she has written, focusing on the courage of women is a new way to reconsider certain private stories, if not history.[1]

Deeply attached to her native region and to the history firmly rooted in the land, she feels a strong affinity with another Piedmontese writer, Beppe Fenoglio, to whom she has dedicated a number of critical studies. In one of these works, she writes about this contemporary author's sense of history:

> The authenticity of Fenoglio emerges intact precisely because of this pure passion of an intellectual faithful to his own origins—whose sense of history is always alive in his pages that deal with both peace and war. But, it is a concrete history that neither follows sociopolitical schemes nor indulges in hagiographies when he speaks about the Resistance as it was. Fenoglio never lowers himself to ostentation and pomp because of his moral rigor, gusto for truth, and spiritual elegance. These same gifts caused him to refute the triumphal rhetoric of the [Fascist] regime without knowing any Marxist texts.[2]

The same concrete faithfulness and profound attachment to one's origins, which Lagorio indicates is characteristic of Fenoglio, are also evident when we examine Lagorio's own artistic production. We sense immediately what Lagorio has learned from Fenoglio when she expresses her opinion on writing: "Only a ferocious and profound attachment to the vital, native lymph can bring a book to life (and this goes also for film). Writing must

77

be an authentic vocation to be confirmed by battles, by struggles, and perhaps by disappointments, but certainly by pain."[3] Elsewhere, she refers to Fenoglio as a direct influence on her decision to become a writer and mentions the background they share and are both inspired by: "I believe what most drove me to write was the surprise, the happiness of having seen my land, the land of labor, of hills, of dreams, the places of my childhood represented above all by Pavese and Fenoglio. . . . Everything instilled in me a geographical courage."[4]

The land she speaks about is the hilly and stark Langhe region in southern Piedmont, where her family had for generations worked the soil. Lagorio writes how she has returned to this region whenever possible to spend vacations at her grandparents' farmhouse. As a young student, she prepared for her university examinations there; as an adult she brings her daughters to the same location. Although Lagorio also lived in the region of Liguria, she wanted her daughters to experience the intense, sweet, chaste, and severe landscape of Piedmont. She wanted them to smell the earth, stalls, straw turned in the sun, and burnt leaves when the earth was prepared for planting.[5] At a conference entitled "Piedmont and Literature in the Twentieth Century," Gina Lagorio was invited as a writer from Piedmont to give her impressions. She began her brief testimony by equating the land of her birth to the land of truth: "Someone like me, who was born in Bra and has lived many years in Liguria, feels, each time I come here, that my truth exists here." She continued by emphasizing that her loyalty to Piedmont is not theoretical but, instead, practical and depicted in several critical and creative works, beginning with her first collection of short stories, *Il polline*. Lagorio had originally entitled the work *Respirare Piemonte* (To breathe Piedmont) and explained that she picked that title because of what she remembered of Piedmont after years of working and living in Liguria: "It meant arriving here, looking at the vineyards, looking at the fields, smelling the odors, eating those certain peppers, feeling that it was a way 'to breathe Piedmont' and, consequently, to be alive still, at least in the memory of the peasant women who had preceded me, through my grandmothers, and to feel that this was my land."[6]

In an article entitled "Donna e fatica" (Women and labor), Lagorio honors the peasant women of the Langhe. She writes of how these tenacious women would work the land beside the men and then also do the domestic work that a house and family necessitated. In describing Fenoglio's effective depiction of his female characters, which was also inspired by the women of the Langhe, Lagorio underlines the ethical parameters that remain a constant of women protagonists in her own writings: "Poor wives who gather the scraps, deformed by labor and maternity, distrustful of what is new, but firm in their heart and arms when defending their roof and land."[7] She offers examples from Fenoglio's short novel *La malora* (Misery), which capture the essence of the "geographical courage" Lagorio often emphasizes when writing about Piedmont. Fenoglio's novel ends with a mother's announcement of death as she prays to a severe God who has violently struck her hopeless world once again:

> Do not call me until you have closed the eyes of my poor son Emilio. Then I will be happy if you call me, if you are happy. And when you do, please keep in mind what I did out of love and be lenient with me for what I did out of necessity. And all of us, who will be up there, will place a hand on Agostino's head, for he is good and has sacrificed himself for the family and will be alone in the world.[8]

Lagorio stresses how this prayer represents the pity common to the peasant women of the Langhe and how these women demonstrate a special understanding for those who are the weakest. She notes that the compassion implicit in the mother's words motivates the courage needed to revolt. She interprets "out of necessity" as all the tremendous power of destiny, along with its inexorable laws, and the women's willingness to accept it with as much pity as possible.[9]

When asked if she was a feminist, Lagorio replied that she did not care for slogans. She recalled the pity and strength of the women that both she and Fenoglio had described, and she believes that women will be at the center of the future—not against men but beside them, responsibly sharing rights and duties. The writer recalls that women were the pillars of the peasant society from which she came. "My grandmother . . . could have commanded an army and I thought back to the women of the Langhe who had been able to close the door in the face of the Germans when there was the need to save a hidden partisan."[10]

Lagorio's less than enthusiastic reaction to feminist slogans is similar to that of another of her favorite writers, Anna Banti. Like Banti, however, Lagorio incorporates the feminine condition as a dominant theme of her work. Banti's collection of short stories written in the 1940s and entitled *Il coraggio delle donne* (The courage of woman) is particularly significant to Lagorio, who writes that the title of the collection carries the central theme of both Banti's and her own writing: "I thought that her [Banti's] theme was precisely the courage of women, and this theme is, I believe, also my own."[11]

Grazia Livi's introduction to Banti's collection highlights motifs that enable us to understand why Lagorio identified with this work from an early date. Livi points out that Banti was the first among Italian and foreign writers of the 1930s and 1940s to write that to be a woman was not a silent patrimony, but one that was capable of generating sudden actions of revolt.[12] Banti's women, continues Livi, far from suffering submissively, are armed and ready to react to the moral and intellectual strictures imposed on them. Livi defines this fortitude:

> It is a courage whose quality is proud, intense, and at times, raving and agitated. It is a courage that, having inverted every preconceived idea of the female sex, does not rely on its legendary malleableness but rather on a woman's own impregnability and on her irresistible desire to be faithful to herself. . . . Therefore, Banti's faithfulness does not mean the subversion of one's own existential condition but rather the affirmation of an irreducible moral value: refusing to surrender or accept the loss of one's dignity, of one's uniqueness; remaining on the alert, combative, proud, firm in the awareness of one's own character.[13]

Although Lagorio's women have taken great steps in liberating themselves from the claustrophobic environment that Banti's women experience, they nevertheless demonstrate a similar pugnacious, moral strength and an equally determined faith. The need for truth distinguishes both Banti's and Lagorio's main characters. Such is the nature of Angela, the heroine of Lagorio's best-selling novel of 1977, *La spiaggia del lupo* (The wolf's beach).[14] Angela is a young woman from a town along the Ligurian riviera; she constructs her life by avoiding pitfalls and by refusing to surrender and by refusing to submit to the code of external respectability. As a child, she lives with her grandfather and mother in a small house on an enchanted beach, "the wolf's beach," so-called because of "a large rock carved on top like a head on a crouched animal ready to leap" (13). The sculpture represents a mythological symbol of defense against the monsters of her childhood fears. Her fisherman grandfather is now too old to go out to sea; her father, an artist and descendant of a noble family, died young; her mother—never recognized by her husband's relatives and therefore disinherited—makes ends meet by working in the city and returns only on Saturdays. Angela grows up alone, wild, and innocent. Until her teen-aged years, her life is characterized by long swims, sheets that wave in the sun, the fresh, salt-smelling rooms of the small houses, the good smell of the local "foccaccia" bread baked with cheese and onions, and a vivid imagination that manifests itself from the first years of childhood: "From her hands everything appears as if it were magic. She needed very little, some crumbs, cuttlefish bones, a little silk, to give form to fantasies that naturally acquired a body from her hands" (15).

In the summer of her eighteenth year, she meets Vladi, a man of thirty who has come from Milan. They fall in love. When Vladi leaves at the beginning of winter, Angela discovers she is pregnant. Vladi is married and, what is worse, tied down by the family business. He does not have the courage to leave the wife with whom he has been since adolescence. Meanwhile, Angela goes to Milan and studies at the art institute of Brera. The child is born and Angela lives for a while as Vladi's mistress. While taking courses in Milan, she undergoes a metamorphosis. She meets politically committed youths and acquires a new self-awareness. When Vladi allows himself to become totally absorbed by his wife and relatives, Angela decides to leave him and dedicate herself to her young baby, Carlino. She returns to the riviera and completes her "sentimental education" by becoming the lover of Penzarocchi, an old, cynical, and corrupt artist. Regarding this relationship, Lucio Felici writes: "The relationship with him risks changing into a spiral of perversion. However, Angela's vitality is stronger, and everything becomes resolved for her through a growing awareness of her own body and a physical maturation that helps her understand herself better and the duty that awaits her."[15]

Angela breaks away from her artist-lover and definitively leaves Liguria for Milan with her child. "She had her strength and her youth for him and for herself: together, in Milan, they would construct their home. Milan was a wounded city but alive. So was she" (215). Lagorio not only succeeds in finding the vital roots of existence but also interprets the difficult birth of consciousness and the formation of a personality. On this note, she writes about her protagonist: "I took Angela by the hand, a child on the wolf's beach, isolated and still intact . . . and I led her through experiences, both happy and traumatic, encounters with characters, both old and young, to Milan where finally I leave her as a woman, alone, free, and capable of responsibly making her own decisions."[16] What saves her is an ability to recognize even in conflict and pain the beauty of life and to know when to recall those things that distinguished and formed her youth:

> The beauty that she enjoyed brought her back to the dreams of an ancient beauty, when Boine arrived in that corner of the world seeking health for his consumed lungs, or Roccatagliata Ceccardi as he hurried along on the last leg of his march toward the life-saving port of his friend Novaro, his pockets empty, the canary in the cage balancing on his shoulder, and the riding-whip, which cut the air like an angry metronome, marking hendecasyllables. (175)[17]

The critic Carlo Bo states that a special and direct notion of poetry saves Angela.[18] Lagorio anticipates this at the beginning of the novel, when she declares that the gift of grace alone allows individuals to visualize what is under and inside things and what no one else sees: "not the things that appear but things as they are for he who lives them, a continuous waiting, celebration, pain, and wonder" (39). Poetry becomes "a miracle that coincides with a breath, that multiplies in a formation of never-ending concentric circles" (39). The writer believes that things can be at the same time both simple and complex; consequently, they may evolve into other phenomena. "Everything flows gradually and continuously, slides into minutes and years, and changes our eyes that look and our mind that understands" (39).

Bo notes that the theme of the novel is Angela's ability to know how to follow and to capture "the waiting, the celebration, the pain, and the wonder" of existence.[19] This theme and the faith in life it evokes echo the words of poet Eugenio Montale, whose artistic expression has its origins in the severe and desolate Ligurian landscape that was an integral part of Angela's development: "It will be a faith whose objective may seem obscure and consists above all in living with the dignity and the hope that life has a meaning that rationally escapes us, but is, nevertheless, worth experiencing."[20]

This belief is also Lagorio's philosophy as she creates Angela. She has nurtured her protagonist on the elements that were part of the rich poetry of the region that fostered the poets Montale, Boine, and Sbarbaro. Lagorio's observation about Montale is appropriate in defining the same qualities that inspired many traits evident in the protagonist of *La spiaggia del lupo:* "Nevertheless, I believe that the fiber of Montale's poetics and the character of his poetry would have been different if his roots had not been nourished by the history and poetry of a harsh and solid region, where beauty has always paid dearly and where the most rooted faith has not been metaphysical, but nurtured by a profound desperation and a profound tenacity."[21] This Ligurian tradition of poetry represents another important point of reference and inspiration in Lagorio's writings. She is faithful to the Piedmontese landscape of the Langhe and to its writers Pavese and Fenoglio; she is also devoted to the severe and rocky landscape of Liguria and to its poets: "However, I am also faithful to Liguria, and I expressed my gratitude to it for all it has given me in my critical works on Ligurian poetry, above all on Camillo Sbarbaro and Angelo Barile, who encouraged me to write and who guided me."[22]

Lagorio interprets the Ligurian heritage in concise and abbreviated language: "a closed tradition of ethical values within a tormented landscape of sea and rocks, of wind and sun."[23] Nevertheless, she avoids the almost inevitable nihilistic side of this landscape and concentrates on the small, everyday problems that people, and, above all, women, continually confront. "Narrating, I tried in my own way to participate in common problems and to avoid the fascination with negation that is so overwhelmingly in the air."[24] The writer receives much strength from the perseverance of the Ligurian people among whom she has lived, and from them she draws the courage needed to engage in work that is difficult for a woman to reconcile with the image of her mother.

The poet Camillo Sbarbaro best illustrates the Liguria that has inspired Lagorio. In the following lines from Sbarbaro's poem, she recognizes the exemplary poetic expression of this arid region: "The skeleton is stone and the earth red and scarce and the grass sparse and strong: and all is rough and dry as if superfluity were devoured by an inner burning."[25] This austere and bare landscape conforms to Sbarbaro's simple, pure, and chaste nature and poetry, which Lagorio emphasizes with the subtitle to her biography on the poet, *Sbarbaro: Un modo spoglio di esistere* (Sbarbaro: A bare way of living). Lagorio implies a style and a way of life that focuses on the essential and refuses the superfluous—an attitude echoed in the works of Fenoglio. What joins these two writers from two regions that are ethnically and culturally different is their faithfulness to a way of existence. Lagorio coins the phrase "secular sanctity" to describe their outlooks on life. The expression implies a sense of pity toward others, a coherent belief, and a simple, strong commitment to truth in one's artistic expression of everyday events.[26]

Lagorio inherits from Sbarbaro and Fenoglio this integrity and a strong sense of the land. Both these aspects are present in her first major work, *Il polline*. Lagorio returns again to Piedmont, and to what she calls "perhaps . . . the most genuine air" in her later novel *Fuori scena* (Offstage).[27] In her recollection of Piedmont and its significance to her and to the novel's protagonist, the successful stage actress Elena, Lagorio poetically defines the land of her origins:

> Piedmont can be a category of the spirit in the sense that there exists for each one of us a geographical horizon that defines us, conditions us, and that is also, above all, a place of the spirit. It is a place where the spirit finds its most genuine shelter perhaps because each one of us needs something to which we can anchor ourselves and filter in ways, such as through the air, smells, and colors, which are most congenial to it.[28]

The writer's description recalls that of fellow Langhe writer Cesare Pavese, who in his novel *La luna e ilfalò (The Moon and the Bonfires)*, treats the return to one's roots and the need to have a place that fosters a sense of existence. Anguilla, the novel's protagonist, expresses such a need: "Your own village means that you are not alone, that you know there's something of you in the people and the plants and the soil, that even when you are not there, it waits to welcome you."[29] Although the principal story of Lagorio's novel is of a woman in crisis with her profession, her lover, and her daughter, the nourishing power of a hometown provides a background to the entire plot. This sense of place gives greater significance to the development of the story's events. Elena has arrived at an impasse in her successful stage career and is on the verge of a nervous breakdown. Her relationship with her rebellious teenaged daughter is also rapidly deteriorating; in addition, she begins to lose the affection of her much younger, unfaithful lover Marco, an actor in her theatrical company. Elena suddenly decides to leave Rome and its artificial theatrical world for her hometown, hoping to reorder her thoughts and feelings in solitude. Her shelter and salvation are in the "village of clear air" (Cherasco), the land of her roots, the place where she finds validity in a more natural setting. While there, she encounters the elderly count Dino with whom she had an idyllic sentimental relationship in her youth. Elena's contact with Dino rekindles certain emotions and an enthusiasm that she believed she had lost, if not forgotten. This encounter is not a nostalgic return to a first love, found miraculously intact, but is something more important and vital. With regard to this relationship, Michele Prisco writes: "It is the discovery of a bond that ties her to her land and with it, the discovery of having arrived at a stage in her life where she is self-sufficient and comfortable with her solitude, her one and true companion."[30] The pure and essential world of her hometown provides Elena with the environment she needs to arrive at a decision: "It was one of those days of light that reveals the beauty of the Langhe in its purity and also inspires a profound emotion in those who were not born here" (75). There is nothing accidental or artificial in the landscape; there is no concession to ornamentation. She experiences the scene as a symbol of what moves within the actions and affections of men.

When Marco comes to take her back to Rome, Elena submissively follows him. Nevertheless, something has changed in her. She will resume her work, her relationship with Marco, and her duties as a mother, but she will do so with a certain detachment. She makes this clear in a conversation with her daughter, Nora, as she reflects upon her escape to the Langhe:

> They laughed together, and Elena for the first time, since she had returned, had the courage to tell her daughter the truth, or what she thought was the truth of her escape: "It's true, I dreamed many times about my return to my hometown. I

no longer know how I lived there. I only remember that I thought about you and also about Marco, as if I were thinking about someone who no longer needed me: he had had enough of me and you were rebellious. I was no use to either of you any longer, I was a nuisance. And then I turned to myself as to someone who has always done what she is supposed to do and for the first time does what she likes in order to breathe peace, without boring or being bored. (102)

The return to her hometown and to the solitude it offers her now becomes an option and an expression of Elena's maturation as a woman. Her reply to Marco, when asked how she imagines her future, now rings with conviction: "Alone, I already told you. With Nora, as long as she is around. Afterward, alone. With friends, my work; if solitude is a choice, and not anguish, it is maturity" (225). Elena's decision is determined by a desire to be faithful to herself and by an innate sense of pride that has prevented her from surrendering. Such was the case when she first decided to leave her hometown and boldly pursue a theatrical career: "Granted, she was poor; the village was a place of exile for a woman like her, and also pride had played in her decision: she was afraid of always remaining a Cinderella next to him [Dino], but above all there was, stronger than any fear, her will to be and make herself free" (187).

Elena has acquired the desire for self-affirmation from the women of her land: "To give up without using the talents one has been given by fortune is only weakness—this was at least what the tenacious and courageous women of her village taught her" (120). Only after years of experience away from the land of her birth, however, is she able to appreciate fully the world of her origins: "The village would have once again had them [Dino and Elena] without masks, in the nakedness of a life already sufficiently lived. They would continue together, seeking beyond the appearances, a sliver of truth and a little love, each for himself and also for the other" (187). Elena's need for veracity and for some validation of her emotions and feelings is expressed through a love that she rediscovers and relives in her search for communion with nature as well as with people. The "village of clear air," therefore, gives significance to her life; it continues to be an immense stage for private stories "like her own and Dino's, which had endured intact against the rush of years, because they had first lived them and then recalled them in the atmosphere of their hometown" (242).

A small seaside town in Liguria provides the backdrop to another of Lagorio's dramas—*Tosca dei gatti* (Tosca of the cats).[31] This prize-winning novel is the story of a humble, middle-aged caretaker of an apartment complex whose thoughts, gestures, behavior, and moods in the few months before her death are recorded in a secret notebook by a journalist whom she had befriended. The severe winter landscape serves as the ideal background for the simple but desperate existence of Tosca who attempts to establish vital relationships with others or with things. Unable to find someone to whom she can communicate her love, she directs her attention and affections to her cats, whom she treats as if they were her children: "One truth was certain in the vagueness of that friendship born from a cold project of analysis; what counts is not the object of love but the capacity to love. And Tosca, in response to the prison of indifference of others, had found an escape in cats. Was that enough? Why not?" (163).

Once again Lagorio concentrates on the small events in her protagonist's life to demonstrate how everyday gestures and words reveal the courage of this woman. Tosca's capacity to recognize the truth, however small it may appear, provides a precise verification of fortitude. Gifted with a fundamental optimism in the midst of so much indifference, Tosca succeeds in giving some sense to her bleak existence. She does so by valuing and remembering even the smallest of affections, which she will miss, as she will her music and dinners. At least, however, she will have beautiful times to recall. "Isn't it better to have something to remember that we then lose than never to have had anything? I say yes" (162). Such a conviction enables her to combat her present state of loneliness. Nevertheless, her capacity to give and receive love is demonstrated on the evening of Italy's victory over Spain in the World Cup soccer championship. For once, Tosca is able to mix with the locals, who have always considered her a bit mad and an outsider ("foresta"), and to share a few hours of euphoria and joy. Tosca's reflections on this evening reveal the tenacity of her nature:

> This evening is testimony that I can recognize myself in others without the selfishness of love and hate. What misfortune I have encountered up to now is not something I've looked for; if I've lost the thread of love with people, my poor cats have helped me perhaps not to forget it entirely; and so cheer up, Tosca, don't let yourself get down; stay at the window and drink the night breeze until daylight. (134)

Although Tosca is childless, she nevertheless has a maternal instinct that induces her to find relationships of affection in order to give, even if it is cats who are her beneficiaries. She draws the strength here to persevere in a life of emptiness and desperation:

> She had attempted sometimes to tell herself that not to exist any longer, not to think and not to suffer, was better than to live the way she lived. But each time

something had stopped her from yielding completely to the temptation of believing in the total uselessness of her life. She had lived for Miciamore, she could live for Poppa or for any other living creature that needed protection. (126)

Until the end, Tosca lives in the faith that affection can still exist and develop with those around her. Mariá, her deceased husband, had lived in faith, because he had always loved everyone. "'And me? I love only cats.' This wasn't true, and she knew it; she even hoped up until the last to make friends with those of the village who frightened her" (226). She allows herself to die in the end, not because she is evicted by her landlord, but because she sees in this eviction a separation from the precarious roots that keep her attached to the world, to her friends, to her cats, and above all, to her beloved memories. Like the women of the Langhe admired by Lagorio, Tosca courageously accepts her hapless destiny with the practical faith that she can affirm herself through love. With the loss of her roof, Tosca sees her ties with others severed and consequently loses her sense of worth. When this occurs, Tosca accepts death with the same dignity that she lived.

The courage of women has proved to be the backbone of Lagorio's poetics. The author has succeeded in transforming the private stories of Angela, Elena, and Tosca, women caught in a harsh environment, into truthful and exemplary editions of social history. The women of the Langhe in Piedmont, a fierce attachment to the land of her origins and the poetic values of Liguria, her aesthetic indebtedness to Fenoglio, Banti, Pavese, Montale, and Sbarbaro provide a life-affirming background for Lagorio's continued fascination with women's unique courage.

NOTES

1. Gina Lagorio, "Il coraggio delle donne," in *Penelope senza tela* (Ravenna: Longo, 1984), pp. 108, 109. All translations in this essay are mine.

2. Gina Lagorio, "Fenoglio: l'epopea della terra di destino," *Rivista milanese di economia,* 13 (January–March 1985): 59.

3. Lagorio's comments are from an interview with Massimo Mida regarding writers and film: "Le buone intenzioni non servono," *Paese Sera,* 19 September 1972, p. 3.

4. Antonio Mungai, "Una donna gatto ci spiega il mestiere di scrivere," *Corriere medico,* Dec. 9, 1983, p. 10.

5. Lucio Felici, "Gina Lagorio," *Otto/Novecento* 2 (March–April 1980): 122.

6. Gina Lagorio, "Testimonianza di Gina Lagorio," *Proceedings of the Conference on Piemonte e la letteratura nel '900* (San Salvatore Monferrato: Assessorato alla cultura del comune di San Salvatore Monferrato, 1979), p. 673.

7. Lagorio, "Il coraggio," p. 115.

8. Beppe Fenoglio, *Opere,* 5 vols. (Turin: Einaudi, 1978), 2: 438.

9. Lagorio, "Il coraggio," p. 118.

10. Ibid., p. 117.

11. Ibid., p. 107.

12. Grazia Livi, Introduction to Anna Banti, *Il coraggio delle donne* (Milan: La Tartaruga, 1983), p. 10.

13. Ibid., pp. 10–11.

14. Gina Lagorio, *La spiaggia del lupo* (Milan: Garzanti, 1977). All references from this edition are indicated in parentheses following the quotation.

15. Felici, "Gina Lagorio," p. 138.

16. Lagorio, "Lagorio," *Corriere d'informazione,* September 3, 1977, p. 3.

17. The names mentioned in this passage—Giovanni Boine, Roccatagliata Ceccardi, and Mario Novaro—are poets in the Ligurian tradition. Mario Novaro was also a discoverer of literary talent and publisher of the magazine *La Riviera Ligure,* founded by his older brother, Angelo Silvio Novaro, in 1895.

18. Carlo Bo, "Attesa, festa e dolore," *Corriere della sera,* (April 17, 1977), p. 12.

19. Ibid.

20. Gina Lagorio recalls these words by Eugenio Montale in her essay "L'amico di Esterina," in *Penelope,* p. 22.

21. Ibid., p. 277.

22. Felici, "Gina Lagorio," p. 122.

23. Gina Lagorio, *Cultura e letteratura ligure del '900* (Genoa: Sabatelli, 1972), pp. 21–22.

24. Gina Lagorio, "Liguria: Una grande finestra sull'azzurro," *Penelope,* pp. 322–23.

25. Lagorio quotes this line from Sbarbaro in her essay *Cultura e letteratura ligure* (30) and in her biography of the Ligurian poet, *Sbarbaro: Un modo spoglio di esistere* (Milan: Garzanti, 1981), p. 9.

26. The following examples are two of several instances in which Lagorio uses the phrase "secular sanctity" when she refers to the moral attitude of both writers. In the case of Sbarbaro, she writes: "Sbarbaro did not have any veil of faith over his eyes, and he rejected any form of humiliation. He was a man who inspected the most hidden forms of nature with the mind of a mystic. If one could speak of secular sanctity—it can be found in the raw prose that, along with his poetry, is his inimitable contribution to our civilization" (*Cultura e letteratura ligure,* p. 32). In another passage, Lagorio speaks of both Sbarbaro and Fenoglio: "Once again we are surprised by how perfectly similar the intent and even the words are with those of the other solitary writer whom we have had the occasion to mention, Camillo Sbarbaro. If we can speak about a 'secular sanctity,' I believe that both have attained it" (*Beppe Fenoglio,* [Florence: La Nuova Italia, 1975], p. 18).

27. Gina Lagorio, *Fuori scena* (Milan: Garzanti, 1979). All references are from the 1979 edition and appear in parentheses immediately after the quotation.

28. Lagorio, "Testimonianza di Gina Lagorio," p. 674.

29. Cesare Pavese, *The Moon and the Bonfires,* trans. Louise Sinclaire (Harmondsworth: Penguin, 1963), p. 8.

30. Michele Prisco, "Elena, attrice fuori scena," *Oggi,* January 11, 1980, p. 46.

31. Gina Lagorio, *Tosca dei gatti* (Milan: Garzanti, 1983). All references to this edition appear in parentheses following the quotations.

GIANNA MANZINI

Gianna Manzini was born in Pistoia, Tuscany, in 1896. She studied literature with Giuseppe De Robertis at the University of Florence. While in Florence, she wrote her first novel, *Tempo innamorato* (1928), and published short stories that demonstrated her extraordinary skill as an observer of animals. After a brief marriage to the journalist Bruno Fallaci, Manzini moved to Rome and formed a lifelong artistic and personal relationship with the critic Enrico Falqui. In 1945, she became editor of the international journal *Prosa,* which developed into an open forum for contemporary writers throughout the world. In that same year, she published her second novel, *Lettera all'editore,* whose innovative structure of a work-in-progress caused considerable critical discussion and debate. Manzini's literary production—twenty-four volumes of novels and short stories—spans six decades and includes *Il valzer del diavolo* (1947), *La sparviera* (1956), *Un'altra cosa* (1961), *Allegro con disperazione* (1965), and, finally, the well-known *Ritratto in piedi* (1971), which earned the Strega award. Her last work, *Sulla soglia,* was published in 1973, the year before she died, and emblematically prefigures the writer's own death.

Gianna Manzini's Poetics of
Verbal Visualization

GIOVANNA MICELI-JEFFRIES

In my own way, I am a casual explorer who happens to
find herself beyond the orbit, envisioning a different plen-
itude, now dark, now dazzling.
—G. MANZINI: *Ritratto in piedi*

Studying Gianna Manzini in the setting of contemporary Italian literature
elicits two essential considerations: one is of the poetic and literary quality
of her prose; the other is of its experimental and innovative character.
Whereas the first aspect places Manzini in the well-established literary
tradition of "prosa d'arte" (artistic prose), the author's tendency to experi-
ment shows her unrelenting exploration of the different, expanded functions of the novel itself.

Manzini's works have not been translated into English, perhaps because
of the peculiar problems that her prose would present in another language.
Critics have often labeled her art as "difficult" and considered her an "elite"
sort of writer.[1] The term *prosa d'arte* refers broadly to certain characteristics
of refinement and linguistic preciousness present in most Italian prose
produced between the two wars. Writing poetic or prose "fragments" was a
well-established practice among collaborators of the literary journal *La Voce*
(1908–1916). It was at the University of Florence, as a student of Giuseppe
De Robertis, editor of *La Voce,* that Manzini was first introduced to the
practice of lyric prose. These "fragments" were mostly short pieces, intensely autobiographical and lyrical, well in accord with Croce's aesthetics,
which fostered a pure and spiritual representation of reality. The codifica-
tion of prosa d'arte took place in the highly influential literary journal *La
Ronda* (1919–1922) and then later in *Novecento.* The concept of a self-
sufficient literature lay at the base of this aesthetic outlook; in addition, the
best of Italy's literary tradition encouraged the search for pure stylistic
dimensions. Pragmatic consideration occupied no place in such a literary
vision. Art remained uncommitted, "free of any moralistic or political

contamination."[2] The literary piece, whether an essay, diaristic confession, or short story, represents a self-contained entity, fully realized and perfected in its own internal structure. Thus, the writer's major preoccupation became the search for a refined and pure linguistic expression capable of sustaining an oneiric and surrealistic perception of reality.

Manzini skillfully exploits the possibilities of her narrative. She searches for internal rhythms and linguistic shades that resemble the "visual fragmentism" and "descriptive impressionism" found in such contemporary Tuscan writers and poets as Tozzi, Cecchi, and Soffici.[3] But, at the same time, she deepens her interest in the structural aspects of fiction, searching for methods that would allow a freer intellectual and emotional interchange between characters and author. For the most part, she accomplishes this open flowing by introducing a circular and diffusive voice that allows the interplay of various narrative levels (dialogue, direct narration, flashback, string of associations), thus creating a crisis of objectivity inside the novel itself. Manzini's novel *Lettera all'editore* (Letter to the publisher) (1945) is a manifesto of her poetics. Structured as a work-in-progress—as Gide's *Faux-monnoyeurs,* Pirandello's *Sei personaggi in cerca d'autore,* and Bontempelli's *Vita intensa*—the novel is self-reflective and constructs its own plot, thus enabling reality to enter fiction and precluding a closed structure. The critic Emilio Cecchi immediately recognized *Lettera all'editore* as an example of Italy's most innovative narrative style and saw it as an attempt to achieve new forms of expression and to create a new type of novel.[4]

In the novel, which opens with a letter to her publisher, the author-narrator discusses her difficulties in dealing with the concepts of unity, linear plot, and objective (historical) time. She confesses that her attitude toward her work has changed and that she is no longer able to distance herself from the story; instead she feels the urge to be actively present and to bring characters, facts, memories, and fantasy into a "dazzling, acute, totally present time."[5] Manzini tends to involve her self—both her life and her art—in her writing, as if the character's situation evokes episodes from her own biography and integrates them into the story. "The true novel lies at the meeting point between the plot and some episodes of my life" (171). This admission does not simply imply that her fiction contains biographical and autobiographical facts, but also that her poetics are constantly regulated by her artistic conscience. For, as she further elaborates in *Forte come un leone* (Strong as a lion), the author believes that writing can foster "an incessant actualization of life"; at the same time, it integrates pure description, "the experience of the fragment," with elevated levels of artistic creativity, "a sense of superior geometry and architecture."[6]

Manzini's stylistic tools are syntactic displacement (progressive and regressive constructions), isolation through punctuation, inversions, interruptions, and suspensions.[7] Her frequent use of synesthesia, oxymoron, analogies, and metaphors gives her prose a distinctive lyric flow. Instead of a simple sketch, she announces "the revolt of yellow infuriating and bubbling at the top of a flower's stem";[8] she describes the sky's "anxious, swollen blue"; she evokes "the white, roaring silence" of statues.[9] Her preference for words rich in meaning, allusion, and especially visual connotation becomes apparent in regularly repeated linguistic signs; the series—*luce, lume, lumino, luccichio, luccicante, luccica* (light, lamp, small light, glitter, shining, shines)—reveals a choice of archaic, rare, precious, learned, and also local Tuscan terms. As the critic Geno Pampaloni perceptively points out, Manzini's linguistic exaltation stems from her "passionate attachment to phenomena. She is not satisfied with reality as it is; she wants to pour something of herself into it; she wants to ignite it with a crown of fires that also adds to its ardor while revealing it."[10]

Most of Manzini's attentive readers and critics agree that her works reflect a combination of "emotion and intelligence, culture and nature, refinement and instinct."[11] Gianfranco Contini states that her highly refined prose goes beyond that of D'Annunzio or *La Ronda;* according to Contini, Manzini successfully integrates "analogical discourse with the melodic lyricism of her monologue" and creates an intellectual theme for this blend.[12] The result is a unique and eminently feminine style. Giansiro Ferrata sees the intense richness of a feminine point of view as the writer's mark of distinction and originality.[13] On the other hand, Anna Nozzoli claims that Manzini's narrative style and choice of characters are so highly conditioned by her interest in a metaphorical representation of reality that female characters fail to acquire "narrative autonomy" or to establish their personalities with realistic and psychological conviction.[14] Although Nozzoli's analysis brings the salient aspects and motives of Manzini's female characterization to light, the critic fails to consider sufficiently the function of the author's "analogical discourse" as an explorative operation.

Manzini's aesthetic vision sees literature as a key to a deeper interpretation of reality. The author's prose stems from a strong belief in the vocation of writing. "Talking about my work"—she remarks in *Sulla soglia* (On the threshold)—"is something that always carries me away, enraptures me, because I believe in it. It is my faith." Her firm conviction is that certain things, whether they be good or bad, can only be written by her: "Without me, nobody could ever know anything about them. This certainty also bestows a responsibility and a right."[15] This seemingly arrogant declaration—expressed with the honesty of a final confession in her last story before her death—illustrates Manzini's missionary attitude toward her work. She proclaims an ontological justification of her own identity and function as a writer. Therefore, at the peak of neorealistic debates, when every Italian writer examined whether literature and art ought faithfully to represent social reality, Manzini expressed her belief that writers must interpret reality in a way that, once written, becomes more transparent, penetrating, and alive than when mistaken for historical events. "Reality, therefore, acquires the clarity that superficial experience obscures. Writers must imprint on reality the shape and clarity that it lacks to become absolute."[16]

Manzini's statement of her poetics is paramount. In the midst of the cultural climate of neorealism, she unequivocally searches for a special clarity. This desire for clearness has an ironic twist in the context of neo-realism, which advocated documentary immediacy and nudity in its effort to desensitize literature from the mystification of Fascist propaganda. In Manzini's vision, however, clarity means more than exact, harsh, and objective exposure of factual situations. The writer wants to observe and represent reality as an ongoing process of discovery and anticipation of meanings and allusions. It is not a coincidence that one of the writers Manzini most loved and admired was Virginia Woolf; from her, Manzini learned "a lesson in endurance" and the ability to perceive deeper regions of "fermenting shadows," where the transparent nature of things is unveiled.[17] Clarity is Manzini's ultimate metaphor, for it is more a condition experienced by the observer than a quality of the examined object; it allows both the writer and the character to dig beneath the surface of things in a perpetual search for that additional something that can be extracted. Clarity is more than a fulfilled epiphany; it is an ongoing quest. The artist rejects traditional linguistic mediums and ardently searches for one that reveals the exploratory process of her characters. In *Ritratto in piedi* (Standing portrait), Manzini declares that some truths bypass logic. "Sudden reflectors place them on stage. And although very concealed and almost forbidden, the center of their truth continues to shine."[18] Thus, her linguistic visualization has a precise function: to uncover layers of reality woven beneath the sign itself and to expose their connections, analogies, and moments of recognition.

In her first novel, *Tempo innamorato* (Time in love), Manzini's use of light leads to an antithetical characterization. There are four major figures in the novel, each displaying strong contrasting attributes, predicaments of their crossed destinies and interdependence. Rita is central to all of them; she is the wife of Raffaello, who commits suicide, and afterward the lover of Ugo, Clementina's husband. The relationship of these couples is at the same time tragic and conventional, but the active presence of the important and unusual narrator gives their lives greater intensity and interest. This unnamed, omnipresent narrator acts as a medium or filter; he or she moves in and out of the events and lives of the other characters by witnessing, assuming, hypothesizing, sympathizing, and apostrophizing as in a confessional novel.

Rita is a beautiful woman who fully enjoys life and is determined to celebrate existence and love regardless of others. In contrast, Raffaello is a joyless introvert who finds himself fighting, indeed negating, all the affirmations of existence that his wife proposes. Clementina is a self-sacrificing creature who is convinced of her lack of beauty and other positive attributes and who spends her life apologizing. Her husband, Ugo, is a man of no particular qualities. Disappointed with life, he abandons Clementina for Rita, who offers beauty and joy.

Manzini characterizes Rita with the splendor of solar tones and brightness, as one who could greet "the light with her eyelashes."[19] She is exhilarated by life, beauty, and the seasons: "She is one of those creatures who, if they open one hand and look at it, are convinced that it will bloom" (94). Therefore, as the title indicates, she bewitches time, as if causing it to fall in love with her. Raffaello, on the other hand, is lightless; he is doomed by his fears and inability to face life as his wife does. His existential problem is his inability to justify or to accept the "generosity" of life. Therefore, he does not understand that Rita is incapable of helping him or of sympathizing with him, because for her "it is so easy to be happy." Instead, he sees Rita's "greedy happiness" as her most unbearable betrayal. His suicide is both an act of liberation and an accusation.

Clementina represents a different opposition to Rita's splendid vitalism. Awkward, gray, and hesitant, she feels like "the dribbled letters left on the blotting-paper in contrast to the beauty of calligraphy" (73). Her world and personality are opaque, her most suitable season is fall, and like Raffaello, she cannot bear the intensity of light. Just as Rita's energy, beauty, and desire for joy represent a threat to Raffaello's stability, so does Clementina's selfless nature and quiet abnegation bewilder her husband, Ugo, who feels "sacrificed, really sacrificed to her goodness" (78). Anna Nozzoli sees the antithetical female characters in this novel more as allegories and metaphors than as "autonomous and self justified roles."[20] But the women are also symbols of light and shadow, and, as such, they signify the outward and inward process of exploring reality. In Manzini's first novel, this method of examination is not yet an integrated dialectic process, since all the characters somehow fail to recognize the validity of signs as necessary paths to self-exploration and full acceptance of life. This narrowness of the characters surfaces in an episode in which Rita observes Clementina and Ugo sitting on a low wall simply playing with statuettes of small sheep. For a moment she desires "to be part of that lifeless play, in that pale resemblance of play, similar to a dialogue with the dusk and with the winter." She chooses however, to lift her face high to capture the light, "satisfied and liberated by her own image of humiliation" (134). The protagonist is not yet ready for an interior journey because she is unable to face the inevitable shadow that eventually leads to her inner self.

An integration of light and shadow in one character appears in the protagonist of *Il valzer del diavolo* (The devil's waltz). In this long story, Silvia, the protagonist-narrator, is an attractive woman going through a process of self-identification and discovery as she notices and takes as a symbol the presence of a beetle crawling on the wall of her immaculate and beautiful bedroom. Disgust and horror paralyze her at first, but the image of her new house infested by hidden, underworld creatures incites her to reflect on the invisible churning of her feelings and restlessness. This process prompts the revelation of her own disruptive and distorting compassion, which she has confused with generous love but which she now sees as her driving and "devilish waltz."[21] In her search for the facts and events that fed her condition, she recalls her succession of lovers only to discover ultimately that her constant offering and giving of love and salvation hid her conviction of "an ancestral slavery" (87) inherent in womanhood. Contrary to Rita in *Tempo innamorato,* who refuses to indulge in self-examination for fear of losing her enchanted time and her joyous disposition for life, Silvia is determined to "light up" the dark labyrinth of her past, and she therefore embarks on the progressive stages of her inward search for emancipating clarity. In Anna Nozzoli's opinion, Silvia is Manzini's "most convincing female portrait," and although metaphor and symbol are still the author's preferred narrative tools, they do not "corrode the autonomy of the protagonist in her liberating quest."[22]

Lia Fava-Guzzetta remarks that the dichotomy of light and dark in *Il valzer del diavolo* also has a temporal equivalent: obscurity is related to the past, which is symbolized by the nightly visits of the beetle, while brightness refers to the present and to the process of clarification.[23] As Silvia discovers the truth about herself and her world, language is charged with intense luminosity. This radiance comes as she sits at an outdoor restaurant overlooking Lake Albano. While observing a group of people partying next to her, she suddenly becomes aware of the intensity of people's colors, weights, forms, and odors. Stripping herself of protective conventionalities, she recalls a similar moment in her childhood when she felt the same "luminous, precise consistency" (76) of reality that permitted her to feel and touch the sight of things. Silvia's final acquisition of "clarity" brings her to a state of self-knowledge that heals her memory and destroys all interest in and need for looking back at the past.

Manzini proposes a different perception and representation of clearness in a later work, *Allegro con disperazione* (Allegro with despair). The protagonist, Angela, is dealing with the memory of a painful past: she had been raped in her youth, and when she later falls in love and marries another man, she is still tormented by the violence of that memory. She has an ambivalent and contrasting relation with light and its "clarity." While she seems to succeed in rescuing flashes of light from the shadows of her past, she is, at the same time, horrified that clarity itself does not offer escape: "It is a trap worse than the shadow itself."[24] In this novel, Manzini further exacerbates the dialectics of light and darkness, of lucidity and confusion in the soul. The protagonist Angela has conflicting feelings: she is suspicious of the "abstract and ambiguous" light emerging from her past; on the other hand, she is unable to accept its shadows. She is, as Ornella Sobrero points out, "the living proof of a torment both cognitive and expressive."[25] As darkness leads to clarity, an osmotic relation occurs in her vision. Manzini plays on language's allusiveness, starting with the musical metaphor of the title and increasingly creating a pervasive atmosphere of ambiguity that reflects the protagonist's oscillations between perception and remembrance. Thus in the beautiful evening landscape of the opening scene, when Angela meets her future husband, the serene sky "seemed a cheat" (11) and its blue "brutal" and "disloyal." As Lia Fava-Guzzetta remarks, Manzini wants to indicate the duplicity inherent in things and events; as a consequence, every meaning seems to want to come out of itself and "meet and intermix with its own opposite."[26]

In *Ho visto il tuo cuore* (I saw your heart), light and darkness also have an indispensable role in guiding the protagonist/narrator, who remains unnamed, to the symbolic discovery of her lover's heart. As the story unfolds around an X-ray of the lover's chest, the narrative structure reveals its analogy with a photograph. When the rib cage flashes, the sight of that "black spot" on the screen represents more than a human organ; it also becomes an emotional revelation: "I see your heart—this stupendous universal lie, this pure light."[27] An ironic quality exists in the apparent simplicity of this declarative sentence. Manzini's verbal visualization develops a crescendo of contrasting images; for as small and as ugly as that "dark" spot appears to her, so much more does "its grave, solemn beating tell of a glittering incognita" (134). In the context of the narrative, seeing implies the ability to penetrate—like an X-ray—protective layers of personality; to violate, in a way, one's secrecy and self-defense; and, finally, to find in the midst of clarity still another inviolable and unknown condition.

Manzini's use of visual signs to interpret invisible layers of reality acquires a new dimension in the novel *La sparviera* (The sparrow hawk), acclaimed by many critics as the author's highest achievement and most ambitious work—one in which structural cohesiveness controls the various narrative levels. The work as a whole reflects the function of representation itself and of words in the creation of images. Through verbal definition and visualization, the writer examines the possibility of creating a mysterious and metaphysical presence; this process activates memory as the privileged source of any discourse and of acquisition of a special knowledge of things. The main protagonist, Giovanni, tries to characterize his own physical ailment, a convulsive chest cough, by giving it a name in the feminine gender, *la sparviera* (sparrow hawk); in Italian, this bird is usually masculine—*lo sparviero*. Its feminization and symbolic configuration summarize the author's long exploration and interpretation of the animal world.[28] The predatory quality of this bird seems to expand semantically to encompass the implacable course of diseases and plagues, since *la sparviera* evokes for the Italian reader *la spagnola, la malaria, la peste, l'asiatica*. Yet this feminization allows for a sense of familiarity, sheltering, and companionship that surfaces in the protagonist's relation with his sparrow hawk.

In the novel's three chapters, Manzini represents Giovanni's life at different times: as a boy in his first experience with the cough; as a young man and promising actor; and as a disillusioned man soon to die under his sparviera's attack. Giovanni's vision grows with his developing awareness of and obsession with the sparviera. As a child in kindergarten under the first spell of the cough, he sparkles, and after another attack his face "lights up and his eyes shine brightly."[29] His face acquires a permanent gilded coloration and reveals the gift of a new insight and a heightened awareness of life itself. Giovanni's encounter with a little girl, Stella, at the party his mother gives to celebrate his recovery, marks the beginning of an ongoing dialogue with and about the sparviera. Stella becomes the boy's confidant, the participant in and recipient of an extraordinary secret reality, and the two engage in an exploration of definitions as Giovanni evokes his sparviera. In the process, he discovers the power and splendor of his memory: "He thought that all he had known till then had been freely given to him. But remembering was another story. Beginning to remember means discovering another perspective, often scary, because it can become a precipice from which nobody, once fallen, can be rescued" (32). When Giovanni and Stella meet again, as young adults and actors in the roles of Hamlet and the Queen, they recapture their intimacy by continuing the same game of defining the sparviera. In a dialogue that parallels the one acted on the stage, the two evoke again the ineffable sparrow hawk through analogies, diffusive correspondences, physical textures, and coloration: "It is strong, true, but its transparent quality prevents one from holding: it betrays you. It might even make you happy. It gives you the illusion of filling you, of satiation and satisfaction, but only makes you feel your own limitations, your human walls. . . . But nevertheless it is rapture that does not allow you to be on the alert, to defend yourself" (87–88). The sparviera's conceptual ambiguity is parallel to its visual ambiguity: "Is it not also something dark, subterranean, and thus gloomy?"—inquires Stella. Giovanni boldly answers: "No: a stupefying clarity; now and then brilliant. Indecipherable" (88).

Manzini's obsessive love for language assumes here a special prominence. The formal aspects of the novel itself lie in the verbal presentation of the sparviera. Manzini accomplishes this structure by minimizing the presence of the narrator and by creating, instead, a symbolic dimension, which intermingles and competes with conventional perceptions of realty. Thus, the creation, evolution, and expansion of the symbolic sparviera are actually the only valid reality for the protagonist. They are his only way of finding fulfillment as a character and as an individual who recognizes (and magnifies) an inner experience that informs his existence. Toward the end of the novel, in fact, Giovanni summarizes all the possible semantic meanings of the sparrow hawk in a confession to his doctor: "This sickness, I am not talking about the pneumonia, all my sickness, has been a sort of construction, which has eventually imprisoned me. . . . I felt it as something shameful, dreadful and yet a condition that is required for placing a certain luminous frenzy at the center of each action: the price of an imaginative life" (167).[30]

The need to substantiate that construction occurs in the final scene, when the protagonist, before dying, sees the face of the sparviera, "beautiful, stupendously invaded by blue eyes, so carved by the memory" (192–93). He seizes it and presses it against his chest and possesses it. Since the sparrow hawk recalls some of Stella's features, the last act symbolizes Giovanni's liberation from his obsession/passion. He ascertains the reality of his vision by integrating the symbol with the person who has been his partner in its creation.

Memory is again the generating force for the biographical novel *Ritratto in piedi* (1971), which also stands as a tribute to the spiritual and physical attributes of the writer's father.[31] A tension develops between the facts stored in the daughter-author's memory and their actualization in her work. This intensely emotional narrative situation occurs mainly through a shift from indirect discourse to a dialogue between the narrator and her father; the author continually apostrophizes him and asks his participation as a witness, judge, and commentator. The dialectic between the writer and the protagonist/narrator, that is between the story itself and its source (the author's memory of her father's life), constitutes the dynamics of the writing process. The author-narrator monitors the protagonist Gianna Manzini, investigates her, and accuses and excuses her; she then forces her to extract and relate the "essence" of her memory of her father. Since the writer searches for words that have the power of recovering intact the image delivered by her sense of recollection, her memory becomes a visual witness of "sparkling truth, revelatory refractions, lightning bolt."[32]

The novel is structured around two basic components of verbal visualization: light and words. Manzini's language repeatedly draws from a semantic pool of luminosity. Her choice of bright denotative words creates a syntactical and visual fermentation: verbs, adjectives, nouns, and adverbs all diffuse their semantic resonances in a process of clarification and discovery. The recurrence of such verbs as "glitter," "beam," "shine," "sparkle," and "dazzle" denotes not only the presence of the father but also effects emanating from him, reaching and affecting nature, objects, and people. Likewise, words such as "splendor," "splendid," "beacon," "sparkle," "diamond," "incandescence," "luminous," "light," "lightning bolt," "beam," and "dazzling" continually echo his presence: "How serene and spacious is his irreducible nobility. . . . His words acquire an indisputable, radiant ratification. . . . Radiant? The word becomes autonomous. It is splendor. What? What is it about? He's taking his famous pocketknife out of his pocket. He shows it to me—a mother-of-pearl handle and an insignificant blade that nevertheless shines. . . . 'My big weapon. My only weapon'" (73).

The portrait of the father is progressively enlarged as it becomes clearer, richer in details, and more complete until it is fully magnified inside and out. In fact, as this enlarging process reaches its apex, the father-protagonist acquires the characteristics of a classical hero, dominating and proud in his physical appearance. "He was always erect . . . his head high, not haughtily but challenging. Loyalty and clarity were declared in his spacious forehead" (72). As a hero worthy of the name, he is courageous, proud, and noble of heart; yet he remains humble and full of pity, disinterested love, and respect for others, especially for the cause of the oppressed (the working class). Born into a wealthy family—the author informs us in the preface of the book that the lineage of the Manzini family goes back to the fifteenth century—he soon divests himself of his possessions to become totally committed to his faith in an anarchic society, free of inequalities, injustices, and privileges. Rejected by his wife's family as irresponsible, he lives alone in a rented room, repairing and selling watches, separated from a wife he dearly loves; he finally dies in Fascist internment.

In this novel, words relate directly to the characters. Each verbal element not only represents signs and means of expression but also regularly redefines functions. In addition, each meaning is expanded either through the narrator's direct intervention or through her father's, who highlights awareness of his own words or those of the others by refusing to allow a definition or interpretation to go by. "Certain words are like fire, a fire that must spread" (96), he tells his young daughter who recalls his "face lit up by the blazing glare" of the brazier. Words act like light catchers; they are the core of Manzini's poetics, which is nothing else but an explorative adventure toward deciphering the "blinking" unknown. Her quest becomes a search for words and, in particular, for her father's words, which "reflect the juice of life and illuminate the future" (181); her desire is to re-create her father's life and his words in her own language. Therefore, two levels of expression appear: the father's uncompromising, crystalline, and precise declarations and the writer's indispensable but admittedly inadequate language, which has to present the objective full-size portrait of an exceptional man. The act of writing eventually captures the crucial experience where father and daughter find their indisputable understanding and where the tension of two languages is released. At the end of the book, the last imaginary dialogue between the author and her father exemplifies their common ideas and their way of looking at things and of interpreting reality: "In every apparition there is an emblem. Everything becomes allusion, or confirmation, or promise. Things, at times, are a veil: even words, even people" (234). Both the writer and her father are themselves "experts" in penetrating layers of reality and external signs, as well as in reading a book: "There are many ways of reading it; but for both you and me there is only one important way" (235). For them, reading means finding, camouflaged behind transparencies (words, signs, images), the trace of the idea (truth), which may be more or less explicit or obscure, and bringing it to light. Thus *Ritratto in piedi*—the representation of the life of the author's father in her layered, inadequate language—stands as a testimony both to Manzini's challenge to her own art (writing) and to the explorative form of her poetics.

Manzini's last work *Sulla soglia* resembles her previous novel *Ritratto in piedi*. She again visits and represents a deceased relative through verbal visualization. This time the writer initiates a dialogue with her mother. The dramatic interchange takes place on the threshold of an emblematic situation bordering life and death. In this concluding narrative, Manzini confirms her quest to discover "the sign of the elsewhere."[33] This search coincides with her belief that a work of art probes the very core of existence itself: "What else is art to me if not an instrument for finding life behind life."[34] As a consequence, her writing becomes an intense and almost absolute search for the linguistic mode capable of expressing a final truth for the author and others (her mother, in particular). In this process, the writer paradoxically attempts to free her words of past inadequacies and, at the same time, to inject them with new validity and meaning.

The challenge Manzini sets for herself in this biographical novella is twofold. She wants to discover her mother and to free her identity from confused, perturbed, and conflicting memories, even those that have been recorded in her previous writings. Therefore, she wants to prove that words are not irrevocable, for although they can metaphorically cause death, they can also resurrect. The writer's task is to shake the words from their mortal rigidity by putting them back "in the plasticity and mobility of the discourse."[35]

The symbolic landscape of the opening scene sets the private reality in which the writer must operate; it shows the protagonist-narrator wandering across intersecting railroad tracks; she is attracted by a sheet of paper filled with indecipherable words and scattered letters, and by the sight of her mother, waving from the window of a "one-way" train. In the author's present historical and poetic condition—"on the threshold" between life and death, past, present, and future, between the written work and that which she must still write, between symbols already chosen and fixed and others she must find—these sights cannot contain mystery or allude to ambiguity. They merely signal their most obvious sense. The intersecting tracks represent crossing destinies, lives that have already interrelated; the one-way train and the mother stand for life itself as it speeds toward its obvious terminal destination. The sheet of paper and scattered letters symbolize the author's work and the literature she so anxiously desires to create: "I must find those letters again . . . set them in order again. For . . . in words I had always found a foundation for existence" (79).

Inside the train with her mother are four other passengers: an elderly musician, an actor, a dignified horse breeder, and a little girl. They are scandalized by the narrator's conversation because she refuses to recognize the final destination of that train. Through their comments, these characters facilitate observation of the mother, whose subtle reactions reveal the psychological portrait of a beautiful middle-class woman, married and separated from an idealist husband whom she loved and to whom she has always remained faithful.

The mother's fundamental ambiguity contrasts with the father's integrity and fully lived life style. But this bias, this "adoption of a decisively male optic,"[36] neither results in a lessening of interest in the mother nor diminishes her validity as a female character. In fact, while the father's figure acquires solemnity and rigidity in his heroic portrayal, the mother's personality becomes more convincing and human, mostly because of the ongoing tension in the author-daughter's attempt to position her in relation to her husband. He remains a living proof of integrity and loyalty to his ideal, while the mother chooses (or is forced to choose by her family) to abide by the conventions of a bourgeois mentality that sees danger and impracticality in her husband's radical life style. Her oscillation between love and admiration for her husband and fearful insecurity about life is the basis for a portrait of a sensitive, lacerated human being trapped in one of womankind's social and historical roles.

In *Ritratto in piedi,* the high concentration of "luminous" lexicon around the character of the father reveals him as the depositary of "light" and as the representation of an uncompromising union between faith and life. In *Sulla soglia,* the narrator views the character and identity of the mother through a sort of opalescent atmosphere, which signifies her conflicting and unresolved position. In fact, while the most frequent analogical image of the father is as a "diamond" or a "beam," the mother's visual connotation is "alabaster." In this context, the father's comment on his wife's splendid complexion is meaningful: "You are an alabaster lamp with a flame inside"

(90). The narrator's words, however, function to lift the "veil" from her mother's character and to expose her innermost self. In doing this, the writer's art becomes a source of light itself that "rescues [the mother] from a perpetual pregnancy of silences" (90) and perplexities. In recalling a dress-making episode that tested her mother's vanity, the writer dramatizes the vital function of words in re-creating life from crystallized remembrances: "Evidently, now that she is my prisoner, she sees again the scene: she does not need any more self help . . . for there is no longer reason for her to feign interest. The white roll of the sleeves has hypnotized her. She has her eyes on my words; and my words are images she falls in love with" (107). The lyric flow of the repetitive synesthesia reveals Manzini's linguistic manner of operating as her words become visual animations of memories; they revive the passion for life, thus neutralizing the signs of decay surrounding the train journey. They are also the truly genetic link between mother and daughter-writer: "Like me, you loved the things that helped you to express yourself and to look like an image of yourself. Those things were for you what words are for me" (105).

Despite the antagonism and sarcasm of the other train passengers, the narrator's confidence and boldness keeps growing as she focuses her conversation on her art and attempts to extend the meaning of her creative work beyond the limits of time. Thus, when a passenger challenges her, implying that "words have some sort of implacability" (90), the protagonist is more than ready to reaffirm her own aesthetic belief that a writer should profit from the irreconcilable and dissonant qualities of words. "The art of the writer sometimes consists exactly in winning or taking advantage of what [the passenger called] implacability." Juxtaposing antithetical words, phrases, and concepts disengages meanings and permits the contemplation of hidden realities. "An effect of opposition is sufficient to make words shine, like a jewel moving in a ray of sun, and to extract from them a sort of productive risk" (90). The contrasting notions of immobility (death) and mobility (writing) inherent in words signify Manzini's final vision that literature can overcome death and foster a continual reaffirmation of life.

Manzini devotes her last two works to the memory of each of her parents. By summarizing their lives, she also portrays her own existence as a daughter and writer; in addition, she recapitulates her aesthetic ideas, while stylistically and linguistically highlighting her commitment to literature and future life. The tradition of artistic prose permeates all her narrative works and consistently maintains an original blend of lyricism and language that sustains her ardent vision of reality. Her unrelenting search for words that emotionally and intellectually re-create existence, energy, and a potential for discovery finds its most fulfilling experience in linguistic signs of "light." Manzini's faith and devotion to writing enable her to conceptualize ineffable and hidden aspects of reality through her poetics.

NOTES

1. Ornella Sobrero, "Gianna Manzini," in *Letteratura italiana: Il Novecento,* 10 vols. (Milan: Garzanti, 1979), 6: 5469.

2. Giorgio Luti, "La Ronda Romana e il suo ritorno all'ordine," in ibid. 5: 3892. All translations of Italian works of criticism and of Manzini's works are mine.

3. Sobrero, "Gianna Manzini," p. 5470.

4. Emilio Cecchi, "Gianna Manzini," in *Storia della letteratura italiana,* 9: 687.

5. Gianna Manzini, *Lettera all'editore* (Milan: Mondadori, 1946), p. 12. All future references to this edition will be indicated by the page number in parentheses following the quotation.

6. Gianna Manzini, *Forte come un leone* (Milan: Mondadori, 1947), pp. 86, 79.

7. Manzini's peculiar use of punctuation to obtain the most rhythmic phrase, as an effective device for displacing, slowing, and contrasting the flow and the emphasis of the narrative elements, is obvious in all her works. She tells of her precocious feelings and understanding, as a young pupil, for the "purely musical value of punctuation; signs that are to help toward a certain mode of reading" (*Ritratto in piedi* [Milan: Mondadori, 1971], p. 51).

8. Ibid., p. 162.

9. Manzini, *Lettera all'editore,* p. 22.

10. Geno Pampaloni, review of *Ritratto in piedi, Corriere della sera* 6 (May 1971): 27.

11. This view is expressed by Sobrero ("Gianna Manzini," p. 5970) and Ferruccio Ulivi ("Narrativa emozionale di G. Manzini," in *Storia della letteratura italiana* 8: 7516). Giacomo Debenedetti also sees Manzini as a writer of opposites: "authoritative and at the same time humble, extremely intelligent and defenseless, complex and evident, rigorous and flexible" ("La Manzini, l'anima e la danza," *Intermezzo* [Milan: Mondadori, 1963], p. 130).

12. Gianfranco Contini, "Gianna Manzini," *La letteratura italiana Otto-Novecento* (Florence: Sansoni, 1974), pp. 361–62.

13. Giansiro Ferrata, preface to Gianna Manzini, *Tempo innamorato* (Milan: Mondadori, 1973), p. xiv.

14. Anna Nozzoli, "Gianna Manzini: Metafora e realtà del personaggio femminile," *Tabù e coscienza: La condizone femminile nella letteratura italiana del Novecento* (Florence: La Nuova Italia, 1978), pp. 67, 69.

15. Gianna Manzini, *Sulla soglia* (Milan: Mondadori, 1973), p. 129.

16. Manzini expressed these views in an interview given to Carlo Bo who was conducting a study on realism, "Inchiesta sul Neorealismo" (Inquiry on neorealism). Reported by Enzo Panareo in *Gianna Manzini* (Milan: Mursia, 1977), p. 52.

17. These remarks on Virginia Woolf appeared first in Manzini's *Forte come un leone* (1947) and were later included in *Album di ritratti* (1964) under the title of "La lezione della Woolf" (Virginia Woolf's lesson).

18. Manzini, *Ritratto in piedi,* p. 51.

19. Gianna Manzini, *Tempo innamorato* (1928; reprint, Milan: Mondadori, 1973), p. 70. All future references to this edition will be indicated by the page number in parentheses following the quotation.

20. Nozzoli, "Gianna Manzini," pp. 67–68.

21. Gianna Manzini, *Il valzer del diavolo* (Milan: Mondadori, 1953), p. 79. All future references to this edition will be indicated by the page number in parentheses following the quotation.

22. Nozzoli, "Gianna Manzini," p. 82.

23. Lia Fava-Guzzetta, *Gianna Manzini* (Florence: La Nuova Italia, 1974), p. 72.

24. Gianna Manzini, *Allegro con disperazione* (Milan: Mondadori, 1965), p. 252.

25. Sobrero, "Gianna Manzini," p. 5489.

26. Fava-Guzzetta, *Gianna Manzini*, pp. 106–7.

27. Gianna Manzini, *Ho visto il tuo cuore* (Milan: Mondadori, 1953), p. 134. All future references to this edition will be indicated by the page number in parentheses following the quotation.

28. Manzini's long-lasting interest and love for animals is well documented in two collections of stories, *Animali sacri e profani* (Sacred and profane animals) (1953) and *Arca di Noè* (Noah's ark) (1960), as well as in several other later stories. Her personal interpretation and exploration of the mystery and poetry that she saw in animals place her among the best contemporary writers of this genre.

29. Gianna Manzini, *La sparviera* (Milan: Mondadori, 1956), p. 10. All future references to this edition will be indicated by the page number in parentheses following the quotation.

30. The author represents illness as a condition that heightens sensitivity and intensifies spirituality, continuing the decadent mystification and symbolism of the same theme as found in D'Annunzio, Mann, Proust, and Svevo.

31. Manzini was the only child of middle-class parents of opposing political views. Her mother separated early from her father, the anarchist Giuseppe Manzini, who later died in Fascist confinement. The writer's love and admiration for her father's unshakable integrity left its mark on her precocious personal and artistic maturation and deepened her commitment to celebrate his life in a book.

32. Gianna Manzini, *Ritratto in piedi* (Milan: Mondadori, 1971), p. 25. All future references to this edition will be indicated by the page number in parentheses following the quotation.

33. Fava-Guzzetta, *Gianna Manzini*, p. 124.

34. Gianna Manzini, *Sulla soglia*, p. 13. All future references to this edition will be indicated by the page number in parentheses immediately following the quotation.

35. This concept of the function of communication in the novel is developed by Guido Guglielmi in his examination "Categories of Time" in his book *La prosa italiana del Novecento* (Turin: Einaudi, 1986), pp. 14–15.

36. Nozzoli, "Gianna Manzini," p. 75.

FAUSTA CIALENTE

Fausta Cialente was born in Sardinia in 1898, the second child of an army officer and an opera singer. During her youth, the writer's family moved frequently to follow her father's regiment and consequently identified with no particular region or city. In 1921, Cialente married Enrico Terni, an Italian composer living in Egypt. They moved to Alexandria and became part of the country's intellectual elite. During World War II, Cialente, then estranged from her husband, aided anti-Fascist efforts with daily broadcasts from Radio Cairo and wrote for a newspaper for Italian prisoners of war. She published her first novel, *Natalia,* in 1929, her second, *Cortile a Cleopatra,* in 1936, her third, *Ballata levantina,* in 1961, and a collection of short stories, *Pamela o la bell'estate,* in 1963. The decade and a half that followed marked Cialente's most productive period with her novels *Un inverno freddissimo* (1966), *Il vento sulla sabbia* (1972), *Le quattro ragazze Wieselberger* (1976), and a second collection of short stories, entitled *Interno con figure* (1976). In addition to her original works, Cialente has translated a number of works from English into Italian. Among them are Louisa May Alcott's *Little Women (Le piccole donne),* Lawrence Durrell's *Clea,* and Henry James's *Turn of the Screw (Il giro della vite).* She is currently writing her memoirs.

Autobiography, Art, and History in Fausta Cialente's Fiction

PAOLA MALPEZZI PRICE

> I don't feel I am able [as a writer] to offer anything other
> than the testimony of my times . . . , it is a duty which
> narrators should fulfill; everyone in his or her own way, of
> course.
>
> —Preface to *Interno con figure*

Fausta Cialente belongs to a small group of Italian writers who, by choice
or necessity, lived part of their adult life outside Italy.[1] Although her
family's nomadic life prevented her from establishing strong ties with any
Italian regional culture or even with the national literary tradition, it
fostered in her a European outlook. She is probably most similar to the
Triestine Italo Svevo, who was also detached from the mainstream of
Italian literature. Both authors communicate in an unadorned style of
writing and portray restless, introspective, and autobiographical characters.
Among European writers, Cialente emulates Gide and Proust in her extensive use of memory and of characters living in a specific environment at a
particular moment in time. Her narrative work consists of six novels and
several short stories. Three of her novels are set in Egypt: *Cortile a Cleopatra*
(Courtyard to Cleopatra), written in 1931 and published in 1936, *Ballata
levantina* (*The Levantines*) (1961), and *Il vento sulla sabbia* (Wind on the
sand) (1972); the other three take place mainly in Italy: *Natalia* (1929), *Un
inverno freddissimo* (A very cold winter) (1966), and *Le quattro ragazze
Wieselberger* (The four Wieselberger girls) (1976).

A chronological examination of Cialente's fiction highlights the author's
gradual progress toward self-revelation and her interpretation of the relationship between art (the world of the intellect) and life (the realm of social
and political activism). In addition, the writer's measured disclosure of
personal truth parallels her analysis of a woman's place in marriage and
society. In her first stories, for instance, characters inhabit a magic or exotic
world; thus, details about personal circumstances are few. Her later novels,

on the other hand, portray individuals who are aware of their importance in historical situations and social settings; the writer relies more on real events and her own life story than on pure fiction. Her last work, which incorporates a significant amount of autobiographical information, blends the main themes of her narrative oeuvre; an exploration of the role of art in society merges with an examination of a woman's role in the world as she describes the author-protagonist, Fausta Cialente, heatedly engaged in the struggles of her time.

Although Cialente's first novel, *Natalia,* lacks the historic perspective of subsequent stories, it assigns to art the prominent role that it will hold in all her fiction.[2] The protagonist of this novel is a young woman engaged in epistolary writing. In her correspondence with the soldier Malaspina, Natalia portrays herself as someone other than who she is, capricious and sensuous, with whom Malaspina falls in love. After marrying the young man, Natalia realizes that a sincere relationship with him can exist only if she destroys her fictitious self. Natalia personifies the conflict between reality and imagination, as well as the failure to discriminate clearly between life and art. A life in the world of art and imagination appears irreconcilable with a woman's traditional role as wife as the novel describes Natalia subduing her creative impulses in order to reenter society and be fully accepted.

Another character in the novel, Valdemaro, helps Natalia find her way back to reality from the world of imagination. A lover of art and unattainable women, Valdemaro is a poet; he also walks the fine line between reality and imagination. His gift for daydreaming provides bizarre interludes in the episodes of Natalia's collision with reality. His visions present a parade of painters obsessed with dead women, pianists with haunted pianos, and saxophonists playing while perched in trees. In the ambiguously "happy" finale culminating in Natalia's reunion with her husband, Valdemaro's intervention reflects the ambivalent role of art in this novel. Natalia's final "rescue" and deliverance to social conformity and bourgeois values seem to affirm the victory of society's most conservative forces against artistic imagination. What a woman's place can be in the world of intellect, one of several themes in this novel, becomes the focus of Cialente's subsequent novels and testifies to the author's deep interest in and evolving ideas on this subject. There are a few autobiographical details throughout the novel. Natalia's father, like the author's, is an army officer; her family moves from house to house, from town to town throughout Italy, like the Cialente family. Natalia's restlessness, her desire for independence, and her flight from her husband's home mirror the author's decision to abandon her family's narrow bourgeois milieu, to marry, and to live abroad.

Cialente's fascination with her new environment and her interest in expatriates uprooted from their native country appear in her first long work set in Egypt, *Cortile a Cleopatra*. Marco, the principal male protagonist in the novel, represents the first of Cialente's many characters without a home and without a sense of belonging to a country, race, or religion. He typifies the rootless, selfless individual whose restlessness at times expresses itself in irresponsibility and indecisiveness. Although in Marco the author presents some of the negative attributes of uprooted individuals, she also shows empathy for him. She herself was a displaced person with no patriotic or religious allegiances. She married an Italian Jew living in Egypt, never professed a religion, and felt life a person without a country.[3]

Although presented in the unimaginative guise of housepainting, art stands in contrast with a capitalistic view of life and has a prominent role as a vehicle for social commentary. Cialente describes Marco's efforts to preserve his freedom from the dangers of capitalism and bourgeois complacency, at the same time highlighting his immaturity and shortcomings. Marco's father was merely a housepainter but, according to his son's affectionate recollection, he "beautified the world" with his brushes.[4] Francesco, a father figure for Marco, also decorates houses, and Marco himself works briefly with brushes and colors as Francesco's helper. Housepainting is placed in opposition to the work of his fiancée's family, the manufacturing and selling of furs, which suggests opulence, comfort, and violence. Marco's antagonism to such capitalistic endeavors, however, results from laziness and lack of initiative rather than from any conscious revolt against an inhumane system. Marco's inability to conceptualize his impulsive aversion reflects his incapacity to become a "writer" or to verbalize his confusion at a critical time in his life: "Marco tried to pencil some words on the oiled and wrinkled bread paper; he wanted to describe these dates, that sky, all that mystery, but he could not" (189). Cialente ultimately punishes Marco for his social irresponsibility by depriving him of the skilled use of the written word.

Another sign of Marco's immaturity is his inability to understand any of the women he meets in the microcosm of the Egyptian courtyard. Women do not play a relevant role in *Cortile a Cleopatra;* they are depicted as struggling to find their identity and survive at the lowest rank of society. Marco's mother, his fiancée, Dinah, and his friend Kikki are facets of the great mystery that women represent for him. Dinah, the furrier's daughter, and Marco's mother, Eve, find in capitalism and religion respectively the rules of conduct for their lives. On the other hand, Eve succumbs to her passion and sense of guilt, and Kikki painfully starts building a future for herself without Marco. Kikki is the predecessor of more developed female characters who achieve freedom from men's tutelage and become independent thinkers.

Cialente published her third major work, *Ballata levantina,* in 1961 after twenty-five years of silence. This novel marks a turning point; it conjoins a deep consciousness of history with a concern for female participation in societal structures.[5] The characters' more lucid and pragmatic view of the world replaces the vague romanticism of *Natalia* and the exoticism of *Cortile a Cleopatra;* henceforth, Cialente's characters will reflect the author's realization that individuals, women in particular, must assume control of their lives lest historical and social factors determine their destiny. Cialente's narrative technique conforms to this idea. In fact, when the main character, Daniela, loses her will to self-determination, the narration shifts from the first- to the third-person point of view.

As her fiction evolves into autobiography—an evolution noticeable in *Ballata levantina*—Cialente uses more memory-related elements as a means to link past and present or to instill a sense of historical continuity in the novel's younger protagonists. Thus, she describes Daniela physically abusing her grandmother's friend Clio in her impatience to learn more about her grandmother's past. Cialente also uses flashbacks to enable her characters to understand at a later time events and situations that are disturbing or confusing at the time of their occurrence. On her trip back to Egypt from a brief sojourn in Italy just before World War II, Daniela muses on how remembering would later help her to understand what had just happened.

> I kept wondering what my trip had really been like. Later I would know, maybe, and the images that were now confused would become clear and pure in my memory; I would see more clearly what all I had seen meant and stood for: the vanity, perfidy, lust, the eternal purposelessness, and absurdity of men against the threatening background of a humiliated country.[6]

Retrospection helps the individual analyze more clearly the troubling aspects of a personal crisis, just as historic distance sheds light on confusing political situations.

In *Ballata levantina,* Cialente tightly connects historical and personal events. Daniela's restlessness reflects Italy's inquietude in the 1930s. The affable and courteous manners of a young acquaintance, Gilbert, charm a confused Daniela in the same way that the vague and illusory message of

Fascism seduces a restless nation. As Mussolini masks the empty word behind his promises, Gilbert succeeds in convincing Daniela of his love, although he remains another woman's lover. On the same day that war is declared in Europe, Daniela puts an end to her humiliating relationship with Gilbert by publicly slapping his mistress. Daniela's shame, retaliation, resultant suffering, and cynicism reflect Italy's tribulations during and immediately after the war.

The character of Daniela highlights the issue of a woman's position in society, especially vis-à-vis love and marriage. Two disparate examples of union between man and woman present themselves to Daniela: the marriage of her foster parents, Livia and Matteo, and the memory of her grandparents' union. The successful marriage between Livia and Matteo, the sole "perfect" marriage in Cialente's fiction, is due not only to the couple's shared political views but also to a reversal of roles in their life together. Livia, a huge, gruff, Fellinian character, is the partner who dominates in her household: she repairs things that break, controls finances, and struggles incessantly with her spade against sand and wind to grow vegetables and flowers. The marriage of Daniela's grandparents, on the other hand, was far from successful. Daniela's grandmother Francesca, an Italian-born ballerina, was abducted "from the stage" by a rich Jew, who kept her in Egypt as his mistress. His refusal to marry her, even after the birth of their daughter, Daniela's mother, made Francesca bitter toward all men, and she tried to pass her attitude on to her granddaughter: "Men are pigs: start there and you'll hardly go wrong." The litany of men's evils would continue: "Men are liars . . . ; they are selfish . . . cowards . . . they are dirty" (80–82). Her final words however, represent a different attitude: "Men are the most important thing in our lives. Men are everything I've told you, and sometimes worse, much worse. But our happiness, our success, our whole life depend on them. A woman without a man is sterile land, and heaven deliver me from her!" (83).

Livia's experience produces a different philosophy about women's relationships to men. Daniela will follow her advice on the subject: "You'll learn not to depend on men, my girl. . . . Learn to get by on your own" (96). Livia bases such exhortations on the belief that men have historically subjugated women; thus, if women now take advantage of men, the latter are to blame: "They've kept them in bed and the kitchen for centuries to get them out of the way as if they were useless for anything else" (96).

In Daniela's story, achieving financial independence is the first of women's victories in their progress toward equality. Cialente highlights, however, the difficulties encountered by a newly emancipated woman. In fact, Daniela achieves monetary freedom but remains emotionally insecure, perceiving the world as an ambivalent place in which "no one ever agrees about anything. Everyone is always a little bit right" (118). Unable to cope with human incomprehension and the burden of decisions, she eventually disappears into the waters of the ancient Nile.

In *Ballata levantina,* women also feel inferior to men in the world of intellect and political activism. Matteo, Daniela's intellectual mentor, writes poetry and anti-Fascist propaganda with equal facility and zeal. Enzo, Daniela's lover who is a partisan working for the anti-Fascist resistance in exile, emerges as a writer in the novel's final pages. His newspaper article about a case of social injustice elicits Cialente's praise for its artistry; Matteo, the book's official critic of art and politics, remarks to Livia: "I must say, he's put it all very clearly" (287). In contrast to men's intellectual achievement, women continue to remain confined to less intellectual roles. Although Livia embodies the courageous, politically conscious woman, her struggles are limited to the taming of her garden and the mundanities of life. In Daniela's case, the ambiguities of a woman's role are even more pronounced. Encouraged by the enlightened Matteo to behave like a modern woman, Daniela is unable to experience fully her independence; she finds herself torn between marriage and freedom, and her involvement in politics remains sterile and passive. The ambiguity of her life parallels the mystery surrounding her death, presented plausibly as either accident or suicide. From a feminist perspective, Daniela's tragic disappearance represents a negative model. As a critic has acutely remarked, it "brings back her adventure under the romantic signs of *eros* and *thanatos.*"[7]

The issue of a woman's role within the family emerges as a main theme in *Un inverno freddissimo,* published five years after *Ballata levantina.*[8] The restlessness of a small group of people living in a squalid attic in Milan mirrors the deep frustrations of post–World War II Italians. The cold, which grows increasingly bitter as winter advances, is a meteorological metaphor for the gradual breakdown of this extended family, which is rocked by the ambitions of one of its younger members. The protagonist is Camilla, a middle-aged woman who has unwillingly assumed the role of leader of the group, since her husband mysteriously disappeared during the war and the other men are either dead, too young, or too inept to make decisions. She considers it her duty to protect not only the health but also the hearts and souls of her family against cynicism, indifference, and selfishness. Perceiving her abandoned condition as sad and tragic, she also must fight these feelings. In the eyes of society and of her own children, she is "inept, a good-for-nothing, who could not make it in life, a sort of wreck" (17). Camilla finds her situation similar to that of Regina, who has been seduced and abandoned by Nicola, Camilla's partisan nephew, who died before he could marry her and legitimize the birth of their daughter. Camilla accepts, therefore, the responsibility of caring also for Regina and her child in the microcosm of the attic.

In this novel, Cialente attacks the institution of marriage, while probing the issue of women's dependence on men. Two other characters in the attic, Matelda and a rich prostitute, stand in contrast to Camilla and Regina, who feel that they have been deceived by men. Matelda and the prostitute exploit men rather than let themselves be used by them. Matelda is Camilla's friend and the wife of a rich but unfaithful husband; like Daniela's grandmother, she thinks little of men: "They are a bunch of selfish people" (44). She remains with her husband because he is rich and she can spend his money on clothes and jewels. On the other hand, the rich prostitute has severed all ties with the past and cares only about her own well-being. Gaudily attired and cynical, she persuades Alba, Camilla's older daughter, to reject her mother's values and begin a life of self-indulgence.

Cialente criticizes here relationships that exist between men and women, while showing the difficulties women encounter in overcoming their subordination. According to Cialente, shunning love or rejecting one's past is not the solution to a woman's quest for independence. The figure of Il Rosso, a farmer whose kindness and burly physique trouble Camilla during her search for tranquillity in the countryside, personifies Camilla's longing for a strong man. Frequent memories of happy times with her husband reinforce Camilla's desire for male companionship and support. In addition, Regina, Camilla's younger counterpart, is unable to reject the tenderness and comfort offered by Enzo, a lonely inhabitant of the attic, who, like her, has suffered the consequences of a tragic love affair.

Love sanctioned by marriage has its representatives in Camilla's nephew and his wife, Arrigo and Milena. The author's scorn for both characters, however, subtly unveils itself throughout the novel and calls into question the bond uniting them. Camilla, often the author's voice, describes Milena as a little bourgeois girl, haughty, selfish, always complaining, and displaying the mind of a shopkeeper. Contrary to the way she portrays other characters who live in the attic, the author refuses to enter Milena's subconscious to reveal her hidden thoughts. On the other hand, Arrigo is given the chance to redeem himself from having married Milena through his interest in music. A violinist in an orchestra, Arrigo is obsessed with music; his passion prevents him from becoming involved, not only in life's daily problems but also in the war that devastates his family and country. Furthermore, his ideas about music—he respects great musicians and rejects any freedom of interpretation—unmask him, in Cialente's eyes, as reactionary and traditionalist. The author finally and scornfully condemns Arrigo to the role of the artist selfishly locked in an ivory tower.

Besides music, creative writing is the other major art form presented in the novel. Lalla, one of Camilla's daughters, is a budding writer who forms a link between imagination and reality and between past and present. She still fondly remembers her cousin Nicola, the dead patriot who taught her to write "with a bare and incisive language, without frills" (31). Her initiatives in both writing and life, however, meet with human vulgarity and indifference. Her encounter with a famous author who had promised to judge one of her short stories ends when, in a shockingly brutal scene, he tries to seduce her. That experience leaves her embittered but also with a greater sense of maturity: "The experience of that day in the damaged house . . . will have to be told one of these days" (197). Like good wine, the event needs to settle for some time in order to be used later in a new and changed form.

Cialente describes in detail Lalla's progress toward a better understanding of life and appreciation of art by focusing on the pain involved in this process. When yet another tragic event occurs in her life, Lalla regards her former creations as futile and even somewhat ridiculous, coming to the conclusion that "they were not worth anything, anymore, those sheets of paper, nor what was written on them" (239). At this time, Enzo in part fulfills his role as intellectual guide, thanks more to his political affinity to the dead partisan Nicola than to any literary superiority. He encourages Lalla to continue in her creative endeavors, stating that "we die, but human creations remain." Her realization not only of the peculiar relationship between life and art but also of the possibility that as a writer she can "make visible what is plunged in the invisible" and interpret and explain life into a "lasting" work also encourages Lalla to continue writing (240).

Un inverno freddissimo marks an important milestone in Cialente's recognition and affirmation of the female intellectual's place in society. Indeed, for the first time in her fiction, a woman rather than a man assumes the role of enlightened artist. Although the male writer in the novel represents a literature at once patriarchal, decadent, and lecherous, Lalla embodies the possibility of new insights and subject matter. In her critical reading of the

female characters of *Un inverno freddissimo,* Anna Nozzoli forgets to examine the character of Lalla and defines the novel as a "woman's *debacle.*"[9] In
fact, the critic concludes, the female protagonists are given only the roles of
mother, wife, and sex object. In Lalla's case, however, writing becomes a
means to escape women's apparently closed worlds. If Camilla is indeed
unconvincing as an emancipated woman, if Regina is too wounded to defy
"bourgeois" values, and if Alba dies in her vain bid for happiness, Lalla
represents the woman of the future: self-sufficient and intellectually emancipated from and superior to her male mentors. By making Lalla's emancipation an intellectual one, Cialente eschews reducing the young woman's
achievement to a trite emotional or sentimental victory over the other sex.

Lalla's project to interpret life and make the invisible visible appears also
to be Cialente's aim in *Il vento sulla sabbia.*[10] Lisa, the narrator, is an older
woman who describes events that occurred thirty years before, when she
was eighteen years of age. She relates her story long after memory has
ended its process of filtering and settling events, her purpose being a
"faithful telling" that will "give justice to the way they [the characters] lived
with their compromises and sins, their mistakes, and their truths" (8).
When the reader realizes that the narrator's and the author's lives reveal
several common elements, the novel assumes autobiographical proportions. Both women had ancestors born under the Austro-Hungarian Empire, a Jewish relative, a matriarchal family, and some evidence of a bourgeois education. Although she still wears the mask of a fictitious narrator,
Cialente shows here a willingness to put part of herself on the stage she has
prepared for her characters. *Il vento sulla sabbia* draws a close relationship
between life and art as each protagonist externalizes feelings and obsessions
in painting, music, and writing. Lisa tells the story of two women, Frida
and Lottie, who enjoyed an intimate friendship during their youth and now
share the love of Stefan, Frida's husband. Besides their love for the same
man, the two women share a passion for painting. Lottie prefers landscapes
and still lifes painted with an unreal, smoky grace—her hallmark as well as
her means to success. Her attempts to paint portraits, however, fail because
of an inability to understand human reality. Just as Valdemaro combines the
poet and the historian in *Natalia,* Frida embodies painter and writer. As
painter, she concentrates on one subject—lilies—attempting to catch their
almost perfect whiteness. In her writing she shows a double interest: art
history and fiction. Lisa, introduced as a young woman hired to type
Frida's two manuscripts, initially finds her employer's study of the origin of
medieval German architecture fascinating; she is bored, however, by her

fictitious epistolary exchange between two women. As she becomes more involved with the feelings of the people with whom she lives and works, Lisa understands how close to reality Frida's written creations are. She also realizes that her suffering results from her husband's love for the "other" woman, Lottie. In her narration, Frida transposes Stefan's romantic preference to a musical context, having him say, in fact, that, while his wife understands music, the other woman embodies music for him.

Il vento sulla sabbia, like *Ballata levantina,* connects the world of art to that of politics; the characters' artistic expressions suggest their political views. This relationship is true especially for the female characters; for the first time in her fiction Cialente clearly enunciates political preferences. Lottie's equivocal paintings, her fragile body, and her melodramatic personality translate into a blind fascination with Hitler's message. In contrast, Frida's artistic versatility, strength, and sensitivity enable her to unmask Hitler's fanaticism. In this novel Cialente also juxtaposes two musicians, representing differing concepts of art and politics. Stefan enjoys only classical music; Filippo, his friend, on the other hand, prefers contemporary forms. Although Cialente hints at Stefan's reactionary politics, she expounds Filippo's attacks upon Nazism as well as his equally fervent criticism of Mozart and Beethoven.

In *Il vento sulla sabbia,* women artists are clearly the protagonists. Besides presenting Lottie and Frida as artists, Cialente depicts the female narrator's evolution from spectator to actor and, ultimately, to relator of the novel's events. Thus, the story of Frida, Lottie, and Stefan gradually becomes Lisa's story as well. Fiction and autobiography, objectivity, and pseudosubjectivity all mingle in a confused pattern, as the older Lisa re-creates the character of her younger self.

Whereas *Il vento sulla sabbia* introduces the first female narrator-protagonist along with specific autobiographical elements, her last novel, *Le quattro ragazze Wieselberger,* represents a true bildungsroman in which the narrator and author are apparently one and the same.[11] By definition, however, novels are works of fiction in which the distinction between relator and author still exists. More extensively than in *Ballata levantina* and *Il vento sulla sabbia,* Cialente's last novel uncovers the narrator's family history before recounting her childhood and adolescence. In the first part, the unnamed teller of the story describes her grandfather—a composer from Trieste—and his four daughters, who share his passion for music; she also brings into focus the family's passionate desire to transfer their allegiance from the Austro-Hungarian Empire to the Italian Kingdom. In the second part, Cialente recounts the most salient episodes of the narrator's adolescence and adulthood, which continue to the end of World War II.

History, social criticism, and autobiography merge into Cialente's account of her family's past. The Wieselbergers' vicissitudes unfold in the social context of the bourgeoisie and in the period between the end of the nineteenth century and the end of World War I. The narrator's love for her ancestors softens her tendency to disparage such sacred feelings as patriotism and nationalism and mitigates her criticism of bourgeois values: "Success, happiness, much money, and successful marriages, blessed also by abundant children." She still unveils the hypocrisy hidden behind some of these values, however, "as if it were an unconfessable shame, worse than a loss at the money exchange, to reveal that marriages may fail and love may prove false currency" (69). The narrator cynically describes how these values are crumbling by the end of the nineteenth century and how her aunt and her mother fall victim to their disintegration. In fact, convinced that their married lives would be as blissful as that of their parents', both Aunt Alice and the narrator's mother, Elsa, blindly take their marriage vows. Cialente ironically underscores the fact that Elsa renounced a promising career in opera "for love." Although both husbands soon prove to be libertines, their wives suffer their betrayals in silence. The narrator shows condemnation and pity for these women who "will never learn that it is not worthwhile to suffer so much, not even for the children's sake," but who, "notwithstanding their sad experience, will educate their children—their daughters especially—to renunciation and sacrifice" (73).

In her 1906 autobiographical novel *Una donna*, Sibilla Aleramo expresses similar feelings toward the fate of women as she depicts the humiliations suffered by the protagonist of her novel. In an attempt to regain her individuality and freedom, this character commits the "unmotherly" crime of abandoning her son as well as her husband. Aleramo then muses: "Why do we idealize sacrifice in mothers? Who gave us this inhuman idea that mothers should negate their own wishes and desires? The acceptance of servitude has been handed down from mother to daughter for so many centuries that it is now a monstrous chain that fetters them."[12] Fausta Cialente entertained a long correspondence and friendship with Aleramo, admiring her involvement in social and political movements as well as her inexhaustible need for love. Although very different in many respects, the two writers are similar in their condemnation of marriage as an institution that enslaves women.

In *Le quattro ragazze Wieselberger*, Cialente unequivocally affirms her conviction of a woman's right to take control of her life, even if it means breaking traditional norms of conduct. As proof of this belief, she presents both the narrator's and her mother's experiences. She points out how Elsa's determination to work as a voice teacher, despite the criticism of her husband and relatives, gave the narrator "the idea that a woman may be or, better yet, may make herself independent" (140). Later, the daughter's encouragement induces the mother to end a humiliating union and live apart from her husband. In recounting her own separation from her spouse, the narrator candidly explains: "I did not deny to myself that my marriage had been an authentic evasion" (210). Aging, she receives consolation and hope for the future in the realization that she forms a link in a chain of women who transmit their values, their feelings, and their hopes from generation to generation. At one end of this chain, she perceives her dead mother and at the other, her daughter and granddaughters.

The second part of the novel recounts the progress that leads the displaced and disenchanted young woman—the narrator-author—to write about life, history, self, and family. Cialente highlights the daughter's rebellion against her school's "stupid essays on specific 'subjects'" (143) and her epistolary exchange with an older cousin, both of which introduce her to the pleasure of manipulating an audience through personal writings. Later, as she becomes more aware of the conflict between imagination and reality in the creative process, the fear of exaggeration or misrepresentation deters her from any realistic description of events. Cialente compares the anguished realization of the limitations of language on the part of the budding writer to the dislike for rhetoric on the part of a World War I soldier confronted with the actuality of the war. Silence seems preferable in both cases. Faced with the repulsive aspects of World War I, however, the young woman rejects taciturn reserve and escapes into an imaginary logo-centric world, accepting the lessons of literary authorities with analogous style and ideas.

Cialente's belief in an intimate interaction between life and art, implicit in most of her fiction, is the result of her experience. In *Le quattro ragazze Wieselberger,* the writer recounts the narrator's involvement in the anti-Fascist struggle through her broadcasts form Radio Cairo and her writings in *Fronte Unito,* a publication for Italian prisoners in the Middle East. The older narrator looks back at those years of passionate political activity and remarks with a touch of irony: "I was no longer 'the writer,' I had even forgotten I ever was; I thought I could never waste any time 'inventing silly stories.'" (229). As she ascribes such a situation to the cruelty of the war, she also recognizes that she was wrong. Cialente's belief in the worth of those "silly stories" results in her decision to continue writing. Henceforth, her fictitious work will deal more and more closely with both historical and personal events. In the final pages of *Le quattro ragazze Wieselberger,* Cialente relates her reaction during a walk on a beach in which the narrator follows her daughter and two granddaughters: "Tears come to my eyes as I continue walking toward the open page of this sea and this sky, behind my three figurines" (263). She strongly feels both hope for the future and a sense of historical and personal continuity.

Autobiography, art, and history—embryonic elements in Cialente's earlier novels—slowly merge and develop as the primary themes of her later fiction. With each subsequent novel the author constructs closer analogies between her family's and her characters' pasts; moreover, the events in her protagonists' lives reflect and parallel historic and social happenings. The ensuing interaction between her characters' private and public lives unfolds as if one had dictated the other by some ineluctable and unwritten law. As she depicts a woman's search for means to express herself in the intellectual domain, Cialente actually tells her own story. Natalia, the confused epistolary writer, evolves first into Lalla, the young woman committed to writing, and, ultimately, into the female narrator-author of *Le quattro ragazze Wieselberger.* Cialente's commitment to writing parallels her social and political commitment. In her last novel, she relates how she has painfully shaken off the yoke of bourgeois mentality: privately, by choosing her life; publicly, by being politically and socially active during and after the war. Cialente ultimately affirms that the right to bear witness to one's time belongs to those individuals who actively participate in their shaping and molding. The artist and the political activist must therefore be one and the same as proof of the indissoluble union of art and life.

NOTES

1. Cialente presently prefers to live in England where her daughter resides. She spends, however, several months each year at her villa "Il grillo" near the city of Varese.

2. Fausta Cialente, *Natalia* (Milan: Mondadori, 1982). The novel was written in 1922, published in 1929 and reprinted in 1982 with some modifications.

3. Cialente recently made the following comment about being Italian: "I never felt Italian because of my origins and the life I led." Interview with Sandra Petrignani, *Le signore della scrittura* (Milan: La Tartaruga, 1984), p. 85 (my translation).

4. Fausta Cialente, *Cortile a Cleopatra* (Florence: Sansoni, 1953), p. 39. All subsequent references to this edition will be indicated by the page number in parentheses following the quotation. All translations are mine.

5. Fausta Cialente, *Ballata levantina* (Milan: Feltrinelli, 1961).

6. Fausta Cialente, *The Levantines,* trans. Isabelle Quigly (London: Faber and Faber, 1962), p. 152. All future references to this edition will be indicated by the page number in parentheses following the quotation.

7. Anna Nozzoli, "Fausta Cialente: testimonianza storica e tipologia femminile," *Tabù e coscienza* (Florence: La Nuova Italia, 1978), p. 122.

8. Fausta Cialente, *Un inverno freddissimo* (Milan: Feltrinelli, 1966). All further references to this edition will be indicated by the page number in parentheses following the quotation. All translations are mine.

9. Nozzoli, "Fausta Cialente," p. 122.

10. Fausta Cialente, *Il vento sulla sabbia* (Milan: Mondadori, 1972). All subsequent references to this edition will be indicated by the page number in parentheses following the quotation. All translations are mine.

11. Fausta Cialente, *Le quattro ragazze Wieselberger* (Milan: Mondadori, 1976). All further references to this edition will be indicated by the page number in parentheses following the quotation. All translations are mine.

12. Sibilla Aleramo, *A Woman,* trans. Rosalind Delmar (Los Angeles: University of California Press, 1980), p. 193.

FRANCESCA SANVITALE

Francesca Sanvitale was born in Milan in 1928 into an aristocratic but impoverished family. The autobiographical elements of her writings reflect her struggle to free herself from the authority of a tyrannical father and her efforts to care for a weak and dependent mother. For approximately twenty years, she lived in Florence where she studied literature with the literary critic Edoardo De Robertis. She presently contributes articles to such literary journals and newspapers as *Nuovi Argomenti, Il Messagero* and *L'Unità*. Her articles from 1981 to 1986 have been published as *Mettendo a fuoco* (1988) in a series directed by Enzo Siciliano. Her first novel, *Il cuore borghese* (1972), represents characters searching for values on which to base human existence. The protagonists of *Madre e figlia* (1980) remain less intellectually motivated and live the tragedy of their fate with determination and intensity. *L'uomo del parco* (1984) preceded a collection of short stories, *La realtà è un dono* (1987), that depicts a generation of middle-aged intellectuals who try to understand reality but succeed only in becoming conscious of an absurd destiny.

Francesca Sanvitale's *Madre e figlia:* From Self-Reflection to Self-Invention

PAOLA BLELLOCH

In *Madre e figlia* (Mother and daughter)[1] Francesca Sanvitale creates a new form of autobiography in which she moves from self-reflection to self-invention and, beyond that, to self-revelation. Her work not only represents a perfect example of the aesthetic, cathartic, and self-revelatory functions of writing but also stands as an imaginative poetic prose that sets the author among the greatest of contemporary writers. The choice of a semi-autobiographical novel allows the writer to reflect upon, reinvent, and relive her past. Having traced the origin of her suffering to a love-hate relationship between herself and her mother and to a rejection of an unloving father, she better understands the fundamental ambivalence in her life and recognizes her desperate need for unity, meaning, acceptance, and love. In addition, Sanvitale explains the psychological complexities of the tormenting situation she lived through with her mother and thereby overcomes the remorse she feels toward her. In fact, by confronting and accepting her feelings, she clarifies their significance and, by analyzing the motives of her actions, she finally justifies them. The act of writing brings together all the scattered pieces of life, both happy and bitter, and gives them their proper place and meaning. The psychoanalytical process alone, however, would not account for the aesthetic qualities of *Madre e figlia* had Sanvitale not found the most suitable form for its content. The structure and the style of this narrative are the perfect reflection of the writer's tormented self, divided between past and present, love and hate. A semiautobiographical genre, an original structure, and an imaginative pictorial style enable the writer to comprehend, forgive, and mirror herself in a beautiful artistic creation.

Sanvitale's novel is more a work of fiction than a traditional autobiography. Undoubtedly, it is based on personal material: the writer was indeed the daughter of an unmarried mother from an impoverished and decadent aristocratic family; she did live in Milan, Florence, and Rome; she worked to support her mother, finally married, and had one son. Sonia, the narrator in the first person and protagonist of the story, however, is more a fictional character than a faithful alter ego of Sanvitale, and her story is more a symbol of the human condition, seen as a struggle for freedom from past and kin, than a faithful account of Sanvitale's own life. The choice of a genre that mixes autobiography and fiction is a response to the author's tendency toward introspection and self-analysis. The definition of her philosophy appears in a letter to a publisher, in which, after rejecting both realism and experimentalism, she stresses a concern with the self and a need to express the equivocal aspects of her life: "The clear recognition of limits—limits of culture, class, character, education, and sentiments—has meant for me the immediate rejection of both experimentalism and realism. Consequently, *I was obliged to accept psychology and narcissism, which constitute, for better or for worse, the ambiguity of my condition.*"[2]

Sanvitale's intellectual interests, as well as her concern with the human psyche and with the unfolding of existence in culture, class, and character, have distanced her from earlier schools of realism, which in Italy had closely mirrored post–World War II reality, and of experimentalism, which in the sixties had emphasized literary form over content and meaning.[3] In fact, her emphasis on spiritual, emotional, and mental faculties gives rise to an ambiguous, fluid, and artistic prose, which differs from the clarity, harshness, and gripping qualities associated with neorealism. On the other hand, her seriousness of intention and the desire to communicate a message to the reader separate her from experimental attempts at originality and from emphasis on form as an end in itself. As a result of this narcissism and propensity for introspection, recounting her life's story becomes a creative, imaginative, and self-revelatory process. According to Paul Eakin, the heuristic nature of autobiographical truth is not a fixed but an evolving content "in an intricate process of *self-discovery* and *self-creation*, and further, the *self*, that is the center of all autobiographical narrative is necessarily a *fictive structure*."[4] The critic's words give justification to Sanvitale's need to search for her real identity and the meaning of her existence. In addition, his comment clarifies Sanvitale's desire to see herself in the mirror of writing and to create an image that embodies, explains, and unifies all of her scattered experiences and contradictions.

Various theorists of the autobiographical genre describe the process of self-reflection and self-invention and forewarn against confusing a narrator with an author, the former being a literary fictional character and the latter being its creator. Marcel Proust in *Contre Sainte-Beuve*,[5] well before French structuralists developed their linguistic and psychoanalytical theories, had already perceived the dual nature of author-narrator and had declared that a book was the product of another "I" immersed in an environment. In 1966, Roland Barthes echoed the same idea: "The one who speaks in the narrative is not the one who writes in real life and the one who writes is not the one who is."[6] Jacques Lacan's theory is even clearer on this point, as he goes even further than his predecessors by interrelating subject, desire, ego, and superego. He conceives the idea of a split ego looking for an identity in the mirror of its writing[7] and creating an alter ego that is the projection of its desire and the fulfillment of its dreams. Lacan's theory elucidates how in *Madre e figlia* writing acts as a narcissistic mirror in which Sanvitale sees a complete image of herself and overcomes her split personality. Through her artistic creation she acquires a deeper awareness of herself and her destiny.

Sonia, as Sanvitale's alter ego, performs a cathartic function when she assumes all guilt, relives her former existence, acknowledges selfishness, and overcomes remorse. The author clearly states that this confrontation with her past motivates writing in *Madre e figlia*. She desires to resurrect her mother and to show after death all the respect and love that she was unable to bestow on her during life: "My mother is worthy of offensive riches. . . . I supported her like a stupid husband, like an offensive and sullen book-keeper . . . as if her life were in my power" (4). Thus Sanvitale's emotions find a natural outlet in the act of writing, which represents a complete and purgative confession of hate and love: "I love her body even old, even dead, even decomposed. Only my mother's body is for me a body of love" (4).

Sanvitale retrospectively reinvents her mother and her past in an effort to arrive at fundamental truth. She revives the historical period, social conditions, and the "palazzo" of her childhood at the beginning of the century. The novel begins with the young Countess Marianna appearing at the threshold of this palace. Through flashbacks into the past and jumps into the future the reader learns that Marianna is the only daughter in an old aristocratic family of the Po Valley. The count, her father, a cultivated and sensitive man, loves and treasures her, as his letters show: "Your room is ready; the garden is waiting for you. Come, my beloved poem" (14). His death, the war, the end of the family fortune, and a broken engagement, however, contribute to Marianna's downfall and lead to her greatest mistake. On a stormy night, an officer appears wrapped in a black cloak on a white horse, like a hero in a fairy tale. Struck by love at first sight, Marianna elopes with him (an unpardonable sin, as the officer was already married). She follows him from city to city until she gives birth to a daughter, Sonia, whose coming into the world destroys forever whatever superficial and selfish love the officer felt. "Love for the Countess Marianna ended in him when he encountered his own eyes in those of little Sonia" (20). This part of the story is a nostalgic evocation of the past and expresses the author's regret for causing the end of her mother's love affair and adventurous, happy existence.

In fact, at the moment when the "Colonnello" abandons them, the mother and child start a miserable wandering life. Poverty and fear, dingy rented rooms, solitude, and humiliations are Sonia's early memories. Incapable of understanding the officer's cruelty, the helpless mother and deserted daughter still regard him as a figure to fear and to love. They both wait for his infrequent visits with joyful anticipation and painful uneasiness; each time they are left frustrated and unhappy as he hurries away after only a few hours and leaves them to their solitude and poverty. As Sonia grows up, studies successfully, and begins to earn her living, however, she takes on the responsibility of caring for her mother. In spite of her good intentions, the more she tries to change their lives and solve their financial problems, the deeper she sinks into hell and despair. Chased by creditors and obsessed by debts, Sonia screams and vehemently reproaches her irresponsible mother until one night, nearly unconsciously, she shakes her and tightens her fingers around her throat. Nevertheless, the mother remains untouched and indifferent, still locked in her unreal childhood world. Exasperated, Sonia finally rebels and deserts her mother, her beloved Florence, and her youth to move to another city, to a different life, and to a new age: "She was leaving the house of tortures, her mother, the city she loved like a human being, and she felt joy and pain at the same time" (133).

As the curtain rises on the second act, Sonia and her mother are together again in an elegant, comfortable apartment in Rome. Sonia, who is recuperating from an abortion, is married to a man she does not love. She behaves overprotectively toward the one son that she does have and assumes her new role as wife and mother in a resigned and listless way. The new situation suggests that Sonia has accepted marriage as a compromise, in order to save her mother; she has sacrificed her freedom in an effort to build a normal life for herself and her family. She helps her ineffective uncle, the decadent Paris, and provides for her mother, who has undergone an operation for cancer and recovered. Nevertheless, she remains unhappy, alone, and unable to have a good relationship with her husband.

The novel provides psychoanalytical insight into the ties between Sanvitale (Sonia in the novel) and her parents; in addition, it facilitates an understanding of her suffering attitude and existential search for answers. According to Freud, a girl who is frustrated in her love for a father reverts to the first stage of affection for a mother. Rejected and humiliated as a child, Sonia does not make the necessary transition from active to passive love, but, by competing and identifying with her parent, internalizes her superego, assuming a man's attitude.[8] The statement "I'll take care of mother" (125) marks the transition from a "feminine" condition of dependency to a "masculine" self-assertive behavior.[9] Later on, Sonia cannot love a husband, since her unconscious probably refuses any dependence on a father figure. Having taken her father's place she can love no one but her mother. Her need to protect and defend her will never disappear: "It is I who defend her as I have always done" (3). Thus she accompanies her mother through a long illness until her death and beyond, when a desire to immortalize her inspires the writing of this novel.

The ambivalence in the mother-daughter relationship pervades the whole work and asserts itself from the start with the title *Madre e figlia*. The conjunction "and" could, in fact, express juxtaposition, antithesis, or a mutual love relationship; it could also signify that each member of the dyad is both mother *and* daughter. It actually encompasses all those possibilities: Sonia's feelings of love and admiration alternate with sentiments of pity and anger, while a desire to share and shape her mother's destiny counteracts the instinct to reject this parent and her past. As the story unfolds, the women reverse their roles. Sonia, the independent, self-affirming, educated, and professional woman becomes mother to Marianna, the old, dependent, self-absorbed, and aristocratic lady who refuses to mature and take responsibility for her actions. This unnatural role reversal and the resulting love-hate relationship with its Freudian undertones lie at the basis of the narrative. The same attraction and repulsion implied in the title permeate the style of the whole novel as Sanvitale plays the dual role of author and narrator. Readers perceive her presence on two different levels. As an author and writer, Sanvitale relives her experience and transforms herself into a literary character; through the eyes of the narrator Sonia, she observes her story developing outside herself like a film projected on a screen.

Other specific structural and stylistic devices also express the fundamental dichotomy of Sanvitale's love-hate relationship. She transforms the narrative from a linear succession of events into a complete multidimensional fresco of life. Her imaginative and poetic prose resembles the technique of Impressionist painters whose contrasting strokes of color create an overall effect of light. Sanvitale similarly unifies scattered and varied memories and reintegrates them in one whole picture. She achieves these effects through a visual style with an emphasis on detail, a synchronized representation of past, present, and future events, and, finally, a shifting stress among the various voices that tell the story.

The writer's pictorial style utilizes such specific images as carefully framed panoramas, frescos, or photos in an album as starting points for a reconstruction of the past and a premonition of future occurrences. She consequently reinvents herself and her mother, giving a fresh interpretation to the events of their lives. In the opening paragraph, Sonia introduces herself as a painter. "On the stage set *I have painted* vases and plants in gray. My mother is luminous in this half-light" (3). The landscapes framed by an open window, a recurrent metaphor, represent visual ingredients that add meaning and depth to the story. In Florence, the bright panorama seen from the miserable room symbolizes space, freedom, and happiness, as Sonia's eyes move from "dust, stains, tiles black with aging filth, torn sheets, frayed rugs" toward "the rectangle of the window where the hill's green curve is etched in the sky" (95). In search of peace, the girl's "gaze sought respite in the rectangle of the sky, which did not change in either luminosity or beauty even when she stared at it for minutes and hours" (95). Sanvitale clearly defines the space where action takes place and characters move; she sets each scene in a frame that serves as a starting point and acts as a commentary. "I would like to tell you this tale with my eyes closed, curled up among *the things* I love with a *background of old bric-a-brac*" (6).

The description of "The Calm and the Storm" in the palace ballroom allegorizes Marianna's life. Sonia sees it on the occasion of her mother's funeral when she meets with her relatives in the salon of the restored palace. The fresco represents the struggle between good and evil. The contrast between life before and after the storm expressed by the strong play of chiaroscuro and by the peaceful shepherd tending his sheep, on the side, and the frightened Agar facing her punishment, on the other, symbolizes the two stages of Marianna's life: her fairy-tale happy childhood and her turbulent lonely adulthood. In the middle of the tempest, frightened shapeless victims of inscrutable forces personify Marianna and Sonia, uprooted from their past and shaken by the cruel winds of life. "The farmer is tumbled about on the ground and clasps his head under his arms to keep from being dragged away. On the wagon, formless and faceless figures writhe in their capes, like bundles" (10). The ever-present dichotomy in Marianna's life is evident in this fresco, which perfectly illustrates Sanvitale's opening statement. "What comes after the First World War is true, what happened before is fiction" (6).

Snapshots also become a visual pretext to re-create the past. Not only do they help Sonia to remember, they reinvent childhood years spent with her father and mother. As the young unhappy girl broods over photos in the family album, she re-creates an ideal time that never existed. The images of her father on his white horse jumping obstacles cause her to dream of a loving parent riding through the desert to meet her. "He comes upon her unexpectedly like sleep and, like a giant messenger, carries her away" (26). Instead of always using a painting, drawing, or photo as starting points for the story, Sanvitale sometimes reverses the procedure by turning memories into pictures. While riding on a trolley, she transforms an observed scene into a concrete representation. "A nurse in a blue uniform comes out of the door and, together with the children grouped around the tram, *turns into a drawing*" (46). Sonia's sick friend Dario, lying in bed, is visualized as a Derain painting with "its suspended air, the trembling light, the window open on the small garden" (35).

Sanvitale's attention to small details further creates the right mood for events in the story. The novel begins with a view of the mother as a young girl framed in the door of a rich, elegant, baroque palace. "The open portal, the flanking Corinthian columns blackened by centuries, the baroque arch, the low inside gate" form the perfect background. The aged, richly decorated, but decadent architecture is the perfect symbol of the family's falling fortune. An excessive emphasis often distorts objects and purposely exaggerates events to make them appear grotesque and melodramatic. Elements like the elopement of Marianna on a stormy night, the infatuation of both women for Shirley Temple, Sonia and the middle-aged, decadent "signor Andrea" dancing at the elegant hotel Hesperia Corona, Sonia's ambiguous relationship with her uncle Paris, some heavy touches of kitsch and of popular culture in the description of rooms or inns, an evening at the opera, the arrival of the circus in town, and a card game in a third-class hotel all create a romanticized, secondary plot within the major story. This technique creates an extravagantly theatrical atmosphere that contrasts with, but does not detract from, the serious intent of the novel. The result resembles a painting whose grotesque details and strong chiaroscuro convey a special message to the reader. In the case of Marianna and Sonia, the pronounced diversity and expressionistic colors used in the descriptions of city, hotel, circus, and movies help to reveal the incongruities of their lives and the plight of two sensitive aristocratic women forced to live in a vulgar materialistic world. "They had a refined and distinguished air, their clothes were worn. They were smiling. In a cartoon they would have said 'good morning,' 'good morning.' . . . They seemed to be propelled by the wind, as if they had *a lighter material density than normal*" (23). The writer nonetheless retains control of the melodramatic plot, at times reminiscent of a soap opera. According to Marco Forti, Sanvitale maintains her hold on the novel's psychological and psychoanalytical skein and draws out its tearful story, first as an objectified flux of conscience, then as *distorted fantasy,* and again as a representation tending toward *expressionism.*"[10]

Sanvitale frequently shifts tenses in the same paragraph in order to accentuate contradictions and strong contrasts in her life. One image from the past turns into its contrary situation in the present or future, as in the following description of her mother seen in turn as a young woman and as an old lady.

> She comes out dressed in lace. Her light kidskin high-heel shoes are buckled around her thin ankles. . . . She is in mourning, dressed as a poor woman, her skirt hem hangs down. . . . She returns in the dress of apricot-colored satin, she leans back with her bare shoulders, smooth and slender, her pearl necklace reaching down to her waist. Under her light old-woman's cardigan, a white scar crosses her breast. The wound is open like a gaping hole. . . . She rests against the back of the chair with the most delicate gesture . . . how graceful she is. . . . Her right eye is paralyzed, open like a black beacon. (4)

This stylistic mechanism reflects Sanvitale's philosophical belief that persons, objects, and feelings are never fixed, clear, and well defined, but are continuously shifting and changing in time into something else, often into their opposites. After Marianna appears on the scene, she quickly begins her metamorphoses. One moment she is a beautiful girl and the next an ugly old woman. Again she first skips on the gravel paths of the palace garden, picking daisies, playing, and singing; then suddenly she is nearly thirty years old, a grown woman sitting in tears at her father's deathbed (7).

This cinematic style of presenting contrasting images in quick succession effectively renders the deep ambivalence at the heart of Sanvitale's poetic vision of life. At the beginning of the novel, the writer uses a similar photographic technique, as she brings the subject alternately closer to the viewer and further into the background. During this transposition, opposite images of the mother appear. She first walks from the back of the lobby toward the street; she crosses the arch; then she stops and steps back into the courtyard, turning into a tiny figure, until finally she comes forward again to meet a hostile crowd. As Sanvitale moves across past, present, and future events, she follows a cyclical rather than a chronological process.

A person or an episode is mentioned, abandoned, then taken up again at some later time, and further developed until it reaches its completeness. This photographic movement continuously holds the novel in its entirety before the reader's eye.

Sanvitale reinforces this cinematic quality of undulation through the use of intersecting voices that tell the story from different points of view. Like many contemporary women writers—the example of Simone de Beauvoir in *Les belles images, Mémoires d'une jeune fille rangée* and *Une mort très douce* comes to mind[11]—Sanvitale is influenced by new linguistic theories and uses the same techniques as her French counterpart. Both novelists structure their works by juxtaposing blocks in the form of dialogues, recollections, events narrated in the third person, confessions, dreams, or interior monologues in the stream-of-consciousness mode. Referring to Beauvoir's early novels, the critic Carolyn Durham indicates that the alternation of first and third persons "marks the individual's dual stature as subject and object, as both consciousness and existence in the world."[12] Durham's comments could equally apply to the structure of *Madre e figlia* and point to the existential character of both writers. Like Laurence in *Les belles images,* Sonia in *Madre e figlia* is at times the speaking subject, the "I," and at other moments, the object being spoken about, the "she."

Various personal pronouns grammatically express the interplay of different voices in the fabric of the novel.[13] Sanvitale introduces her mother, herself, and their story in the first person. In addition, she intersperses dialogues all through the novel in which major characters, solicited by Sonia, tell their stories. When Marianna tells her daughter about the death of her beloved father, his long letter in which he addresses Marianna in the second person occupies four pages. "Close your eyes, Marianna, and give me your hand" (11). On page fourteen, the narrator finally switches to the third person, as if she wanted to distance herself at last from the story. At her mother's funeral, the narrator refers to herself for the first time as "the daughter of the countess." From this point on, she narrates the story in the third person except for a few of the writer's incidental remarks. This play with personal pronouns gives a multidimensional quality to the novel that acts like a crystal, reflecting light from many facets. Sanvitale accomplishes her act of self-invention through the strong contrasts of her pictorial style, the synchronized representation of past and future events, and the different angles from which the story is told by the author, the narrator, and other characters. The sense of instability and fluctuation is well expressed and visualized in the curving lines and illusive shadows of soft, rounded, baroque, and rococo surfaces, which the writer loves to describe:

The facade of the palace is smooth, musical; where the portals open it curves like a wave. Around the arched void toward the staircase, curls of stone intertwine, lost like dribbles on the smooth surface, and appear again like ribbons around the windows that seem almost simulated. . . . We enter with Marianna breaking the rococo curve that frames the sides. The almost breathlike beauty of this small-town architecture becomes in me an ache for something inexpressible and therefore lost. (8–9)

Although Sanvitale artistically portrays her life in strong dramatic colors, she still confesses her failure to grasp its fundamental truth. When she tries to remember, "what was true and what was false get mixed up." In fact, she admits that she "cannot easily set Countess Marianna in the year 1901" (6). Nevertheless, self-revelation finally occurs in the form of dreams. Sanvitale herself (addressing the reader directly: "*Listen* to me"), compares her writing to dreaming, which allows the unconscious to surface with its revealing nightmares. "It is a trial similar to torture: I fear it and desire it at the same time. It is a fierce desire because it seems to me that the truth I seek during the day is really located in sleep—in the void, that is" (57). In fact, Marianna and Sonia reveal their real selves to Sanvitale during their sleep when they are beyond the limits of chronological time and well-defined space, "the logical and historical consecution that my head does not hold" (58). Dream metaphors facilitate the revelation of the real essence of a character. "When I enter the darkness of sleep I know, suddenly, that *there* is the enigmatic den from which I should extract data with toil, because it is there that the meaning of my life, and therefore also Sonia's and Marianna's, lies nestled, and appears and disappears" (58). Freud states that images are superimposed in dreams and that the phenomena of condensation and displacement make references to time erratic.[14] Sanvitale's style closely reproduces the oneiric process, presenting the reader with a series of epiphanies outside any chronological order. As in dreams, the writer remains free to play with narrative time, reliving memories from the past and anticipating events in the future.

The ultimate revelation comes at the end of the novel by way of a futuristic dream and an apocalyptic vision. The mother appears as a venerated old queen against a metamorphic background. This setting changes from a steep rocky mountain to a rococo royal palace, where people in later life will find their eternal home. Sanvitale, who, up to that moment, felt responsible for the life and death of her mother, decides to end her story with the account of this revelatory dream, which reintegrates the elderly Marianna in her rightful position and transforms her into a queen returning to an ancient palace. "A few days ago I had a beautiful dream that I believe is a *suitable conclusion* to this tale of my adventures" (228).

The composition and typographical setup of *Madre e figlia* reflect this oneiric substructure even under a superimposed order. Free from the constriction of chapter titles, Sanvitale, in spite of jumps forward and backward in time, divides her book into four parts, which broadly correspond to four periods in her life. The first eighty-three pages deal with Sonia's childhood; the next forty-nine pages relate to her adolescence in Florence; the following sixty-five pages portray her married life in Milan and Rome; the final thirty pages conclude with her mother's illness and death. Blank spaces, however, separate the various episodic blocks within the major sections. Each of these blocks introduces different incidents in the form of a description, recollection, dialogue, letter, or life history of such secondary characters as the uncles Paris, Giacomo, and Federico. Every unit of action constitutes an individual short story within the novel and connects to the following one by association. For instance, the desire to re-create imaginatively the mother's life in the first block causes Sanvitale to reconstruct, in the second, the provincial town where she lived in 1901. The vision of Marianna at her father's deathbed prompts the dialogue between her and Sonia on that same subject years later. These distinct, self-contained episodes closely interrelate like strokes of color that combine to produce a special overall effect.

In *Madre e figlia,* Sanvitale not only re-creates her own existence but also brings life to all the other characters of her story, especially to her father and uncles, who appear as victims of a destiny that transcends them and that they do not understand. Rather than cold intellectual figures bent on talking about their destiny as in *Il cuore borghese (The Bourgeois Heart),* the characters in this novel live out their ideas to their extreme conclusions. Their predicaments involve readers in an existential experience that goes beyond romantic plot and grotesque scenery, as they create a mirror that permits both writer and audience to recognize themselves. Sanvitale reveals this new desire to understand herself and to communicate directly with the public in an interview for the magazine *Uomini e libri.* Discussing *Madre e figlia,* she explains her evolution and stresses her sense of urgency. "During eight years of silence, I developed a new attitude toward *narrative as a mirror of oneself* in the world and vice versa: now I think only of the *joy of communicating;* no longer am I bound by the solitary task of building models of society."[15] In fact, Sanvitale tries to involve readers in her story by addressing them directly in the second person. "I would like to shut my eyes and tell *you* this story" (6); or "Have *you* ever seen a provincial town?" (5); or "*Listen to me:* when I go to bed" (57); or again "I would like to tell *you* still more about Countess Marianna" (228), up to when she begs her readers not to leave: "I'm sorry that, like me, *you* too close the book and detach *yourself* from my emotions. *Don't go away. Don't think* about anything else . . . *you* must know . . . I had a dream. Please *listen* to it" (228).

When asked whether *Madre e figlia* was an autobiographical novel, Sanvitale expressed the wish to save "the artifice of writing, because without that we lose poetry forever."[16] Indeed, the attempt to define autobiography as a literary genre becomes problematic. According to James Olney, autobiography is a mode of writing that can be infinitely varied.[17] Other recent critics maintain that the line between autobiography and fiction is difficult to draw. Paul De Man doubts that autobiography depends on reference "as a photograph depends on its subject or a 'realistic' picture on its model . . . the autobiographical project may itself produce the life . . . and be determined by the resources of the medium."[18] A comparison with Simone de Beauvoir, one of the first contemporary women authors of autobiography, helps to understand better Sanvitale's achievement. Both writers portray a deeply troubled mother-daughter relationship, and the act of writing produces a cathartic effect through the confrontation of self (author) and other (mother). Whereas the French writer treats this material in a didactic way, creating a realistic account of her mother's illness and death in *Une mort très douce,* the Italian author produces a metaphorical novel that transposes reality to an imaginative and more universal level.

Sanvitale understands that only art can shed real light on the self and that autobiography, at its best, takes the form of fiction. She proves the validity of Nabokov's words on the possibility of revealing the true essence of life through art: "Neither in environment nor in heredity can I find the exact instrument that fashioned me, the anonymous roller that pressed upon my life a certain *intricate* watermark whose *unique* design becomes visible when the *lamp of art* is made to shine through life's foolscap."[19] In like manner, the memorialist essentially acquires a true understanding of life through the act of writing. In *Madre e figlia,* the protagonist's struggle for independence, her suffering, failures, and successes find a perfect form of expression. Sanvitale creates the most appropriate structure and style for her subject and allows the "lamp of art" to shine through her life.

NOTES

1. Francesca Sanvitale, *Madre e figlia* (Turin: Einaudi, 1980). All further references to it will be indicated by the page number following the quotation. Translations from *Madre e figlia* and other Italian sources are mine.

2. From a letter quoted by Gino Pampaloni in his presentation of the first edition of *Il cuore borghese* see p. 25. (Florence: Vallecchi, 1972) (on the novel jacket).

3. Marco Forti, "Francesca Sanvitale o la perenne crudeltà della favola," *Lunario Nuovo* 4, no. 18–19 (1982): 30. In this article, Forti praises Sanvitale for reacting against an experimentalism that could easily become a gratuitous literary game.

4. Paul John Eakin, *Fictions in Autobiography: Studies in the Art of Self-Invention* (Princeton: Princeton University Press, 1985), p. 3.

5. Marcel Proust, *Contre Sainte-Beuve,* published in 1956, was written in 1896–1919 and translated by Sylvia Townsend Warner with the title *On Art and Literature* (New York: Meridian Books, 1958) and with the title *By Way of Sainte-Beuve* (London: Hogarth Press, 1984). In it, Proust says: "Le moi de l'écrivain ne se montre que dans ses livres et on est écrivain quand on est dans la solitude" ("The writer reveals himself only in his books and is a writer only in solitude.")

6. Roland Barthes, "Introduction à l'analyse structurale des récits," *Communications* 8 (1966), translated as "An Introduction to the Structural Analysis of Narrative," *New Literary History* 6 (1974–75): 261.

7. Jacques Lacan, "The Mirror Stage as Formative of the Function of the I," in *Ecrits: A Selection,* trans. Alan Sheridan (London: Tavistock, 1977), pp. 1–7. Lacan sees literature as a mirror that sends us back to our ego in its gestalt or total unity.

8. Sigmund Freud, "Femininity," Lecture 33 of *Introductory Lectures on Psycho-Analysis,* 1933 (1932). *The Standard Edition of the Psychological Works of Sigmund Freud,* trans. and ed. James Strachey, 24 vols. (London: The Hogarth Press and the Institute of Psycho-Analysis, 1953–1974), 22: 5–182 (hereafter referred to as SE followed by volume and page numbers). If different, the date of writing is given after the date of publication.

9. Sigmund Freud defines the concepts of "feminine" (equal passivity) and "masculine" (equal activity) in "Femininity" and in "Female Sexuality" (1931), SE 21: 225–43.

10. Forti, "Francesca Sanvitale," p. 32.

11. All three novels were published by Gallimard respectively in 1966, 1958, and 1964.

12. Carolyn A. Durham, "Patterns of Influence: Simone de Beauvoir and Marie Cardinal," *French Review* 60, no. 3 (1987): 346.

13. Emile Benveniste, *Problèmes de linguistique générale,* trans. M. E. Meek, as *Problems of General Linguistics* (Coral Gables: University of Miami Press, 1971). Benveniste develops the theory of personal pronouns. Other French structuralists who studied and gave different definitions of the "narrative voice" are Jacques Lacan, Roland Barthes, Jacques Derrida, Mikhaîl Bakhtin, Luce Irigaray, Julia Kristeva, Hélène Cixous, Marguerite Duras, and Annie Leclerc.

14. Sigmund Freud, *On Dreams* (New York: Norton, 1952). First English edition *The Interpretation of Dreams* (1900); SE 4: 1–338; SE 5: 339–625. Freud explains that dreams lack the dimensions of time and space and are characterized by condensation and displacement, as well as association and visual symbolism.

15. Interview: "Ognuno di noi è pieno di storie da raccontare," *Uomini e Libri* 16, no. 36 (1980): 36.

16. Ibid.

17. James Olney, "Autobiography and the Cultural Movement: A Thematic, Historic and Bibliographical Introduction," in *Autobiography: Essays Theoretical and Critical,* ed. James Olney (Princeton: Princeton University Press, 1980).

18. Paul De Man, "Autobiography as De-Facement," *MLN* 94 (1979): 920.

19. Vladimir Nabokov, *Speak, Memory: An Autobiography Revisited* (New York: Putnam's, 1966), p. 25.

DACIA MARAINI

Dacia Maraini, one of the most prominent cultural feminists, is not only the founder of the experimental theater La Maddalena but is also a prize-winning novelist, poet, literary and film critic, film writer, historian, and political activist. Her works of fiction—*L'età del malessere* (1962), *La vacanza* (1966), *Diario di una ladra* (1972), *Donna in guerra* (1975), *Il treno per Helsinski* (1984)—all deal with women's struggles for genuine freedom and react to centuries of stereotyped women. In the 1970s, Maraini worked to found a woman's cultural center in a poor neighborhood of Rome and campaigned in favor of legalized abortion; in the 1980s, she became involved in connecting the disarmament movements of other countries with the Italian effort and in understanding feminism in an international context. She has lectured on the feminist theater in Brazil, Holland, Spain, and the United States. Her contemporary interest is a series of plays about women in historic Italian court trials, including one about a prostitute who was killed to save a man's reputation. In an interview in November 1981, Maraini said that Marxist premises and the attempt to analyze the roots of cultural and social discrimination against women are the two currents that have informed Italian feminism from the beginning.

Dacia Maraini's *Donna in guerra:*
Victory or Defeat?

ANTHONY J. TAMBURRI

Donna in guerra (Women at War)[1] covers a brief period of a couple's relationship. Vannina, an elementary school teacher in Rome's periphery, grows increasingly weary of her unsatisfactory marriage. Giacinto, her mechanic husband, is a seemingly kind and pensive individual whose traditional perspective fails to recognize a woman's needs. Their life together initially appears to be without problems, until a summer vacation unexpectedly exposes Vannina to a world entirely different from the one she knows.

Written in the form of a diary, the novel reflects not only Vannina's personal experiences but also the overall condition of women in Italy.[2] Examples that illustrate themes of social injustice surface, and gender stereotyping invariably comes into play. Vannina's brief association with an underground Leftist group accentuates a sociopolitical scenario. Although proclaiming themselves revolutionary thinkers concerned with people's rights, the men in this ideological organization show themselves to be increasingly insensitive to the plight of women. Vannina herself witnesses labor exploitation of the worst kind in the slums of Naples, where she conducts interviews with housewives engaged in poorly paid piecework. While it is almost impossible to isolate the common denominator in literature written by women, the most recurring remains the motif of conflict. When these authors or their protagonists identify with others, they demonstrate sympathy for those involved in some form of class struggle.[3]

Informing her text with a strong feminist charge, Maraini adopts a narrative technique that noticeably deviates from the canon. In order to demonstrate the need for an end to patriarchal stereotyping of women, she adopts a narrative technique of reversal. She eschews narration as the dominant mode of communication, and her vocabulary often reflects an everyday inventory of slang and vulgarities.

Presented as a diary, a medium long associated with women writers,[4] *Donna in guerra* differs from the canon in that it favors dialogue over narration. The use of dialogue sets the events of the story in the immediate present. Narration, on the other hand, usually implies circumstances already completed, and the passages of conversation interspersed within "serve simply to dramatize the events and characters in order to make them more vivid,"[5] thus animating the writer's world. Narration, then, ordinarily offers a vantage point from which the reader judges events in their totality, namely, the usual perspective of hindsight. Dialogue, conversely, deprives the reader of hindsight by the very fact that situations remain firmly embedded in the present. In the case of a highly dialogical work,[6] readers must assume a more active role, as dialogue plays an originative role in the dissemination of information rather than merely reinforcing what the author might otherwise communicate through narration. Direct discourse supposedly represents an objective fact heard by the author who undertakes the role of a reporter faithfully recording verbal exchange. At the same time, the technique forces the reader to act as an impartial and attentive observer and literally requires greater involvement.

This stylistic method combines with the first-person presentation of the narrator and underlines the urgency of the author's communique. The diaristic form alone normally provides a confession, a description of an individual's life, and a narrator's perspective. In the case of *Donna in guerra,* readers also have the advantage of another point of view. They actively become "producer[s] of the text"[7] and draw inferences from the dialogue in order to make better sense of the words. This author/reader coproduction of the "unformulated text"[8] charges the novel with a more forceful message.

The issue of gendered roles is immediately presented and remains constant throughout the work. Giacinto is already off fishing early Sunday morning, and Vannina, having gotten up to make him coffee, cleans the house and puts the rest of his fishing gear in order. The only reported words are hers—"What do you want to eat?"—and quickly establish her in the role of home making wife. The couple is on vacation, yet both take it for granted that she will rise early and provide for his needs. Other details distinguish their respective conditions when Vannina emphasizes her bodily features. After dozing off, she awakes to an unexpected discomfort. "I woke up with a sharp pain, a silent and deep one. Something hot was wet on my thighs. I stuck a hand under my skirt. I withdrew it stained with blood" (3).

Menstruation, therefore, characterizes the dichotomy between the sexes from the very beginning. In contrast to mythical and primitive notions of the menses as impure,[9] Vannina refers to it as a wholesome and comforting phenomenon.

> So begins my vacation: a stream of beneficent blood, the joy of the outdoors, the strong odor of basil. School is far away. Giacinto will be back later with the fish. The house is in order. Ironing shirts, preparing the sauce, cleaning pots are all put off until this evening. Now I don't want to think about anything. I'm content. (4)

Vannina's solitary happiness occurs in that realm of female "otherness" that so often threatens the male.[10] The conventional female duties of house-cleaning, cooking, and the like are now parenthetically placed between the joy of excursions in the open air and the postponement of day-to-day concerns.[11] Giacinto's absence has allowed Vannina to briefly abandon her traditional role.

The first three entries are dedicated to Vannina and her tasks during the couple's vacation. The fourth annotation deals instead with Giacinto.

> Giacinto is asleep. He's there curled up nude on the bed, hiding his penis between his knees. His back curved, his head tucked between his shoulders, his folded legs express an obstinate defense. Against what, I don't know. . . . I bend over to kiss him. He awakes suddenly. He looks at me as if I had come to steal something from him. (6)

Sleeping unclothed in a protective position, he shields himself from his wife. When she finally embraces him, he abruptly opens his eyes, as if he fears losing a personal possession.

In one respect, Giacinto's unexpected alarm serves as a counterpoint to Vannina's temporary feeling of freedom; relaxed in the chaise lounge, she disregards her so-called duties. She stands momentarily as the "other" vis-à-vis the male, whereas Giacinto's obstinate defense implies tension and fear in the face of a woman's independent status. Thus, their mutual attitudes underscore the male/female dichotomy. In the courtyard, Vannina expresses a certain ease with her sexuality as she demonstrates no surprise at her bodily function. In fact, she expects nature to follow its course and, in a sense, takes pleasure in the moment. Giacinto, on the other hand, covers himself up, as if someone—here his wife—"had come to steal something from him." The three contiguous episodes that open the novel set the tone, but from that point on, the couple's relationship undergoes a transformation brought about, for the most part, by Vannina's multiple and varied experience with the people she meets.

Suna, the first of a series of catalysts for change, possesses a strong feminist stance despite her sometimes contradictory behavior.[12] In one of their first revealing conversations, Suna points out Giacinto's self-serving, exploitative nature.

> —[Giacinto and Mario] talk about women to each other.
> —Solidarity among men.

—When I arrive they stop talking, they become serious, obnoxious, then if I go to sleep I hear them laugh, talk, drink, they can go on until two or three in the morning; Giacinto's another person with him, he becomes a little boy, he jokes around, he tells a bunch of tales.
—He's distracted.
—That's his nature.
—Do you think he loves you?
—I don't know.
—Would it bother you if he didn't give a damn about you?
—Yes.
—You think you love him, because you submit yourself to him, you look after him, you take care of him, you put yourself beneath him, but it's not love.
—What is it?
—Duty, you're in love with your duty.
—I couldn't live without him.
—You don't get along sexually.
—Not well.
—You see.
—Giacinto says that sex counts very little when two people love one another ("quando si vuole bene").
—He says it because it's convenient for him.
—He's sincere.
—And what do you think?
Nothing. I didn't think anything. I didn't know how to answer. What Giacinto does I make mine. I have never even thought of contradicting him. I believe he's better than me, that he's right, that what he says is good for both of us. (89–90)

The dialogue between the two women highlights the subject of solidarity between men. When Vannina enters the room, the men's silence implies a separation indicative of a tension—"they become serious, obnoxious"— due to a total lack of communication. Suna also discusses the concept of love versus obligation in her conversation; indeed in this case, a sense of duty derives from without rather than evolves from within. In addition, the question of instinct vis-à-vis social conditioning arises when Suna states that the distinction between the two sexes is social and political rather than biological and ontological.[13] The two women finally allude to sexual activity; the couple's physical interaction totally depends on Giacinto's desire, and it is he who essentially defines this aspect of their marital life. They engage in intercourse only when he decides to do so, and Vannina, despite her lack of desire, concedes.

Sexual activity remains the feature that ties the novel's characters to-gether. As a writer, Maraini demonstrates a lack of inhibition in her use of descriptions and usurps a technique often associated with pornography and the objectification of women for the very purpose of indicating such objectification. The portrayal of specific carnal acts constitutes another aspect of her overall narrative technique. While it is "dangerous [i.e., limiting] to place the body at the center of the search for female identity," biological imagery is important insofar as "factors other than anatomy are involved in it. Ideas about the body are fundamental to understanding how women conceptualize their situations in society."[14] Indeed, Maraini does not limit herself to a description of the female but places equal emphasis on the male body and, in so doing, informs many of these anecdotes with a message that transcends sexual imagery per se.

Sex is indeed a metaphor in *Donna in guerra,* and as such it defines the very essence of the individual.[15] Giacinto's relationship with Vannina and his reaction to her desires blatantly reveals his self-indulgence. Since sex for him is only a source of physical pleasure, she becomes completely objectified and, consequently, is denied any sexual gratification.

> We ate the charcoaled fish. We made love. Quickly, as usual, without giving me time to reach climax. Then he fell asleep in his usual contracted position of defense with his legs and arms folded under his chin. I tell him to wait for me. He tells me that if he doesn't do it right away he loses his desire. He's in a hurry to get an erection. To have himself swallowed up, to get red hot, to slap flesh against flesh . . . as if by hesitating he might lose something. . . . So I'm left hanging, panting, tense. He runs, chased by a fear of I don't know what. (11)

Just as Giacinto eats because he is hungry so does he copulate in order to satisfy a physical urge. No emotional or sentimental tone qualifies his participation. Instead, just as one would do after a big meal, Giacinto rolls over and falls asleep. The book presents several similar scenes, and in all these instances, Giacinto assumes his usual defensive position and exhibits his fear of losing something, an inexplicable phobia that Vannina cannot define. These references reinforce the dichotomy of the sexes, which is underscored by Vannina having to bring herself to an orgasm "like a painful sprain."[16]

This marriage eventually becomes one of violence and violation. Vannina realizes how precarious her situation is and tries to remedy it. Giacinto conversely begins to manifest characteristics of a dominant male, demanding a demure, obedient, subservient wife.[17] Although Vannina behaves this way in the opening scenes of the novel, she changes as the story unfolds, and Giacinto reacts negatively to her gradual feminist awareness. He bemoans her new status and laments the "loss" of her good nature.

—You betray your nature, my love.

—What nature?

—You have a good nature, soft, sensitive, and you want to make it become something hard, aggressive.

    —Am I aggressive if I don't want to make love with you?

    —You're aggressive against yourself, you do violence to your character. . . .

    —I only wanted to please you.

    —It was right because you loved me.

    —I wanted to be a good wife.

    —And you have been, but now you're changing, you reject the best part of yourself.

    —The best because it's convenient. (237)

At this point, Vannina is clearly aware of her situation. Her last utterance echoes Suna's earlier criticism of Giacinto's statement "sex counts very little when two people love one another";—she had retorted, "he says it because it's convenient for him" (89–90).[18] Vannina now expresses the same understanding when she responds "the best because it's convenient." She sees that the preservation of Vannina's "best part" is in his interest, not hers. In fact, when they make love in a moment of apparent reconciliation, Giacinto, as usual, thinks only of himself.

The majority of men in the novel consider sexual gratification a male's prerogative. In their eyes, enjoyment by the woman is either inconceivable, or at least shameful. Vittorio, the political activist, ironically propagandizes these notions when he directs his revolutionary message primarily at men. If he tolerates Suna's participation, it is mainly because she contributes money to his cause. During his activist period, he conveniently indulges in a relationship with Mafalda, who acts as both his ideological confrere and his sexual partner, although he abandons her at the border when they flee to Switzerland. By chance, he meets Dominique, whom he subsequently marries. Paradoxically, she is young, pretty, rich, and, most important, a virgin—all characteristics that a Leftist movement would find ideologically suspect. In his conversation with Suna, he clarifies his ideas on women.

    —What does your mother do? [Suna asks]

    —Nothing, she stays at home.

    —Do you have a maid?

    —No.

    —And so how can you say she doesn't do anything?

    —Well, she stays at home, she does housework.

    —That is she prepares lunch, she makes your bed, she washes your clothes, she irons your shirts, she goes shopping for you, she cooks, she washes the dishes doesn't she? . . . Do you have any brothers or sisters?

—Six, two are still small.
—And who watches after them?
—My mother.
—Has your mother ever had a lover?
—What are you talking about? If you saw her you'd understand that yours is a bourgeois question, out of place, that mother of mine is an old lady, hardly a woman.
—Exactly, an old lady, without genitals and without a brain, an old lady who wipes all your asses.
—Illogical logic, typically feminine . . . one can't reason with you. (72–73)

Vittorio possesses a totally patriarchal concept of love that accepts corporeal fulfillment as a man's right but completely disregards female sexuality. His characterization of his mother incarnates the historical paradox of women's biological needs and reflects Millett's analysis of this condition.

Women have been confined to the cultural level of animal life in providing the male with a sexual outlet and exercising the animal functions of reproduction and caring for the young. Thus the female has had sexuality visited upon her as a punishment in a way of life which, with few exceptions, and apart from maternity, did not encourage her to derive pleasure from sexuality and limited her to an existence otherwise comprised mainly of menial labor and domestic service.[19]

Vittorio sees his mother with a limited vision and delineates his attitude when he describes her as an old lady who is hardly a woman.

Violence toward women occurs in a variety of physical and psychological ways. Early in the novel, one of Santino's brothers participates in the gang rape of an eighteen-year-old English woman. After the youth recounts the story at the dinner table, his father expresses his proud approval of his son's act. Another character, Faele, who is in love with a German woman who chooses his friend Peppe instead, seeks revenge against his friend by attempting to rape Peppe's mongoloid sister. His cruel and grotesque plan backfires, however, when the handicapped child proves quite familiar with certain sexual acts. This aspect of the story emphasizes the concept of sexual socialization, which assumes the female will be subservient to the male's desires. The implication is that the child gained her sexual knowledge from the male members of her family—her father, brothers, and cousins.

Vannina's negative experiences are not limited to her home. When she goes by herself to the movies she is harassed. In the theater, two men think she is a prostitute and each tries to fondle her. On her way home, two other men approach her in a car and immediately ask her price. When she responds that all women out after dark are not prostitutes, they assault her and take her money. More significant examples of violence take place within the household. Two scenes illustrate the patriarchal concept of the male as the exclusive head of the family; in both instances Giacinto insists on making love. Although the couple's relationship degenerates significantly, Giacinto's behavior remains constant throughout, and he continues to remind his wife of her duties. The subordinate role of his partner encourages these scenes, which contain strong instances of verbal violence.[20] In one case, Giacinto draws her physically into the bedroom and underscores their uneven relationship through his indifference to her lack of desire.

> —Let's do it anyway.
> —I don't want to.
> —All you have to do is lie there, what's it to you?
> —That's what I don't want.
> —You've always done it.
> —I don't want to.
> —See, you've changed, I was wrong, that shithead set you against me; you lost your nature, you've become stubborn, irritable, like that slut Suna, you've ruined yourself, and your kindness, your kindness I liked so much, where the fuck did it go? (234)

More than demonstrating an uneven relationship, Giacinto's insistence particularly exemplifies male objectification of a female and society's expectations for an obedient, docile "body-servant."[21] His description of the recently changed Vannina opposes the model of the obedient ("set . . . against me"), sweet ("your kindness . . . where the fuck did it go"), and demure ("stubborn, irritable") housewife who is always at her husband's beck and call.

The most offensive case of male presumption and violation of women occurs when Giacinto argues with Vannina's refusal, stating that motherhood is the essence of a female's nature. "A woman needs to have a child . . . a woman without children is like a cat without kittens, who cries, flings itself about in a frenzy, bites its tail in a sorry way" (246). Determined to have his own way, Giacinto commits conjugal rape two nights later. Although Vannina is already asleep without any contraceptive protection, he quickly mounts and impregnates her before she can fully understand the consequences of the act. In light of Giacinto's quick orgasms in previous scenes of the novel, a slight touch of irony characterizes her description of the event. "He did it *so quickly* that I didn't have time to react" (249). This case of domestic violence more significantly sheds light on the general condition of societal brutality against women. The consequences of this experience are paramount for Vannina. Not wanting a child, she must now rely on a doctor to perform an illegal abortion. A brief and precise entry in Vannina's diary ("7 dicembre," 267) focuses on the male doctor's actions.[22]

Although Maraini uses sex as a metaphor of one's character, she also believes that an individual's personality is not an innate biologically evolved phenomenon. Character, and in particular, sex roles, results from socialization.[23] While Suna's various discussions highlight this perspective, more specific ideas concerning the woman's plight intertwine in this context. When Vannina returns to school after her summer vacation, she enters the classroom and finds a group of boys pretending to rape one of the girls.

> Two boys were holding Maria Stella by her arms and feet, while two others had gotten on top of her. One was on top of her contorting his body with a ridiculous and exaggerated movement, pumping his behind forward and backward. . . .
> The other was sitting astride her neck so that his pants squashed her face. He was swaying back and forth, red and sweaty, yelling:—Suck suck you whore. . . . The boy's eyes . . . were fixed toward the other boys and girls, looking for approval.
> The girls were all grouped on one side and they were giggling, amused. (255–56)

The socialization of the male's sexual domination begins at the earliest of ages. The majority of the children accept this spirit of domination. The boys, unconcerned with the act itself, look toward the group for approval; the girls, seeing one of their own lie victim, are overwhelmingly amused by the situation.

In her conversation with Maria Stella, Vannina now reveals her newly found liberation. She questions the girl and simultaneously exposes the overall social status of women.

> —Rape, do you know what it is?
> —I donno!
> —Rape is a violent act a man or men perpetrate against a woman, or a little girl as in your case, do you understand?
> —They screw her then.
> —And why do you think the other girls didn't come and help you?
> —Because they're sons of bitches.
> —Could it not be because they think the boys have a right to do these things? . . .
> —Do you think that if you were a boy, even small, they would play the same trick on you?
> —No, what's the difference, the female acts like a woman and stays on the bottom, the male acts like a man and gets on top and fucks her. (257)

Rape is defined as an act of violence that men perpetrate upon women. Yet in the eyes of this little child, it is permitted; as far as she is concerned, what the male does is what he should do and what the female does is what she should. The literal position of top and bottom metaphorically represents the general pattern of domination in a patriarchal society. Vannina's reference to overbearing actions, physical force, and lack of tenderness also recalls her own experiences with brutality in marriage. (At this point in the novel, Vannina has already been raped by her husband.) And in contrast, Vannina now defines love, as she continues her conversation with Maria Stella.

> —And do you think one makes love like this?
> —I donno!
> —With arrogance, squashing and laughing, without concern for the other person?
> —They're sons of bitches, teacher.
> —Love is something you share together, with kindness, with tenderness, without overbearing actions and both people have to be happy, don't you think so? (257–58)

The rapport that exists between Vannina and Giacinto has never been anything more than a physical one; Giacinto has usually been the initiator.[24] Love has never been a part of his motivation, intercourse for him is only a physical release. Nevertheless, *Donna in guerra,* an extreme expression of the woman's plight in early 1970 Italy, assumes no antimale stance. Although Maraini makes blatantly evident the problems inherent in gender stereotyping, she does not advocate separatism. Suna, the most enlightened of the female characters, does not incarnate the ideal feminist. Her strong feelings for Santino deprive her of the necessary courage to renounce their relationship, however precarious it may be. Conversely, while the adult males tend to reflect overbearing patriarchal attitudes toward women, Vannina's brief affair with Orio makes it clear that Maraini does not unequivocally condemn men. Of primary significance is his age; at fourteen years old, he has not yet been totally indoctrinated into the patriarchal society in which he lives. It is during this affair, in fact, that Vannina has her only positive experiences with both physical and emotional love. Describing intercourse with Orio, she writes that he "moved patiently, slowly, aware of my rhythm. And I with him" (103). She then reproachfully reveals everything to Giacinto: "You, when you make love, think only about yourself, you don't give a damn about me; Orio, with all that he's a boy, paid more attention to me" (104).[25]

The message then may be considered twofold. First of all, *Donna in guerra* illustrates the difficulties women experience in a totally male-oriented society. If a woman does succeed in liberating herself from an oppressive situation, the overall problem of gender stereotyping remains unsolved. Giacinto's final supplication to Vannina after her abortion highlights this dilemma. He asks her to return, promising to forgive and forget the mistakes he continues to see as hers. Secondly, then, solutions to the plight of women require the cooperation of both the male and the female; otherwise, women will always find themselves in perilous predicaments. This is the subtext of many of Vannina's experiences; for the most part, she acquires a sense of peace and calm either in the company of other females or with those males, e.g., Orio, who have not been totally coopted by patriarchy. Thus, the title *Donna in guerra* refers precisely to the continuing struggle women must wage against patriarchy, just as Vannina, by freeing herself from Giacinto, has won a battle but not the war.

NOTES

An earlier version of this essay was delivered at the Florida State University Conference on Comparative Literature and Film: Gender (Tallahassee), January 1986.

1. Dacia Maraini, *Donna in guerra* (Turin: Einaudi, 1975). *Donna in guerra* was translated into English as *Woman at War* by Mara Benetti and Elisabeth Spottiswood (Brighlingsea, Essex: Lighthouse Books, 1984). Because the English translation was not readily available when this essay went to press, all translations are mine; the numbers in parentheses refer to the Italian edition.

2. The story takes place in southern Italy, where women have always lived in a much more restrictive social environment. For an analogous account of a woman's plight in the South, see Sibilla Aleramo's novel, *Una donna* (Turin: Sten, 1906), now available from Feltrinelli (Milan, 1985). Two sociological books dedicated to the woman in the South are Ann Cornelison, *Women in the Shadows* (New York: Vintage Books, 1977), and Charlotte Gower Chapman, *Milocca: A Sicilian Village* (Cambridge, Mass.: Schenkman, 1971).

3. See, Elisabetta Rasy, *Le donne e la letteratura* (Rome: Editori Riuniti, 1984), p. 35; Kate Millett, *Sexual Politics* (New York: Doubleday, 1970), p. 38. One finds similar characteristics in Aleramo's novel *Una donna*, where the narrator-protagonist associates her plight as a woman with the socioeconomic plight of the oppressed. Augustus Pallotta also indicates similarities between these two novels in his brief overview, "Dacia Maraini: From Alienation to Feminism," *World Literature Today* 58, no. 3 (1984): 361.

4. See Susan Gubar, "'The Blank Page' and the Issue of Female Creativity," in *Writing and Sexual Difference,* ed. Elizabeth Abel (Chicago: University of Chicago Press, 1982), pp. 81–82; Anna Nozzoli, "Sul romanzo femminista degli anni settanta," *Nuova DWF Donna Woman Femme* 5: 69; and Rasy, *Le donne*, p. 93.

5. Wolfgang Iser, *The Implied Reader: Patterns of Communication in Prose from Bunyan to Beckett* (Baltimore: Johns Hopkins University Press, 1974), pp. 235–38.

6. I use this term in its strictest sense, i.e., a narrative work with an abundance of direct discourse, and not in the Bakhtinian sense of intertextuality.

7. Roland Barthes, *S/Z,* trans. Richard Miller (New York: Hill and Wang, 1974), p. 4.

8. Iser, *The Implied Reader,* p. 34.

9. See Gubar, "'The Blank Page,'" p. 83; Millett, *Sexual Politics*, p. 47.

10. Millett, *Sexual Politics*, p. 46.

11. This female "otherness" is analogous to Giacinto's fishing excursion; for the amateur fisher*man*, being outdoors in a relaxed situation is equal to, if not more desirous than, the actual task of catching fish.

12. Suna is involved in a relationship with Santino, a totally self-absorbed male. As he does with others, Santino exploits Suna financially and physically.

13. For more on this concept, see Monique Wittig, "The Straight Mind," *Feminist Issues* 1, no. 1 (1980): 103–10. For her, "'man' and 'woman' are political concepts of opposition [due to] a historical situation of domination" (108).

14. Elaine Showalter, "Feminist Criticism in the Wilderness," in Abel, *Writing and Sexual Difference,* p. 19.

15. As readers, we are not privy to the two laundry women, Tota and Giottina, engaging in sexual activity. They do, however, speak constantly of the sexual "perversity" of the rich and nonresidents of the town. Such insistence on the unusual acts of the rich and nonresidents transcends their physical meaning and indicates instead the spiritual and moral "perversity" of the individuals in question.

16. One may interpret Vannina's masturbation as a symbol of the woman's self-sufficient nature. The adjective *doloroso* (painful), however, has a negative connotation. The pain may result from Giacinto's insensitivity to both her physical and her emotional needs.

17. With regard to the "nature of woman" and her position in society vis-à-vis man, John Stuart Mill wrote in 1869 that "what is now called the nature of woman is an extremely artificial thing—the result of forced repression in some directions, unnatural stimulation in others. It may be asserted without scruple, that no other class or dependents have had their character so entirely distorted from its natural proportions by their relation with their masters" (*The Subjection of Women* [Cambridge: MIT Press, 1970], p. 22). Similarly, Engels demonstrated the historical roots of male domination of women in *The Origins of the Family, Private Property and the State* (1884; New York: International Publishers, 1942), where he stated: "In Euripides, the wife is described as *oikurima*, a thing for housekeeping (the word is in the neuter gender), and apart from the business of bearing children, she was nothing more to the Athenian than the chief housemaid" (55).

18. Here, the use of "si vuole bene" is significant. Although the expression *volere bene* translates "to love," its connotations are of the spiritual and emotional aspects of feelings, and although it is readily used by lovers and husbands and wives, it is also used by relatives, between parents and children, for example. *Amare* is used to describe the passionate love one finds between "physical" lovers.

19. Millett, *Sexual Politics*, p. 119.

20. While Maraini engages in a liberal use of slang in both her sexual descriptions and conversations, the crude and vulgar language is generally attributed to the males. The females, despite their explicit sexual descriptions, tend to use a more euphemistic mode of speech. This is especially true in the cases of Tota and Giottina, who prove extremely generous and precise in their descriptions of the sexual practices of the rich.

21. Mill defined the home as the center of a system he considered "domestic slavery"—a system where the woman's only lot in life was "that of being the personal body-servant of a despot." For more on Mill and his disagreement with some of his contemporaries, see Millett, *Sexual Politics*, pp. 89–108.

22. Maraini does not deal with abortion as a moral issue; the characters never engage in any political or philosophical discussions about it. Instead, she places emphasis on the physical consequences for women. Thus she underscores the violence against women with a description of both the operation itself and the husband/lover's reaction to it (237, 253).

23. Millett discusses this concept at length in her *Sexual Politics,* pp. 214–33.

24. On the few occasions Vannina wanted to make love, Giacinto always made excuses. When they did engage in sex, he behaved in his usual manner.

25. Analogous is Vannina's brief encounter with Fidelio, her student, at the beginning of the novel. A poor, underprivileged boy, he walks five miles a day to school. This brief relationship is solely emotional, but it hints at future themes. Like Orio, Fidelio is also too young to have been corrupted by society.

ARMANDA GUIDUCCI

Literary critic, political writer, feminist, and social commentator, Armanda Guiducci has a long list of published works and professional activities. She has been editor of several cultural periodicals—*Ragionamenti, Arguments, Opinione, Passato e Presente, Tempi Moderni*—and has contributed to many others, including Cesare Pavese's famous journal *Cultura e Realtà*, dedicated to the social importance of art. Active in political groups, Guiducci was an early organizer of the Circolo Turati and writes for the literary pages of *L'Avanti*, Italy's socialist newspaper. She has also directed cultural programs for Swiss television. Her books range from literary criticism to poetry and have earned her such prestigious awards as the Citadella for *Poesie per un uomo* (1965), the Pisa for *Il mito Pavese* (1967) and for *A colpi di silenzio* (1982). Guiducci's feminist writings—*La mela e il serpente* (1974), *Due donne da buttare* (1976), *La donna non è gente* (1977), *All'ombra di Kali* (1979), *Donna e serva* (1983), and *A testa in giù* (1984)—have not been translated into English.

Armanda Guiducci's Disposable Women

FIORA A. BASSANESE

Written in the charged atmosphere of the 1970s, Armanda Guiducci's feminist books address the issues facing women in a traditional patriarchy, where being female is tantamount to being invisible. Guiducci's protagonists are not angry protestors who scream their rage at an unjust sexist society and shout war cries at the male-dominated world, but are instead the truly silent majority, conditioned to resignation and relegated to the shadows of history and culture. The writer intends to give voice to these women of silence, allowing them to emerge from obscurity and speak themselves into visibility. Intentionally created to function as both distinctive narrators and universal prototypes, Guiducci's emblematic protagonists represent the female situation understood as a cycle repeated from generation to generation, since the beginning of time. The title of Guiducci's first fictional work, *La mela e il serpente* (The apple and the serpent) (1974), is connotative: it is about one woman, as indicated in the subtitle (Self-analysis of a woman), but it is also about Eve, the first woman and the symbol of everywoman. In this work, the first-person narrator delves into both the conscious and the unconscious self, seeking to understand her continued adherence to a tradition of oppression and conditioning, concluding that a woman's struggle for self-affirmation is as much personal as it is societal. This protagonist explores herself and her roles, coming face-to-face with the obstacles to self-fulfillment presented by the environment and by history itself. For Armanda Guiducci, the female condition in society is inherently inferior.

Women's status as a second sex is clearly demonstrated in the two companion pieces, *Due donne da buttare* (Two disposable women; 1976) and *La donna non è gente* (Women are not people; 1977). Conceived as instruments for the affirmation of the profound humanity of the dispossessed women of Italian society, these testimonies of pain and invisibility speak to the universality of each individual experience. Guiducci's narrative strategy manipulates the confessional genre by presenting unpolished and unsequential monologues that reflect women's unfamiliarity with self-expression, thereby giving speech to silence. Muted words and unheard lives find a voice in Guiducci's first-person narratives, which are both fiction and biography and represent untrained, nonliterary voices appropriate to women who have been traditionally excluded from power, position, and expression. In the preface to *La donna non è gente,* the author explains her fascination with the impoverished, socially marginal peasantry and offers her literary design, which is feminist and polemical:

> These women, deprived of all voice by a series of subtractions—by history, by the proletariat itself, by feminine emancipation—which reduces them to the zero point of femininity, what do they think in the silences of their unexpressed voices?
>
> I sought to face these silences, these minds, these voiceless voices without resonance.[1]

While all Guiducci's confessions are based on actual interviews, her two companion books are stylistically dissimilar and depict distinctive environments. Whereas *La donna non è gente* is nonfictional in tone and structure, *Due donne da buttare* has the texture and form of a novel, utilizing literary devices such as imagery, symbolism, and specularity to reinforce the writer's feminist message. Although Guiducci appears as interviewer and narrator in her rural study, she retreats from the pages of her urban creation, allowing the two protagonists direct access to the reader to whom they communicate their words (being) without an authorial presence. No intermediary witness, advocate, commentator, or editor explains or interprets; to elicit meaning, the reader must deconstruct Guiducci's text, interpreting the verbal and metaphorical signs connecting the two narratives.

Due donne da buttare portrays urban females as protagonists and oppressed victims. Less destitute and far more sophisticated than their country sisters, the narrators of these two confessions—a prostitute and a housewife—are externally antithetical but in deeper thematic and figurative levels of the text they emerge united, like two heads on opposite sides of a coin. Ideologically they bond because both are equally silenced and exploited by history, tradition, and patriarchal definition. The housewife chained to her familial roles and routine and the former call girl tied to her past are both products of a similar environment and conditioning. Invisible to the society at large, neither would be considered a worthy exemplar of the traditional fictional heroine. Yet, through her portraits, Guiducci does create antiheroes of a negative narrative, allowing them to "speak themselves" into literary existence by verbalizing their individual biographies and thoughts in words that denote rather than betray them.[2] By finding her voice, Guiducci's protagonist escapes anonymity and becomes an active participant in culture; she can finally be heard.

Through the confessional instrument, a woman's being becomes her text. The symbolic connection between female lives and their language defines Guiducci's two companion volumes but was already suggested in the earlier work, *La mela e il serpente*. The common denominator is the issue of gender, for "the female subject is always constructed and defined in gender, starting from gender."[3] Guiducci explores sex itself as the instrument of self-definition. In *La mela e il serpente*, masculine and feminine identity originates in biological difference and its social consequences in Western patriarchal society, a view that underscores the narratives of *Due donne da buttare*. But the voices Guiducci cites do not speak in unison. Urban housewives, peasant mothers, and young hookers are separated by class, personal experience, and status; what unites them is their shared womanhood, which identifies them far more profoundly than any other single element. Guiducci points out that millennia of segregation and isolation have formed a peasant class outside the dominant urbanized culture of modern Italy, which she terms "hegemonic";[4] yet peasant women experience the same prejudices faced by the urban protagonists of *Due donne da buttare*, who are in the mainstream, familiar figures in their communities, and recognizable throughout the Western world. One reviewer has aptly noted that *Due donne da buttare* is "a duet that insists on a single note: the marginality and social inferiority of women."[5] Earlier, in *La mela e il serpente*, Guiducci presented a woman's physical identity itself, her biology, her reproductive capacities, and her organs as the source of her marginality and segregation. A woman's very body is perceived as her inferiority and symbolized by menstrual blood; this primary sign of sexual identity is a "predestination to pain, to her role as a daughter of Eve."[6]

The narrating voices of *Due donne da buttare* are both individualistic and prototypical; their differences only serve to reinforce their gender similarities, thematically and metaphorically. The selection of two superficially antithetical protagonists, a middle-aged housewife and a young prostitute, is actually a clever device to point to society's essential misogyny, which dehumanizes women by categorizing them in antipodal moral terms: good and evil, virtue and vice, innocence and corruption, grace and sin. In Western culture, these ethical poles are embodied in the archetypes of mother and whore. Clearly a distortion of the ontological self, which exists in the permutations of gray rather than in a black-and-white polarization, this symbolic dichotomy is nevertheless endemic to Italian society, fostered in part by the Catholic veneration of the Madonna as the Ideal Woman, whose halo crowns the heads of all "good" mothers and daughters.[7] The resulting double standard indicates a startling attitude toward the opposite sex; if the wife is esteemed, then the prostitute is obviously despised; nevertheless she is sought and desired. In *Due donne da buttare,* Guiducci proposes the female view of this cultural attitude—the traditionally silent voice—and argues that neither Madonna nor prostitute is actually respected by the hegemonic male. Both the model wife and the unrepentant hooker are equally exploited emotionally, sexually, and economically. Guiducci ascribes to the Leftist view that such oppression is based on the patriarchal desire to "ensure both the sanctity and inheritance of their families [the Madonna's role] and their extrafamilial sexual pleasure [the whore's function]" by controlling female sexuality to suit male needs.[8] The author enlarges the scope, however, suggesting that both sexes are trapped in these artificial categories, leading to psychological cleavage and emotional dissatisfaction.

> Men, it seems to me now, have split women in half—even themselves, poor things; they've split their very own sex in half. They want a wife and then they run to a prostitute to relieve themselves, because a wife, so they say, doesn't do certain things. . . . They've split sex in half, respectable sex and bad sex, and then they run around like wild men from one piece of woman to another.
>
> I feel sorry for these wives, because they never have a whole man. And as for us [prostitutes], we never get a whole man either, only man's animal side. Men split in half, women split in half.[9]

Nevertheless, these half-men are the oppressors of both categories of half-women, as the author demonstrates in the confessions of her two characters, both of whom are defined by their relationship to males. Stellina, the former call girl, quite literally sells herself to satisfy male fantasies; her body is her product. A social outcast because of her profession, she quickly points out that all women sell themselves to males, either by the hour or for an entire lifetime: "If you overlook all the hypocritical morality that divides women into respectable ones and whores, as long as money jingles in men's pockets, it seems to me all women are bought" (94). She rejects marriage as a state of lifelong servitude to one male in which a woman's condition consists of "always saying thanks, always yes, and pretending love"; she prefers the prostitute's style of living—"A screw is better, with free and clear money" (93). Stellina is nevertheless dependent on male clients for her presumed independence, in direct opposition to her belief in a self-made freedom. Eventually, this prostitute abandons the profession for love and takes the more conventional job of saleswoman, only to succumb to emotional dependency. The middle-class housewife is also victimized by the bonds of love and money, albeit in the more traditional guise of marriage.

Having accepted the social dictum that a woman should remain at home and dedicate herself to the happiness of her family, Guiducci's wife finds herself locked into a role that identifies her but provides little fulfillment or recognition. She significantly remains nameless and is defined as a person only in relation to her husband (called Tonio) and sons (including Tonio, Jr.). It is they who give meaning to her existence. As a daughter of Eve, she has become anonymous. Like centuries of women, she has been erased as an individual, confined to her domestic walls, and assigned a series of routine gestures and unchanging actions. She has accepted these tasks unconditionally as her natural biological destiny. Like her foremothers, Guiducci's wife associates housework and service with love, only to discover that the fairy-tale ending does not apply to her. Unhappy forever after, she views her family's indifference as rejection. In the treatise *Donna e serva* (Woman and servant), Guiducci notes that homemakers validate their sacrifices and find meaning in housework by associating it with love, not labor, only to feel betrayed by the self-serving egotism and indifference of their mates and children. "It becomes the annulment of a hard-working pledge."[10] The denial of love becomes the negation of one's efforts and consequently one's existential purpose. Caught in a vicious circle, the housewife keeps on cleaning and cooking in an attempt to regain affection and acceptance, only to witness the devaluation of her efforts. This situation is necessarily aggravated by the loss of sexual attractiveness as she ages. The wife who loses her physical appeal is considered a parasite eating her husband's hard-earned bread, becoming the binomial "woman and servant" in her own eyes as well as his.[11]

The insidiousness of this situation is captured in the fractured language of the housewife's confession. Unable to verbalize objectively her sensations and intuitions through logical discourse, she does succeed in subjectively communicating to readers in her breathless ungrammatical ramblings. The meaninglessness of her punctuation reflects the senselessness of her chores. She nonetheless devotes her days to eliminating dust, buying food, preparing tasty meals, and washing dishes, adhering instinctively to her routine, conditioned to please. On the surface, she appears to believe in a biologically determined fate. Dividing men and women into separate spheres, Guiducci's housewife accepts inherent differences between the sexes and acknowledges her gender as the ineludible source of her pain.

Through a series of recurrent images, Guiducci builds a biologically determined identity for her character, both as a sexual being and as a wife/mother. Maternally, a woman's role is to nurture, both physiologically and emotionally, finding meaning in this altruistic function, to the point "that being nourishment becomes the only way for her to relate and to perceive herself as a presence in the world."[12] Outside of this generous selflessness based on self-denial, subordination, and guilt, the housewife has no identity. In her narrative, her first expressed preoccupation concerns the purchase of bread for the family meal; this quest is elevated to epic proportions, a struggle against the hurdles of urban life and her own lethargy. "How many streets I traveled last Monday no bread no bread not a crumb a desert without bread. I absolutely must buy bread a half kilo of rolls. . . . *Buy bread.* I'll underline it three times in my head now. Heaven help me if my mind wanders" (7). Obtaining bread is the symbol of her familial mandate to nourish with food and devotion; she is required to provide this staple, which denotes spiritual as well as physical sustenance, or she will be found wanting. Actually, *she* is the bread on which her family feeds. The food she prepares is eaten while she herself is consumed. Figures of speech relating to nourishment, both affirmative (toward others) and negative (directed at herself), abound: her "damned house" "eats [her] life" and "gnaws" her fingers (7); her children "sucked her alive milk bones marrow everything" (27); even "the State sits on the backs of housewives and grows fat there" (49).

Just as food represents a social role and personal function, it is also oxymoronically lethal: poison nourishment. The nurturer is unable to find food that will be lifegiving. In the same manner, she cannot fulfill her other role as keeper of the hearth, due to the eternal battle against dust and dirt, aggravated by the modern menace of smog, pollution, cancer, plastic foods, and temperamental appliances. A visit to the local supermarket is a descent into Hell, a labyrinth of disease, death, and adulteration sheathed in plastic where she sees reflections of herself.

> If I see myself with that idiotic cart hours and hours rummaging cans studying price tags all slobbered all smudged sausages ham in plastic salame in plastic bacon shrunk in plastic dried up herring in plastic antipasto compressed in plastic deviled eggs colored filth all crushed in plastic this is expensive no maybe this is and all those wooden dried fish decapitated frozen mountains of plastic mountains of cans ground meat maybe rat meat in aspic disgusting intestines ground

frozen maybe rat maybe cat who knows mountains of peas closed in cans peppers tomatoes closed in cans *like me* [my emphasis] closed fleshless sealed suffocated and I push my cart hours and hours spent rummaging inside all this horrible food my stomach turns thinking of it. (28–29)

Having drawn her own simile, the wife *is* food, but deformed, dessicated, unnatural, colored, ground up, and, most of all, imprisoned, whether in plastic or aluminum or in her hermetically sealed can-house; in a smog-infested city and under a gray sky, the middle-aged homemaker washes an endless supply of dirty dishes, dreaming of distant times and lost possibilities. Images of freedom and wholeness in nature, dominated by the solar seascape of youthful memories, are antithetical to her dreary enclosed reality. "I would lie down close my eyes and zap! the sun would enter. Better than a man. All that warmth on me. Marvelous" (8). Guiducci's message is clear: the natural self, in harmony with the physical world, is associated with a premarital, virginal self; marriage causes a separation from nature and enclosure, drying up the woman's natural juices until she changes into "a dry branch on a tree that never ceases to blossom" (55). The tree of life and femininity is denied her. Her sap is indeed sucked out, her life force gone. Significantly, a fine soprano voice that would rise in youthful song disappears after marriage, leading her to the voicelessness of women locked in the patriarchy.

The housewife's nightmares are extensions of her day-to-day reality. Whereas in her girlhood sleep she dreamt of unattainable sweets and the white bread that presently torments her, she now dreams of gingerly dining on a serpent's "cut-off little green head on the plate . . . as if nothing were the matter" (33). She associates eating the snake's head with dirt and the adulteration of food, unaware of the dream's sexual implications and its transposition of gender roles; no longer nourishing, she is nourished on a primal phallic symbol. Her conscious visions are far more frightening. Tormented by the elimination of grime, the preparation of foods, and the onset of menopause, Guiducci's housewife battles against invincible enemies. Dirt conquers her known universe and contaminates all; manageable dust has given way to "sticky black" smog that she cannot eliminate. Air and water pollute and saturate animals, fish, and vegetation with disease so that her cooking is like "preparing poisons and funeral dinners" in a "kitchen crematorium among corpses made-up yellow and red put in the oven taken out then your children get cancer" (33). Time destroys her body with complete indifference. "Everything falls toward the earth down chin double chin muscles bosom even internal organs fall downward what a total awful collapse" (59). The body, made for life and love, is overcome by disease, moving toward the earth that represents both fertility and death. "Living is soiling" (34), she declares, joining the despoiling qualities of the environment to the human tendency to produce garbage and dirt. Called upon to clean the mess of others, she is overpowered by the filth that mercilessly propagates radioactive waste, garbage, insecticides, excrement floating on the waves and infecting drinking water, dead rats, cats, and dogs, as well as chopped up babies and multitudes of condoms flushed down toilets, clogging the pipes and sewer systems, all forming an immense army of "universal filth . . . choking the world polluting the sea infecting the skies sucking you all" (66). The housewife's final vision is an Armageddon, an apocalyptic explosion of dirt, filth, grime, and poisons that denotes her hysteria, not a divine revelation.

Bordering on the archetype of the mad housewife, Guiducci's protagonist expresses herself in "the obsessive, implosive mental elements capable of 'exploding' into nervous disorders that whirl around somewhat unrelentingly even in the head of a 'normal' housewife."[13] Dirt, smog, rats, roaches, disease, cancer, toilets, condoms, and sewers are the icons chosen to represent frustration and alienation; they are Guiducci's metaphors for the negative elements of feminine domesticity. Valued only for her homemaking skills, the protagonist passively rebels against her lot by elevating the abhorred objects of her cleaning efforts to the stature of omnipotent cosmic forces, which she can only combat with faulty weapons at best: detergents that corrode her hands, washing machines that vomit dirty water, corrosive detergents, tasty foods filled with carcinogens. This vicious circle of "sameness" further erodes her feelings of self-worth and human dignity.

Guiducci's heroine is on the edge, seeking inner balance, and yet remains painfully aware of the ease with which she could precipitate a fall. She tells tales of friends who turned to alcohol to forget and stories of acquaintances locked in asylums where visions of dust and dirt persecute them: Adelina's mother who never stopped dusting; Ester who kept washing her hands until they were raw in order to avoid contamination. "Depicting wifehood as a cause of condition of madness, [women writers] develop extended metaphors linking normal households and insane asylums, not only using real insane asylums but also picturing individual rooms, suites, floors, and entire houses where women are driven mad by dehumanizing gender norms."[14] Having become "little more than a piece of furniture" (31), Guiducci's protagonist is imprisoned in her institutionalized role. After years of marriage, her husband Tonio aggravates her existential despair.

Having grown tired of his mate, he browbeats her as a sponger and a loafer. He denigrates her contributions, because they are quickly consumed or erased and unquestioningly taken for granted. Husbands, children, the community, and society expect a wife to provide comfort, attention, and serenity, as well as good food, clean underwear, and sexual availability. In time, these tasks form a meaningless routine of cleaning, cooking, washing, shopping, and copulating—"always and only on Sundays like holy Mass" (30). Since biology rather than personal initiative receives credit for feminine accomplishments, the housewife cannot find fulfillment in her rote gestures.[15] She becomes a prisoner of prevailing gender norms and acts as her own obsessed jailer.

The condition of the prostitute remains curiously specular to that of the respectable wife. The patriarchy encloses both in their homes: whereas the "good" woman's destiny requires service to a male within four domestic walls, the whore services men's lust in the privacy of concealed rooms. Dehumanizing and unpraised routines based on repetition condemn each of them: the wife cooks and cleans day in, day out; the prostitute offers her body in a series of mechanical sexual acts with faceless males. Valued only for their sexuality, the madonna-wife reproduces children in the marital union whereas the whore avoids offspring and endlessly reproduces the physical act itself. Discontented with their lots, they react with obsessions and phobias. The homemaker wages an eternal war against dirt; Stellina experiences a continuous need to eliminate feelings of stickiness and sliminess that act as barriers of filth separating her "from other people and never leave" (70). While loathsome dirt consumes the former, such ever-growing cleansing supplies as soaps, gels, douches, and creams become a constant preoccupation of the latter. Both are daughters of Eve, receiving their biblical legacy of uncleanliness.

This thematic specularity depends partly on the social division of women and love into two distinct categories along conventional theosophic lines. Love is either *eros* or *caritas;* women are either virtuous or wicked. Embodied in wifemother and whore, these patriarchal categories result in the isolation of both feminine types. While social custom confines the wife to a home (viewed as her natural environment), society approves the hooker's choice to separate herself from a dangerous world of violence and crime. Like the homemaker, the call girl finds herself defined by her functions and anatomy rather than by her humanity, to the point of losing her sense of self in the routine replication of carnal unions that violate her integrity. In her narrative, Stellina employs a synecdoche to evince this awareness of loss.

> I was no longer *I,* and I was no longer my body nor that passive body I wanted to be, I was even separated from that stretched out passive body, I was an anonymous piece of cunt reduced to the most bestial of objects. It was there between my legs by chance, but it didn't belong either to me, Stellina, or to anybody else anymore. It was like a steak on the butcher's counter, chopped away from an animal that doesn't interest anyone, and everybody can buy it and chew it up for themselves. . . . For a moment, I am no longer I, I become that thing again, on that bed. (112)

As an instrument of erotic pleasure, the prostitute experiences reification and reduction at the hand of her clients along with the realization that the half-man she services becomes equally degraded in the relationship. "That man was reduced, like me, to a raw organ, an exasperated member. We were two copulating organs, separated from our bodies, our feelings, both of us were two things, only two genitals . . . alone, separated from everything" (112–13). Having become "meat," Stellina represents the erotic equivalent of the nourishing wife.

As food for males, both women are consumed by their belief that, as sexual beings, they exist for men alone. This gender socialization leads to the female internalization of "a male image of their sexuality *as* their identity as women."[16] The housewife's misery assumes an additional dimension in her struggle against the wrinkles, fat, and years that will render her undesirable and, thereby, devoid of purpose and place. "For an old woman the home is the best of tombs wrinkles better not show them in public they're your fault even the gaze of the man who loved you . . . even that gaze becomes hostile" (55). The homemaker is only partially aware that the intertwining of female self-image and judgmental male gaze constitutes her personal evaluation. The constant sexual attention she received as an adolescent predisposes Stellina to an early realization of this condition. The future prostitute consequently learns to associate female anatomy with individual worth and resolves not to cover her sexuality with cobwebs— "beauty, a body, what other resources does a woman have?" (88).

For Guiducci, biology is not the only gender determinant. A critic of patriarchal models, the author attacks the impositions of bourgeois morality and capitalist values on the definition of self-worth. To accentuate the rapport of capitalism to female reification, Guiducci employs a series of commercial similes. Stellina learns to interpret female bodies as exchangeable commodities. Male discourse teaches her to view herself as a marketable good whose "treasure" consists of her erotic zones. Men tell her that she really has good merchandise, that she is well supplied, that she has first-quality wares, and that "it would be a pity not to put them on shelves" (87). Quite logically, she puts a price tag on her merchandise, knowing "that a woman's game-time is brief, that these goods don't last long" (87). Her sister's marriage, "the most horrible sale I've ever witnessed" (91), to a rich but revolting "daddy's boy" convinces Stellina to take the plunge into prostitution and officially enter the sexual marketplace.

Unlike the housewife who seeks validation through the male, Stellina seeks it *as* a male by disassociating herself from traditionally acceptable female roles and assuming attitudes normally considered masculine. She differentiates between "a screw and love" (74); she enjoys making money, having it, and then spending it; she thrives in a competitive environment that leads to her financial independence. Having ingested petit bourgeois values, money represents security, happiness, and gratification, all the more so in a society where women are exploited and underpaid. Like her parents, Stellina idolizes lucre. "The fact is, money is money, time is also money, and money has the marvelous property of filling in the greatest void, the biggest empty purse, and finally, whether it's a little pig or a bank window, money piles up" (90). Money sates her gnawing hunger for material possessions and stability, understood in physical terms as nutrition to fill her "empty stomach." Significantly, a childhood passion for a piggybank remains with her well into maturity. As a girl, the toy and its coins gave her intensely voluptuous pleasure; as a woman, the ceramic pig stands guard next to the phone she uses to conduct business and represents the embodiment of her craving. The piggybank is the sign of Stellina's physical self: passive rosy flesh used to gather money. Stellina is proud of her earning ability and takes delight in her buying power as long as she does not consider their origins— the sale of her physical self.

Preferring prostitution to marriage, Guiducci's protagonist still suffers from the inability to integrate her practical approach to the profession and her emotional reactions. Although she depersonalizes her body, she still suffers from a feeling of contamination that does not affect her clients. It brands her "like a trademark" (96), separating her from the rest of humanity like an invisible wall "made of contempt": "I walk on this side [of the wall] and I'm dirty, immoral, animallike—another breed of woman, another breed of humanity" (109). Stellina belongs to the category of whores that patriarchal society censures for their active sexuality. This condemnation, however, inculpates only the female participant in the mercenary sexual act. Having internalized these social attitudes. Stellina finds herself immersed in a state of transgression, caught between two conflicting codes. On the one hand, she has been trained to view youth and beauty as negotiable currency; on the other hand, custom and religion preach feminine passivity, chastity, submission, and self-sacrifice. So, while she can earn great sums of money, she cannot escape from her internal sense of guilt and vileness, manifested in her obsession with physical hygiene. By the same token, her virtuous counterpart is the victim of capitalist rhetoric.

Blameless, the wife is nonetheless persecuted for being exactly what she is—a middle-aged homemaker. Influenced by current economic perceptions and distorting messages received from the media, Tonio berates his spouse for laziness and dependency. Does she not have all the modern appliances to do the housework? Does she not live off *his* work? *his* salary? *his* kindness? As Guiducci suggests in *Donna e serva,* the figure of the housewife in the modern industrialized world is a throwback to the past; her productivity remains unsung because it is unseen. "The time she spends immersed in the home has a quality that has no issue or importance in the industrialized outside world: it is saturated with an ambiguous emotional quality."[17] Defined by biologically based gender roles, the housewife receives a repressive upbringing that leads her to abdicate her autonomy— and thereby her power—to the men who surround her. In real terms, the prostitute does the same by becoming an object for male enjoyment, subject to her patrons' whims and requests. Whether for an hour or a lifetime, both protagonists submit to the power, money, desires, and control of men, understood as individuals, groups, and institutions.

Armanda Guiducci represents a male/female association in terms of violence, both passive and aggressive: from petty rebuffs of an irritated husband to assaults upon and murders of hookers. Law and custom promote institutionalized violence and promulgate this attitude through language, gestures, and deeds. Prostitutes, in particular, are victims of linguistic violation, which Stellina relates to a masculine taste for filth. "Men seek us out because in their mouths, in their minds, in their hearts, they have this dirty, disgusting taste for sex . . . it's from that disgusting taste for sin. . . . So, all the obscenity in the world is unloaded onto a prostitute's stomach" (98). Given a series of defamatory appellations, the whore is doubly dehumanized in her body and in language. She receives such animal names as "sewer rat" and "bitch" to diminish her position on the evolutionary scale and to justify using her as an object created for masculine consumption. Worse still for Stellina are the indelible words spoken in the heat of male passion. Etched in her memory, these have replaced true communication. If speech is the means for knowing and understanding, Stellina has discovered and comprehended the baseness of human nature at its lowest manifestations. "I don't have real words, the kind people exchange, behind me. I don't have normal words. I have a foul heap of words that are not words: subwords, insults, slanders, frightening masturbations. . . . Better still, coitus. It's incredible how certain men use words as a way to copulate— crude disgusting words that make them mean and excite them. Naturally, you need to humiliate the woman. To use words that humiliate a woman" (111). Comparable to Tonio's gaze, Stellina's words illustrate male ascendancy: these women judge themselves through the verdict given by a jury of nonpeers and find themselves culpable. Conditioned to passivity, they do not revolt but internalize their angers and pain, creating such psychological status as depression, frigidity, and compulsive behavior.

Having been split into two mutually exclusive and dichotomous categories by the hegemonic (male) culture, women continue to sunder their personhood according to gender-defined roles rather than along the psychoanalytic lines suggested by Freud. Thus, Stellina divides herself into emotional and physical halves. Her reason, ambition, and intellect are termed male, as is her ability to "produce" services that bring in money and purchase desirable goods. This interpretation follows distinct patterns of gender stereotyping that ascribe the mind and its processes, as well as an active nature, to the male of the species.[18] Stellina's "feminine" side includes the emotional and physical selves, which is further subdivided into a copulating organ and the remaining detached body. In order to survive, she suffocates her emotional and spiritual dimensions and chooses money as her ultimate attachment rather than the feelings of love, devotion, and self-sacrifice typical of the wife-mother. Her frigid body conforms to this choice and remains detached both from the depersonalized men she services and from any recollection of her activities. Whereas her colleagues use drugs because they cannot separate their physical sensations from any sentimental involvement, Stellina's aloofness becomes her anesthetic. She fears the fate of Sonia, who experiences orgasm, or Marisa, who remembers everything and suffers. Like the housewives who escape into madness or alcohol, prostitutes opt for heroin. "In order not to feel anymore, you shoot up before and after" (83). Recalling her reaction to surgical anesthetics, Stellina rejects drugs because of their numbing qualities and the resulting loss of total control. She is proud to feel nothing, to be sexually insensitive, unaware that anesthesia is merely the temporary suppression of pain, not its elimination.

Stellina's frigidity, like the housewife's compulsions, is an attempt to retain control and to have some measure of say. Both women, however, face their fundamentally disposable condition. The housewife is conscious of the ease with which wives are discarded and replaced with younger brides or mistresses, while Stellina must admit that any prostitute can replace another in the mercenary exchange of bodies for cash. "You have to accept the fact that you're interchangeable (you or somebody else, once you're all on the auction block men can pick whomever they want)" (83). This interchangeability and reification wear Stellina down at a seemingly unconscious level. Crediting Gèc's love and insistence for her transformation into a "respectable" woman, she barely acknowledges her own need to become a complete and integral woman again who is personally and socially admissible. "I see Gèc waiting for me after work—he's really waiting for me—my heart skips a beat into normalcy. He's waiting for me, good Lord. I'm no longer interchangeable" (73).

The reentry into an exclusively feminine identity provides Stellina with a sense of wholeness but opens her to its risks and pain as well. When she rejects prostitution for love of Gèc, she experiences the union of love and sex and rediscovers body and feeling. But she can never wash away the impression of uncleanness or erase the memory of the past that now invades her consciousness, for she is permanently encased in the category of the fallen according to her own estimate. She cannot be reborn. This return to traditional behavioral norms is accompanied by subservience to a respectable economic position. No longer a salable object, she now sells objects at a job that exhausts her and pays poorly, for "money flows between men, and women, no matter how much they slave, are always paid with the salaries of the weak" (99). Guiducci's subtle use of linguistic specularity— the metaphor of the branch reappears with its allusions to fertility and beauty—clarifies that in time Stellina will rejoin the vicious circle of economic and emotional dependency experienced by the housewife. If the latter has become a withered branch in her maturity, the former sees herself as alive, although segregated. "They say that a broken branch can still sprout leaves" (123). Detached from the tree of acceptable womankind, the "madonnas," she retains her fertility, her youth, her desirability—characteristics doomed to disappear with time. Through language, the author suggests the inevitable decline facing the young prostitute: she too will grow old and wither. While the housewife is eaten and consumed by her duties and children, Stellina will be devoured by her history. Guiducci's word choice is again specular: "The most terrible thing about memories is that they have the suction hold of leeches, and not a drop of your blood escapes them. . . . What disgusting creatures! Memories are just like that. They suck me alive" (111).

Within the context of European feminism, Armanda Guiducci reinforces the belief that the individual self is indeed political. The soliloquies of *Due donne da buttare* are concurrently personal and universal expressions of the female condition in the patriarchy, a condition that is simultaneously temporal (the presence of urban industrialized Italy) and atemporal (the cross-generational repetition of activities and attitudes). Guiducci's critique is directed, in part, at the contemporary oppression of women advanced by bourgeois materialism but also at the ceaseless feminine servitude of marriage, which results in the subordination of women's bodies to the desires and exigencies of men. Although grounded in European Leftist feminism, the author goes beyond its concerns with the hegemonic middle class in her exploration of the archetypal figures of Madonna and whore. By deconstructing these male-formulated configurations and reconstructing them in feminist terms from the inside, Guiducci "has come to repudiate an interclass perspective in order to specify, first on the theoretical level, and then within the area of narrative expression, the profound dichotomies existing within the feminine role."[19] The tales of private woe and psychic cleavage recounted by the housewife and the prostitute support the view that each woman is an everywoman whose individual experiences reflect and register the collective lives of her sisters. Women are joined in gender and Guiducci's use of female imagery reinforces the truth of this connection. In the conversational patterns, broken ungrammatical sentences, fragmentary phrasing, and obsessive imagery of these confessions, Armanda Guiducci creates a female discourse, giving voice to the silence of centuries. If men "have the money have a handle on the world" (15), women can escape total oblivion through expression, giving voice to silence and words to the previously unspoken. To quote the housewife, "it's necessary to dream isn't it I'm not ready to throw away yet like this I'm not in my coffin yet" (19).

NOTES

1. Armanda Guiducci, *La donna non è gente* (Milan: Rizzoli, 1977), p. 7. All translations are my own.

2. By allowing these protagonists to "speak themselves" into existence, Guiducci proposes a peculiar form of *écriture féminine*, as suggested by French feminist theoretician Hélène Cixous in her formulation of the theory of a feminist manner of writing: "Woman must write her self: must write about women and bring women to writing, from which they have been driven

away as violently as from their bodies. Woman must put herself into the text—as into the world and into history—by her own movement." This quotation is taken from Cixous's manifesto, "Laugh of Medusa," as quoted in Ann Rosalind Jones's article "Inscribing Femininity: French Theories of the Feminine," in *Making a Difference: Feminist Literary Criticism,* ed. Gayle Greene and Coppélia Kahn (New York: Metheun, 1985), p. 85.

3. Teresa de Lauretis, "Feminist Studies/Critical Studies: Issues, Terms, and Contexts," in her *Feminist Studies/Critical Studies* (Bloomington: Indiana University Press, 1986), p. 14.

4. Guiducci, *La donna non è gente,* p. 9.

5. The reviewer is Michele Sovente, writing for *Il Mattino,* 16 September 1976, quoted in Armanda Guiducci, *A testa in giù* (Milan: Rizzoli, 1984), p. 154. The addendum to this novel contains several important reviews of Guiducci's feminist works.

6. Armanda Guiducci, *La mela e il serpente* (Milan: Rizzoli, 1974), pp. 18–19.

7. For a discussion of the importance of Marinology in Catholicism, see Marina Warner, *Alone of All Her Sex: The Myth and Cult of the Virgin Mary* (New York: Knopf, 1976). The Marian model of virtuous femininity is prevalent throughout traditional Italian culture, across class and geographic lines, and is shown in Gabriella Parca's scientific survey of Italian males: *I Sultani* (The sultans) (1965; reprint, Milan: Rizzoli, 1977). Parca's sampling of 1,018 representative males shows that Italians divide "women into two categories: those that necessitate, or demand, respect, and 'the others.' He will choose his future wife from the first group; the others are used to satisfy his sexual instincts" (50). As a result, Parca concludes that sex and feelings are severed, divided between the two female categories, but rarely joined in a single woman. Armanda Guiducci offers an identical analysis of this phenomenon in the young prostitute's narrative in *Due donne da buttare.* Similarly, in the housewife's story, the narrator echoes Parca's findings that the male's ideal is a "beautiful woman, who seldom speaks, is sweet and sympathetic, is intelligent enough to understand her husband, unpretentious, family oriented, honest, and virtuous, free of makeup and possessed of a calm disposition . . . a woman who has no life of her own but lives in terms of her mate" (135; my translation). The book's statistics are telling: 66 percent of Italian males want to marry virgins; 71 percent frequent prostitutes before (and often after) marriage; more than half of those interviewed admitted to adultery. Guiducci's two confessions speak to both sides of this double standard and its subversion of the female identity.

8. Michele Barrett, *Women's Oppression Today: Problems in Marxist Feminist Analysis* (London: Villiers, 1980), p. 45.

9. Armanda Guiducci, *Due donne da buttare* (1976; reprint, Milan: Rizzoli, 1980), pp. 96–97. All selections from this book will be indicated by page number in the text and are my translation. The title of this "novel" could also be translated as "Two throwaway women"; the adjective implies ease of discard as a characteristic of the female condition. In the supermarket scene, the parallel between consumer goods and the housewife's condition emphasizes this "throwaway" quality.

10. Armanda Guiducci, *Donna e serva* (Milan: Rizzoli, 1983), p. 17.

11. In *Donna e serva,* Guiducci makes several references to the importance of sexuality in the rapport of male to female. Echoing Parca's conclusions, Guiducci suggests that centuries of frequenting prostitutes and bordellos have led men to associate sexual gratification with payment to the women who provide it: "In the masculine psyche, support remains justified by the pleasure principle. I repeat, it crosses into the age-old designs of prostitution. As for the wife who no longer enjoys sexual favor, this support will eventually be thrown in her face as a burden—a useless and almost senseless overload. . . . Support then becomes a weapon of intimidation, threat, and affront directed at the woman" (72; my translation). *Due donne da buttare* presents the psychological states of both wives and prostitutes—the main recipients of male financial support. Degraded and dependent, the housewife's confession signals the slide

from being loved to being consumed by a long and unrecognized life of giving, leading to physical abuse, servitude to males, and domestic bondage.

12. Silvia Montefoschi, "Ruolo materno e identità personale," *Nuova DWF donnawoman-femme* 6–7 (1978): 154. The entire issue is dedicated to "Maternity and Imperialism." Montefoschi's article on maternal identity is predominantly psychological in nature, as are many of the contributions in the issue.

13. Guiducci, *Donna e serva,* p. 84. Although this book is a feminist sociological investigation, several recent studies have explored the figure of the mad housewife in literature, most notably Sandra M. Gilbert and Susan Gubar's *Madwoman in the Attic* (New Haven: Yale University Press, 1979) and Annis Pratt's *Archetypal Patterns in Women's Fiction* (Bloomington: Indiana University Press, 1981).

14. Pratt, *Archetypal Patterns,* p. 51. In *Women and Madness* (New York: Avon, 1973), Phyllis Chesler has noted that the frustration of being powerless leads to neuroses and mental breakdowns, with asylums functioning as mirror images of the female experience (39).

15. In her study of "feminine creativity," *I profili della luna* (Rome: Bulzoni, 1982), Mariella Comerci speaks of the immanent and repetitive nature of women's work. "It does not produce things, but serves to 'reproduce': giving birth, nursing babies, bringing them up are not activities that imply achievement as an individual but are imposed functions that are endured as biological fate" (57).

16. Catherine A. MacKinnon, "Feminism, Marxism, Method, and the State: An Agenda for Theory," *Signs* 7, no. 3 (1982): 531. Gender socialization is an important aspect of this study.

17. Guiducci, *Donna e serva,* p. 15.

18. For more information on gender stereotyping, see Mary Ellmann, *Thinking about Women* (New York: Harcourt, Brace and World, 1968). In the housewife's confessions, a similar distribution of characteristics can be found. Tonio pities his wife's inability to think and organize (male traits) in ironic terms: "Poor thing you don't know how to get organized and the grand industrial invective begins on how a man would do this and that" (51). Both husband and wife divide their psychological makeup into standardized cultural perceptions of reason vs. emotion, farsightedness vs. shortsightedness, public vs. private spheres.

19. Anna Nozzoli, *Tabù e coscienza: La condizione femminile nella letteratura italiana del Novecento* (Florence: La Nuova Italia, 1978), pp. 158–59.

ORIANA FALLACI

Oriana Fallaci was born in Florence on 29 June 1930. Her family was anti-Fascist and during the Nazi occupation she fought in the underground movement, Corps of Volunteers for Freedom. She was honorably discharged from the Italian army when she was fourteen. She began her career by working for an Italian daily newspaper and has been a journalist ever since. She has traveled around the world, reporting on revolutions and royal marriages. She has interviewed such famous people as Henry Kissinger, William Colby, Indira Ghandi, Ayatollah Khoumeini, and Nguyen Van Thieu. She presently writes for magazines in Europe and South America. Her novels are *Penelope alla guerra* (1961), *Lettera a un bambino mai nato* (1975), and *Un uomo* (1979); her works of nonfiction are *Il sesso inutile* (1961), *Gli antipatici* (1963), *Se il sole muore* (1965), *Niente e così sia* (1969), *Quel giorno sulla luna* (1970), and *Intervista con la storia* (1974). Although most critics tend to associate Fallaci with Italian feminism, she herself emphatically refuses any alliance with the movement and sharply separates from it on the issue of abortion.

Oriana Fallaci's Journalistic Novel:
Niente e così sia

SANTO L. ARICÒ

Although Oriana Fallaci is best known as a political interviewer, she is also recognized as an ardent practitioner of New Journalism.[1] According to the critic James C. Murphy, this innovative approach allows the journalist's opinions, ideas, and commitments to permeate the story. Correspondents become so intensely involved that they attack their assignments with missionary zeal. Murphy refers to this subjectivity as activism in news reporting.[2] Fallaci's effort to write *Niente e così sia (Nothing and Amen)*, her report of the war in Vietnam, is a classic example of such activism. The personal nature of her account runs counter to more conventional journalistic objectivity, and her bias colors the narration. Her anti-American and pro-Vietcong feelings are a matter of public record, but during her stay in wartorn Vietnam, Fallaci's perceptions undergo a noticeable transition and this change develops into one of the most interesting aspects of her book.[3] The zeal with which she embraces her assignment is obvious. She spends nearly a year on location, compulsively covering dangerous situations, interviewing fighting men at the bloody conflict in Dak To, flying on a bombing mission in order to experience a pilot's emotions during combat, and almost losing her life during the battle of Hue. Indeed, Fallaci's absorption in her professional pursuits consumes her so completely that any comparison with traditional reporting appears misleading.

Departing from customary methods of gathering data, Oriana Fallaci practices a distinct type of writing. Murphy points out that some scholars consider New Journalism to be a literary genre.[4] Such an interpretation sees the writer's exposé as more than just a forum for viewing and experiencing incidents through the medium of her own individuality; it is also nonfictional prose that uses the resources of fiction. Her work stands as a classic example of what Seymour Krim labels "journalit" and classifies as the de facto literature of our times.[5] In his article "The New Confusion," William L. Rivers proposes that writings in this modernistic style add "a flavor and a humanity to journalistic writing that push it into the realm of art."[6]

Fallaci's virtue as a writer lies precisely in showing the possibility of something strikingly different in journalism and in furthering efforts to replace earlier types of fiction with a new brand of literature. Her total immersion in the Vietnamese conflict explains a large part of the popularity that her book attracted. Her writing exerts, however, an even greater impact when she elevates factual statements to artistic invention, demonstrating that it is possible to write accurate nonfiction while using literary devices such as traditional dialogues and stream-of-consciousness.

In 1972, Tom Wolfe hailed New Journalism's replacement of the novel as literature's main event and detailed the historical development of this movement. According to Wolfe, authors like Truman Capote (*In Cold Blood*), Gay Talese (*Honor Thy Father*), Norman Mailer (*Armies of the Night*), and John Sack (*M*) write journalistic novels, using the same techniques that gave the literature of social realism its impact. Discovering the joys and power of faithful portrayal, these writers applied their new knowledge to the richest terrain of the novel—the manners and customs of society. Wolfe points out that in the 1960s journalists began employing the techniques of realism—particularly those of Fielding, Smollett, Gogol, Balzac, and Dickens. "By trial and error, by 'instinct' rather than theory, journalists began to discover the devices that gave the realistic novel its unique power, variously known as its 'immediacy,' its 'concrete reality,' its 'emotional involvement,' its 'gripping' or 'absorbing quality.'" Wolfe proposes that this extraordinary dynamism derives its force from just four devices: scene-by-scene construction, full record of dialogue, third-person point of view, and the portrayal of everyday details in the lives of people to round out character development.[7]

Although Fallaci makes use of the literary conventions of mood development, interviews, character portrayal, satire, and humor, she mainly relies on the four techniques of realism that Wolfe summarizes. By doing so, she changes what would have been an objective record of an armed conflict into a fresh form of art. According to Wolfe, the first characteristic that sets dramatic fiction apart from documentaries is scene-by-scene construction. The writer relates a series of events by moving from one situation to another, resorting as little as possible to sheer historical narrative. Although novelists have relied heavily on this method, its role in classical journalism has been minor. In the new style, however, background building is paramount to storytelling: it eliminates any similarity to detailed documents; it explains, too, why journalists undertake extraordinary feats in order to obtain the information needed to construct a scenario.[8]

The first scene that Fallaci describes is one that takes place after her arrival in Saigon on 18 November 1967. She uses the classical approach of juxtaposing sights that catch her attention en route from the airport to her hotel. At the Than Son Nhut terminal, she indicates the setting's main features: "Jet fighters, helicopters with heavy machine guns, trailers loaded with napalm bombs, stood in line with unhappy-looking American soldiers."[9] She notes salient aspects of the countryside on the way to Saigon: "Guarding the road leading into town were sandbag fortifications surrounded by barbed-wire fences and ending in turrets with rifles sticking out" (2). The author next concentrates on the vital signs of life in the city itself and highlights jeeps full of American soldiers, trucks with cannons leveled, convoys carrying ammunition boxes, rickshaws plunging into traffic and swiftly pedaling on, water sellers scurrying about, their merchandise swinging from bamboo sticks across their shoulders, minute women in long dresses, their loose hair waving beyond their shoulders like black veils, bicycles, motorcycles, shoe-shine boys, and filthy, reckless taxicabs.

Fallaci reveals surprise at not immediately seeing the full impact of the war, and her commentary reinforces her technique of accumulation. "There was a chaos almost gay in this Saigon in November of 1967. . . . It seemed more like a postwar period: the markets filled with food, the jewelry shops stocked with gold, the restaurants open and all that sunshine" (3). The tranquil atmosphere at the hotel creates the impression of a relaxed city that is oblivious to its country's agony: "Even the elevator, the telephone, the fan on the ceiling were working, and the Vietnamese waiter was ready to respond to any gesture you might make, and on the table there was always a bowl of fresh pineapple and mangoes" (3). One final observation summarizes her overall impression: "Dying didn't occur to you" (3).

Fallaci uses the same procedure as she constructs the scene at Battery 25 when she visits an army chaplain, Father Bill. The besieged outpost occupies a barren plateau surrounded by North Vietnamese positions and receives a steady barrage from enemy artillery. "On the bare earth, all you could see were artillery posts, five or six trenches and a hundred dirty soldiers who needed a shave" (274). Father Bill, who regularly enters the encircled area by helicopter in order to minister to the men's spiritual needs, explains that the North Vietnamese, who occupy all the surrounding hills, bombard the American position with mortars twice a day and attack it once a week. The priest quickly prepares an altar by placing a cardboard box on two empty howitzer shells. The recruits assemble in the open space and Mass begins, lasting for about twenty minutes. During that time, two

Phantoms drop napalm ten kilometers to the southeast, causing black clouds to darken the blue sky. Farther away to the northeast, cannons thunder. There is, however, absolute quiet at Battery 25, where Father Bill raises his cardboard beaker, calling on the Lord and leading the men in prayer. "All this took place in the most complete serenity, the most absolute silence. In the same silence the boys got up, stood in line, and Father Bill gave them communion: laying little hosts like peppermints on their tongues" (276).

In her personal reflections, Fallaci wonders incredulously why the North Vietnamese did not fire during the service. Since they are able to see clearly the American position with or without field glasses, the writer concludes that enemy gunners chose not to initiate action until the men had finished their prayers. "It seems absurd, I know, but I think they really did want that, because as soon as Mass was over, when Father Bill had hardly put away his crucifix and his jars, the first mortar fire fell. Right into the camp" (276).

The re-creation of scenery and atmosphere is central to Fallaci's technique. Her mimetic ability and talent for acute description enable her readers to receive as full an experience of the war as possible, short of actual, physical presence. The portrayals of Than Son Nhut Airport, Saigon, Dak To, Battery 25, and many other locations bring people and situations alive in a way that makes conventional journalism seem bloodless. Fallaci differs from traditional reporters, who have also been writing anecdotes for years, by her literary technique of building scenes, which she does throughout the book.

The second technique of realism that Wolfe identifies as part of journalistic literature is fully recounting a dialogue. The skilled novelist allows characters to develop action, plot, and personalities in free colloquial exchanges rather than in descriptions or explanations. This device also defines each protagonist quickly, efficiently catches the reader's attention, and creates a sense of proximity to what occurs in the story.[10] Fallaci capitalizes on this tactic by having her subjects' words carry great portions of the story and by developing their uniqueness through these conversations or simple monologues.

Immediately after her arrival in Vietnam, Fallaci made arrangements to go to Dak To.[11] During her first night there, a mortar attack forced her to seek safety in one of the bunkers on Hill 1383. Although it was a light bombardment that lasted an hour, she had time to listen to a group of soldiers conversing about draft dodging. The journalist's restatement of this conversation casts a new light on the character of many soldiers, as well as their real attitude toward the conflict:

"You see, he told me he had to take care of his mother and so he managed to stay in Los Angeles and built himself a swimming pool."
"Well, Jack was even smarter."
"What did he do?"
"He started drinking and drank himself into an ulcer, so they turned him down because of the ulcer."
"Roll on the ulcers!" (14)

According to one of the men, his friend Howard was the most skillful at obtaining a deferment:

"When they asked him if he liked girls he said: 'Goodness no, everyone knows I go for boys.'"
"Is he a queer?"
"Of course not. You crazy? But if you say you're queer, they turn you down flat, didn't you know?"
"No, dammit. Suppose I said it now?"
"Too late, buster. You should have thought of it sooner. I should've, too." (14)

During the battle of Dak To, the North Vietnamese controlled most areas around the American positions and shelled them day and night. Most of the firing came from Hill 875, which seemed impregnable. Any attempts to overrun the enemy emplacement resulted in failure and major casualties. American soldiers whom the North Vietnamese had pinned down there were accidentally bombed by their own aircraft trying to dislodge the opposition. When help finally arrived, the full impact of losses became evident. Fallaci's recordings catch the anguish and depression of the wounded as they are prepared for evacuation. One of them grabs her, laughing hysterically: "The order was to take the hill. Take the damned hill! But we couldn't, you see, we couldn't!" Another, half naked, shakes and stomps around, slapping his forehead, sobbing: "I hate them! I hate you! You bastards! You pigs!" Others try to calm him and lead him off to sick bay, but they cannot. A black man sits quietly eating a bowl of soup and weeping as he recalls the heaps of dead after that bomb: "You didn't know where to go, you didn't know where to hide. You slept with the corpses. I slept under Joe. He was dead, but he kept me warm. Give me a cigarette. Have you ever slept under a corpse that kept you warm?" (25).

The soldiers in camp 1383 had received the brunt of the attack and, in many cases, fell victim to depression in these trying circumstances. Fallaci captures the men's intense agony and frustration by simply restating their words. A young Puerto Rican from New York vents his despair. He neither knows what communism is nor understands why he should fight for the benefit of a distant nation in southeast Asia. "I don't know what the hell this communism is and I don't give a damn and I don't give a damn about these fucking Vietnamese. Let them fight communism themselves. There's not a single South Vietnamese here" (15). When a corporal tries to silence him, the soldier not only angrily refuses to be still but also heatedly recalls his father's anger after he had volunteered. "And he was right! He said: 'You're a fool; let the rich boys go.' They never do, you know. My father's a workman and let me tell you something: it's always the sons of the working people that die in wars. Never the rich boys, never!" (15).

Rather than describe each fighting man in concrete terms, Fallaci gives glimpses of their inner selves by relating their free and spontaneous statements. The writer is able to communicate a frame of mind by reporting revelations of their fullest and most intimate sort. This gives the narration its atmosphere of accessibility and nearness; it, together with scene construction, separates the writer's work from traditional journalism and makes it technically more like a novel.

According to Wolfe, seeing the world through someone else's eyes is the third characteristic of journalistic literature. Eye-witness accounts permit both Fallaci and the reader to experience sights from the vantage point of an observer. This slant avoids the limits of exclusivity invoked with a first-person perspective, and also generates a climate of intimacy through its full exposure of a character's mind and emotional life. Wolfe's term was "chameleon," i.e., taking on the coloration of whomever or whatever was being written about.[12]

Most instances of this technique occur when François Pelou, director of *France Presse,* describes for Fallaci major events that she had not witnessed herself. During a conversation with him about Buddhist self-immolation, Fallaci expresses a desire to witness one. Her colleague reacts negatively to the request but then proceeds to describe a burning that took place in Saigon in July 1966, which he witnessed while he was on his way to a press conference. After hearing the noise of an explosion and seeing flames rising up, Pelou approached the fire and recognized a young monk in the flames, sitting with his legs crossed in the lotus position. "Around him there are kids playing, women crying, and two nuns who stare emotionless. Though everybody seems to respect his decision, the traffic is hardly disturbed by the show" (65).

Pelou attempts to save the burning victim who begins to move and twist with pain; fellow monks, however, block his efforts to aid the victim. Except for the covering of his shoulder, the victim's skin slips away from his arm and hand. After a nun places burning material back on the suffering person, Pelou quickly removes it once more, only to have it thrown back by the religious. "The whole thing is grotesque, this coming and going of burning clothes, while it's obvious that the poor monk has lost any will to die. Now he waves his hands, all his body clearly asking for help" (66). Pelou and other newsmen eventually succeed in extinguishing the flames and getting the monk to a hospital, where he finally dies. This third-person point of view exposes the horrible suffering endured by the victim and also suggests the influence of chemical drugs and brainwashing to keep the individual resolved during burning. Pelou believes that no willpower on earth can keep a person standing still during such agony. "Not to mention another kind of drug—the one we call brainwashing. Get it into the head of a monk of seventy or a nun of seventeen that the destiny of Vietnam depends on his sacrifice and he'll agree to be roasted straight away" (66).

In another conversation, Pelou expresses his thoughts on the insanity of dying in combat and his belief that incidentals frequently distract from an actual slaughter. He illustrates this with two anecdotes that deal with his experience as a Korean War correspondent. The first story deals with a heated engagement between a French battalion and North Korean units. Action began early in the morning and lasted until six in the evening. During the subsequent period of calm, Pelou interviewed a group of men. At a certain point, however, an artillery shell landed amidst these very soldiers. "It fell on them and the bodies shot out in pieces. A head in one place, a foot in another" (158). Rather than experiencing grief at the sight of severed members, the journalist explains that his attention was caught by a helmet flying much higher than the heads or feet and completely absorbed him: "Up, up, up till it was nearly still and turned a somersault and came down in a spiral, down, down, till it hit the ground with a resounding thud" (158).

The second incident occurred during the same period. After one particular battle, many of the dead remained exposed to the elements in subzero weather. Only after a few days could military personnel begin the grizzly task of retrieving frozen bodies. It was unbearably cold and the corpses were statues of ice, crystallized into absurd positions. Their awkward postures made it impossible to align them horizontally in containers. "You couldn't lay them out in a normal position, before putting them into the plastic bags. And so you were forced to bend the arms and legs till they broke like a glass—crack—and then you had to jump on the body and crush it well" (158). Pelou explains how workers begin to perspire and how the sweat froze into snow on their faces. An unexpected detail again detracts from the morbid scene. One particular soldier appears relaxed and unruffled by his labor. "He wasn't working hard. In fact he didn't even try to stretch out their arms and legs; he just gave them a wack with a stick and that laid them out. And as he hit them, he sang: 'Mona Lisa . . . when you smile, Mona Lisa . . . I love you!' " (158).

Third-person point of view considers reality through someone else's perceptions and exposes a person's intimate feelings. In the description of a Buddhist self-immolation, the reader is presented with Pelou's frantic attempts to save a human life and his frustration as all rescue attempts fail. Pelou's earlier experience permits him to formulate a personal philosophy of death. Nonetheless, the incidental details in his two Korean stories—a spiraling helmet, a soldier's failure to perspire like everyone else, and his irreverent song as he performs his horrible duty—distract from the actual fact of death, while simultaneously creating a surrealistic atmosphere of the macabre and absurd.

Wolfe refers to social autopsy as the fourth technique that distinguishes journalistic literature. The writer pays close attention to the minute manners and other trappings of a subject's life and, consequently, presents a comprehensive picture that communicates insight into personalities and situations. Symbolic details represent entire patterns of behavior and positions in the world. Recording of such incidentals is not embroidery; it contributes as much to the power of realism as any other literary device. It resembles third-person point of view because it also casts unexpected clarity on a character.[13]

Fallaci's use of social autopsy takes various forms—brief informative details, humor, mood, portraits. She best utilizes this approach, however, when she paints a word picture of particular people whom she encounters. In each case, her sketch places emphasis on what she perceives as the character's principal trait. Physical features reinforce her observations, correspond directly to each person's inner spirit, and satirize obvious weaknesses.

The press officer at Dak To with limited intellectual vision: "He has a small ridiculous mustache on his dumb mouselike face and looks as if he'd been born in his helmet. Probably he sleeps in it" (12). In his pants pocket, he keeps a box of color slides that he shows everyone: his girl in a nightgown and without it, naked, photographed while he was on leave in Honolulu. "Showing us the slides he scratches himself. How depressing to think that we shall have him around for most of the time" (12).

The mysterious silence of François Pelou's accountant, Than Van Lang: "When you happen to look his way and see him, he comes as a surprise; he seems to have materialized that very moment" (35). He never gets up, never speaks; he only writes with long, slim fingers and an old-fashioned pen that he dips in an inkwell. "The movement carrying the pen to the mouth of the inkwell is so strangely slow that it seems as if it weren't happening at all" (35–36). Nothing upsets or bothers him; he shows no emotion, even in the face of death. "An invisible wall round his desk isolates him from us, and beyond that wall his eyes move only to look at François. Secretly, though, while the face remains impenetrable. A thin, yellow, ageless face" (36).

General Loan, who has the reputation of being the cruelest individual in Vietnam: "The ugliest little man I had ever seen, with a tiny twisted head screwed on to his meager shoulders. The only thing you noticed about the face was the mouth—so large and so out of proportion" (88). According to Fallaci, one looked directly down to the neck from the mouth because the chin fell away so fast that one wondered if it had existed. His eyes were not really eyes; they were eyelids that were scarcely visible through the slit. "The nose, on the other hand, was a nose but so flat it was lost in the cheeks, which were also flat. I looked at him and felt a kind of uneasiness" (88).

The gross policeman dressed only in underwear who receives Fallaci and another journalist at central headquarters: "Fat, barefoot, sweating. He looked at us as if we were a couple of criminals, pulled up his pants and spat on the floor. Then he stood admiring the spittle, scratched himself down to his genitals and pushed us toward a desk" (113).

Catherine, the French journalist whose false timidity camouflages an aggressive nature: "Catherine, with that little each-man-for-himself face of hers. I shall never understand that girl. You look at her and feel, immediately, that you want to protect her: so blonde, so worn, so tiny" (114). A second glance, however, quickly changes the initial reaction. "You feel that you want to protect yourself—from her. Perhaps it's her eyes—pitiless, cold. Perhaps it's her fingers—large, knotty, always held forward like the claws of an eagle" (114).

The impractical and mistaken patriotism of Barry Zorthian, director of the Joint United States Public Affairs Office of Vietnam and considered one of the most important men in Saigon: "Mr. Zorthian . . . has a large nose, a large belly, a large faith in this war, and an unshakable conviction that the United States must teach civilization to poor people who have never heard of democracy and technological progress" (71).

The superficial and convenient Catholicism of the adoption agent Tran Ti An, who takes Fallaci to an orphanage: "She has a pretty face of old ivory and owns a factory that makes chemical products, a house full of china and servants. She deals with adoptions and she looks like the charity ladies who think they'll get to heaven on bazaars and good works" (192). Fallaci had gone to see her about adopting a child. When she informs her that she is neither a good Catholic nor a bad one, the lady seems irritated. When she hears that the writer has a chapel in her country home, however, she appears satisfied "as if someone with a chapel was automatically on the right side of the angels" (192).

The highly intelligent American lieutenant Teaneck from Oklahoma who saved Fallaci's life at the Battle of Hue: "He has a wide, red, Indian face mixed with some other race—high cheekbones, thin nose, Asian cheeks" (172). He does not fit the stereotype of the unthinking, ignorant foot soldier, who simply obeys without thinking. On the contrary, he labels Fallaci a liberal who has unfairly disparaged American soldiers in favor of the Vietcong. "It's one thing to take risks with a return ticket and another to take risks with a one-way ticket. Like me" (175). He questions her fairness and justice, objecting to the journalist's partiality. "The fact of being in the war doesn't authorize you to despise us and respect them. Because when you escape, as you did today, you owe it to us mediocre men. To us Ugly Americans. To us who fire for your sake, to save your life and your conscience" (175).

The coldness and impenetrability of Vietnam's president Cao Ky: "He's a Vietnamese like plenty of others, neither tall nor short, neither strong nor frail, and physically distinguished from the others only by a black mustache that stands out on his dark amber face." Fallaci sees his profile as unattractive and closed in by a sad, arrogant expression; his glance is direct but at the same time somber and melancholic. What he says, however, is greatly interesting to her and makes a profound impression. Ky is the only one on his side of the barricade "who dares admit he belongs to a powerless, inefficient, corrupt regime. I'm the only one who says the Americans are here not to defend us but to defend their own interests and set up a new colonialism" (200–201).

Before her subjects even speak, Fallaci points out physical features that often indicate their personalities and provide a key to their emotional constitution. Scarcely a detail does not illuminate some point of their temperament. These clues, in combination with the writer's evaluations and comments, constitute the very essence of her literary portraits. The relentless and meticulous accumulation of these character profiles not only reveals Fallaci's private interpretations of each protagonist but also projects a comprehensive panorama of Vietnamese society during the war.

According to Seymour Krim, journalists enjoy a definite advantage in their attempts to re-create reality if they use every conceivable literary avenue open to them.[14] Oriana Fallaci does so and particularly profits from the techniques of realism that Wolfe outlines. By observing the facts of a ruthless conflict and selecting them with an artist's touch, she captures the deeper half of reality, which old-time journalism excluded, and structures a narrative with skills that had always been associated with novels. If for some reason Fallaci had written a fictional sketch, changing names and location, she would have disgraced the reality of what she had seen. She ascertains, however, the veracity of all her data while simultaneously structuring her information in the manner of narrative prose writers. The result is a form that looks like fiction but unquestionably remains reportage. The impact of *Niente e così sia* lies in its portrayal of reality and the realization that its subject matter has not been imagined.

Oriana Fallaci combines her talent as a reporter and interviewer with a proven ability to write novels. The end result of her efforts, however, is not "fictional" literature. Such a label would suggest that the author has made up her story. It is true that *Niente e così sia* is indeed "imaginative," but that is not because Fallaci has distorted data but because she has presented them in a full manner instead of in the style of cold, clipped, factual newspaper journalism. She has brought out the sights, sounds, and feelings surrounding the raw material of her report, connecting them in an artistic manner that does not diminish but gives greater depth and dimension to the information.

Krim proposes that writers like Hemingway, Fitzgerald, Wolfe, and Faulkner were "in the most radical sense *reporters* whose subject matter and vision were too hot or subtle or complicated or violent or lyrical or intractable or challenging for the mass media of their period." He proposes that twenty or thirty years ago writers of talent necessarily expressed themselves in fiction because only this form was able to bypass the narrow framework of journalism and provide a channel through which invented characters with made-up names in imagined situations could express their creators' world.[15] Fallaci, however, takes part in a movement that reverses this trend. Her success lies precisely in the ability to communicate directly an investigation of the war in Vietnam as if she were writing a novel.

Fallaci accepts the ideal that art remains at all times the highest condition to which a person can aspire. In fact, she speaks openly of her burning desire to write novels after having dedicated so much of her life to the professional aspects of journalism.[16] She projects the full weight of this desire and belief on the war in Vietnam, creating in the process an imaginative nonfiction that profits from acceptable literary techniques, especially those of social realism. In 1972, Tom Wolfe wrote: "I think there is a tremendous future for a sort of novel that will be called the journalistic novel or perhaps documentary novel, novels of intense social realism based upon the same painstaking reporting that goes into the New Journalism."[17] Fallaci's *Niente e così sia* stands as a classic example of this imaginative truth writing—a genre as creative as fiction used to be, which uses the staples of the older art, in particular the four techniques outlined by Wolfe, when it needs or wants to, but expands them into deeper and more authentic worlds of contemporary reality.

NOTES

1. Oriana Fallaci, *Intervista con la storia* (Rizzoli: Milan, 1974), trans. John Shepley as *Interview with History*. This work contains most of the writer's famous interviews. For an analysis of her interview techniques see Santo L. Aricò, "Breaking the Ice: An In-Depth Look at Oriana Fallaci's Interview Techniques," *Journalism Quarterly* 63, no. 3 (1986): 587–93.

2. James E. Murphy, "The New Journalism: A Critical Perspective," *Journalism Monographs*, no. 34 (1974): 3.

3. See Santo L. Aricò, "Oriana Fallaci's Discovery of Truth in *Niente e così sia*," *European Studies Journal* 3, no. 2 (1986), 11–23.

4. Murphy, "The New Journalism," p. 4.

5. Seymour Krim, *Shake It for the World, Smart Ass* (New York: Dial Press, 1970), p. 359.

6. William L. Rivers, "The New Confusion," *The Progressive*, no. 35 (Dec. 1971): 28.

7. Tom Wolfe, "Why They Aren't Writing the Great American Novel Anymore," *Esquire*, December 1972, p. 158.

8. Ibid.

9. Oriana Fallaci, *Niente e così sia* (Milan: Rizzoli, 1969); trans. Isabel Quigly as *Nothing and Amen* (New York: Doubleday, 1972), p. 2. All further references to this translation will be indicated by the page number in parentheses following the quotation.

10. "Dickens has a way of fixing a character in your mind so that you have the feeling he has described every inch of his appearance—only to go back and discover that he actually took care of the principal description in two or three sentences; the rest he has established in dialogue" Wolfe, "Why They Aren't Writing," p. 158.

11. The Battle of Dak To, named after a village in the area, took place ten miles from the Laotian and Cambodian border near the mouth of the Ho Chi Minh Trail.

12. Tom Wolfe, "The New Journalism," *Bulletin of the American Society of Newspaper Editors*, Sept. 1970, p. 19. A corollary to this eye-witness technique is the interview. Subjects openly answer Fallaci's skillful questions in the first person and reveal themselves. The interview tangibly exposes a person's feelings and consequently produces the same results that use of third-person point of view obtains.

13. Wolfe, "Why They Aren't Writing," p. 158.

14. Krim, *Shake It for the World*, p. 344.

15. Ibid., p. 348.

16. See Patrizia Carrano, *Le Signore Grandi Firme* (Florence: Guaraldi, 1978), p. 75.

17. Wolfe, "Why They Aren't Writing," p. 272.

CAMILLA CEDERNA

Camilla Cederna was born in Milan in 1921. She holds a degree in classics from the University of Milan. In 1945 she was one of the founders of *L'Europeo,* a leading cultural and political magazine. In 1958 she started working for *L'Espresso* as an editor and reporter but in 1980 joined another leading weekly, *Panorama,* where she presently works as an editor and featured columnist. Her journalism and writing have always reflected the manners, customs, and changes of Italian society. Her early works—*Noi siamo le signore* (1958), *La voce dei padroni* (1962), *Signore e signori* (1963), *Fellini 8½* (1963), and three volumes of *Il lato debole: Diario italiano* (1977)—range from ironic descriptions of upper middle-class society in Milan to pungent portraits of such personalities as Federico Fellini and Arturo Toscanini. The period of widespread social unrest and violence in Italy provided the impetus for a real-life police thriller, *Pinelli: Una finestra sulla strage* (1971), and a scathing indictment of the Italian president, *Giovanni Leone: La carriera di un presidente* (1978). During the past few years, Cederna's *Casa nostra: Viaggio nei misteri d'Italia* (1983), *De gustibus* (1986), and the autobiographical *Il mondo di Camilla* (1980) continue to describe people and events that play a major role in shaping Italian culture.

Camilla Cederna:
Portrayer of Italian Society

GIOVANNA BELLESIA

Camilla Cederna's literary production has reflected the manners and customs of influential segments of Italian society for four decades. In the 1950s and 1960s, her newspaper columns provided insight into the country's cultural, social, and political life; her work in the 1970s implicated the highest offices of government in scandalous activities; books written in the 1980s return to her earlier orientation and again expose the inner dynamism of a nation. Her first books, *Noi siamo le signore* (We are the ladies), *La voce dei padroni* (Voice of the big bosses), and *Signore e signori* (Ladies and gentlemen), contain ironic, pungent descriptions of the upper middle-class in Milan, as well as lively, humorous, and penetrating portraits of important personalities. Although Cederna depicts Italian life in an acute and nonconforming manner, she also exposes truth, especially in those instances when government officials try to camouflage it with cover-ups, payoffs, and continuous lies. Cederna's thirst for justice provides Italian readers with such powerful denunciations of corruption that Cederna may be compared to Bob Woodward and Carl Bernstein, whose *All the President's Men* publicized the Watergate scandals.

From the beginning of her career, Cederna's combination of literary techniques and journalistic skills has allowed her to describe people and events with a lively and humorous style. In 1960, Cederna interviewed Federico Fellini and included a copy of the written dialogue in *La voce dei padroni*. Her portrait of the director gives the impression of a real presence. She briefly highlights the physical characteristics that best communicate his gentle and perceptive temperament: "His eyes and ears, which seem to be sleeping, keep recording, while a tiny and kind voice comes out from that big body."[1] She even allows readers to choose how to react to him: "Some would be reminded of the voice of Pinocchio's talking cricket, others of the voice of Monsignor Sergio Pignedoli, auxiliary Bishop of Milan" (*Voce*, 139). Her final comments pinpoint the essence of his charm and talent:

"Fellini neither warns nor preaches. He is instead a delicious and ironic storyteller, an improviser full of humor. He is helped by his naturally histrionic nature and by his sweet, drawled accent from Romagna, mixed with less caressing inflections from Rome" (*Voce*, 139). Cederna's interest in Fellini continued and in 1963 led to the publication of a book about $8\frac{1}{2}$, one of his best known films. The narrator explains how he first conceived the idea for this movie and what the final outcome was. *Fellini $8\frac{1}{2}$* extraordinarily documents how the director works and lives, while also presenting an additional illustration of the writer's ability to describe vividly people and events.

In her portraits, Cederna not only outlines the salient features of a subject but also conveys her emotions and impressions. She carefully chooses imaginative words that match her acute power of observation. She indicates specific details that invariably correspond to personality traits. Her laconic sketch of the famous pianist Arturo Benedetti Michelangeli highlights the impenetrability of his character through an unusual comparison with physical nature: "Arturo Benedetti Michelangeli: this great moonlike virtuoso, marble faced, with an abstract look and a rare smile" (*Voce*, 126). In a similar way, in her collection *Signore e signori*, she communicates a humorous and satiric vision of Lyndon Johnson during his presidential campaign: "Johnson is very tall, a little bit flabby, with a cunning pink and gray face that looks like rubber, since it can distort and return so quickly to normal when he speaks. Johnson has very long ears; his right hand is double the size of his left because of the many handshakes that he gives and receives."[2]

Cederna's portraits bypass typical journalistic reportage. She goes beyond merely accumulating facts when she interjects penetrating comments on the personalities she interviews. Her reaction to Carla Fracci, Italy's leading ballerina, underscores her sensitivity to the celebrity's emotional and spiritual composure.

> And even after the weariness of the applause, at that table Carla Fracci offered the rather rare example of a perfectly calm young woman: in fact, one realizes that she had reached absolute control not only of her muscles, which have become very intelligent and obedient, but also of her nerves, her low and pleasant voice, the movements of her heart and thoughts. (*S & S*, 215)

The same artistry characterizes her representation of Pope John XXIII who continued to smile while asking his guests to excuse him for talking to them while seated. The writer fuses the obvious discomfort caused by his serious illness with the simple spirituality that motivates his every step. "His eyes seemed to say, 'anyway, you know that I am ill,' while his lips said, 'Jesus Christ too used to sit on a mound or stone while talking to his disciples; therefore, allow his humble pope to do the same'" (*S & S*, 120).

Cederna often begins her paragraph with a striking quotation or a pointed comment and then proceeds to explain the reason for her choice. When Spanish-born Queen Fabiola married into the royal family of Belgium, the writer introduced her picture of the queen by citing a literary character. "'One should always be very kind to young women because one never knows who they will end up marrying,' Lady Montdore, one of Nancy Mitford's heroines, used to say." A clarification immediately follows. "This is an important social precept, which, unfortunately, some of the most elegant and now very dismayed ladies from Madrid must not have pondered. They are now in Brussels, loaded with presents and hoping in vain to receive an invitation to the king's wedding." (*Voce*, 71).

A similar writing technique attracts her readers' attention when a series of questions from colleagues and acquaintances punctuate her own experience with Arturo Benedetti Michelangeli and changes her from interviewer to interviewée.

> "So, what's he like? Same as he looks? Lucky you. Very pale, unsociable, cold? Charming, I bet. His hands, what about his hands? Just like Chopin, isn't he? Like a poet when he talks? Did you get something that belonged to him? You can't imagine what I'd do for it. . . . Tell me, quick, come on." Here I am, for once being intensively interviewed myself after having met with Arturo Benedetti Michelangeli. (*Voce*, 127)

Cederna's portraits also include impressions of her subjects' environments and homes. During the exchange with Mike Bongiorno, host of the most popular game shows in Italy, she appears more interested in the setting than in the person:

> "I am talking with him more than twenty years after his triumphal beginning with 'Quit or Double?' when they called him 'Mr. Mike.' . . . Bongiorno remembers 'these golden years' in his luxury apartment, where a whole floor is designed for entertaining, one living room after another and, at the end, his office."[3]

Similar details provide an introduction for her visit to the singer Adriano Celentano: "His mother was cooking (peppers with anchovies), his cousin was dusting (ficus plant leaves), his aunt was motionless (watching an old movie on TV), his fiancée was reading (cartoons), and Adriano was sleeping (because he had stayed up late the night before). So before talking to him, I had time to look around the apartment" (*S & S*, 280).

In her later political writings, Cederna writes as a journalist who communicates with her public in a generally serious manner and only sparingly intersperses humorous portraits. Nevertheless, traces of irony periodically appear. During an interview with President Giovanni Leone of Italy, she asked him if he was a religious man. He answered that he did not always go to Mass, and Cederna compared the tragic overtones of his responses to Mimi's melodramatic plight in *La bohème*. The verbal exchange ended with a light touch of satire when she labeled him a "garrulous and untruthful 'late-blooming tree.' "[4] Her comments on Leone's wife, Vittoria, who allows no photographs while she smokes, drinks, or eats, comically underscore the reasons for her vanity. "The first lady must not appear to have any bad habits and must always give a perfect image of herself; woe betide if she is seen chewing an olive or with smoke coming out of her nose."[5]

When describing her working methods before the 1970s, Cederna reveals that she had aimed to present people the way an entomologist describes ants—cataloging stereotypes, behaviors, forms, habits, and details.[6] Focusing on a particular characteristic and then conventionalizing it accounts for her ability to transform an everyday event into a fascinating experience. Her picture of clinging people ("l'appiccicosa") evokes a type easily recognizable in society. "Do you mind if I come too . . . if you don't mind . . . maybe I bother you, then just forget about it . . . so you'll ask them if I can come too" (*S & S*, 150). The acquaintance whose smile or snide remark always manages to humiliate another individual ("la carogna") also figures in this repertory. "You can even get your hair cut short, lucky you. With your chubby cheeks, so beautifully plump" (*S & S*, 133). Cederna's commentaries ring true, and their accuracy gives them their impact. The self-inviting routine and the snide maliciousness becomes hilarious in print.

This cataloging technique also explains the writer's humor. The comic quality of the report on Queen Elizabeth springs in part from her reference to "the wandering Englishwomen of Bellagio and Fiesole" as if they were a special breed.

> It is logical, in fact, that the queen of England would not follow the latest fashion from Paris, but rather be furnished in pure English style, with colors suitable for British rosy cheeks, with a "vieux-jeu" charm that has always been the vaguely melancholic charm of the wandering Englishwomen of Bellagio or Fiesole, and that she should have organza petals on her head, silks that look like chocolate wrappers, and a handbag hanging from her arm (she must always have both hands free to caress a child, to shake other hands, or to receive an unexpected bouquet). (*S & S*, 561)

Cederna's spirit of irony shows itself in the use of words like "arredata" ("furnished") instead of "vestita" ("dressed") or her many far-fetched associations and similes. The humor in the passage about Mike Bongiorno ensues from grouping the game-show host, two singers, and a leading political party in the same category, and in comparing the celebrity to Fiat chocolates: "He remains 'the everlasting,' and he surely is one of the longer-lasting phenomena of our society, like Celentano, Claudio Villa, and the Christian Democratic party; and his strength, even if his shows change their names, is that he never changes, like Fiat chocolates, always the same . . . and always good."[7]

Many of Cederna's articles written for weekly magazines have been collected into books. The three volumes of *Il lato debole: Diario italiano* (The weak side: An Italian journal) contain the essays she composed for *L'Espresso* from 1956 to 1976. They reflect the changes that took place both in Italy and in the writer herself during those years. The subtitles succinctly summarize the general trends of Italian society. The first volume, *Gli anni ricchi del boom* (The rich years of the boom), covers from 1956 to 1962; the second volume, *Le radici della crisi* (The roots of the crisis), spans from 1963 to 1968; the last part, *La tragedia in piazza* (The tragedy in the open), goes from 1969 to 1976. In her introduction to the first volume, Lietta Torna-buoni appropriately defines Cederna's production as a catalog of all those behaviors, slang expressions, stereotypes, and trends that compose the minor history of a country.[8]

By the 1960s, when the writer had acquired a reputation as chronicler of the upper middle-class in Milan, some of her work already showed signs of political and social commitment. She recently stated, however, that her association with high society never impeded her from observing less fortunate classes. In 1961, she visited the slums of Rome to witness the acute misery and hazardous conditions of the area.

> The weddings of the powerful and my participation in the frivolous and gallant high society never prevented me from going to see the opposite side of society, the people who live in poverty, ignored by most Italians and by their newspapers. In fact, when I tell a society lady that I am going to Rome to see the slums, she asks me what they are. After finding that out, she says that they are all Communist lies.[9]

In her columns, Cederna occasionally wrote about serious social problems or reported on an international event, but in 1968 her life and writing changed radically when she began to focus on political repression and injustice. Italy was torn apart by a period of widespread social unrest and violence in the 1970s. Deeply aware of this new reality, Cederna took a firm stand on controversial issues. In *De gustibus,* she discusses her almost physical compulsion to denounce injustice: "I consider it my civil duty to sign a petition that I believe in: the intellectual must sound the alarm when others remain silent (although I do not consider myself an intellectual, but rather a person who, not suffering from political estrangement, has been trying to fight corruption for years)."[10] Cederna became disillusioned when the "good bourgeoisie" failed to fulfill its role as a moral and enlightened ruling class. Although she understood the reasons for this dereliction of duty, she did not condone it. She is the heir of eighteenth-century Milan, which was at the center of the Italian Enlightenment. The city's citizenry inspired high ethical standards, played an active role in the pursuit of justice, and used its resources in the process. The writer adheres faithfully to this tradition.

Cederna proved her political commitment by writing three of the most controversial books of the 1970s: *Pinelli: Una finestra sulla strage* (Pinelli: A window above the massacre); *Sparare a vista: Come la polizia del regime DC mantiene l'ordine pubblico* (Shoot on sight: How the police maintain public order for Christian Democrats); *Giovanni Leone: La carriera di un presidente* (Giovanni Leone: The career of a president). During this time, Cederna's three publications earned her the reputation of a subversive propagandist and resulted in several trials for public defamation and libel.

Pinelli: Una finestra sulla strage analyzed a judicial inquiry into a tragic bombing of the Banca dell'agricultura in Milan on 15 December 1969 in which ninety persons suffered injuries and fifteen died, and which led to one of the most dreadful court cases in recent Italian history. The terrorist attack occurred during a very bitter phase of that year's strikes and delicate talks between workers and management. The Italian power structure concealed many of the facts of the bombing, but every detail of circumstantial evidence, including a series of absurd decisions on the part of both the court and the police and the mysterious deaths of at least twelve witnesses during the intervening months, pointed to the origin of the bombs. They came from the Fascist lunatic fringe on the Right whose interests would have been served by any collective panic disrupting negotiations between the major industries and unions.

Within a few hours of the killings, however, the police had decided to place the blame on the most defenseless group of all the parliamentary parties—the anarchists. Several men were promptly arrested on the basis of evidence that soon proved unreliable, and the trial of the chief man among those accused, Pietro Valpreda, was consistently postponed for three years. Another suspect, Giuseppe Pinelli, fell from a window in the Milan police headquarters during his interrogation. At first, officials spoke of suicide; they then switched to other versions, which were all incompatible with the fact that karate lesions were discovered on the body and that an ambulance had been called before the time of Pinelli's alleged suicide. Cederna arrived quickly on the scene and immediately noticed the contradictory reports of the witnesses.

The writer's indefatigable reportage began at that point. She questioned dozens of witnesses and lawyers, denounced the corruption of magistrates, and assembled a sensational dossier in the form of an antipolice thriller. In a two-year series of articles, the writer single-handedly shaped public reaction and kept nationwide interest alive in this frightful Italian-style Dreyfus case, which many people would have preferred to shelve and forget. Her book achieved the improbable; against every obstacle raised by a conservative court, the case was reopened, Valpreda was finally declared innocent, the corpse exhumed and reexamined, and proceedings were instituted against police officials.

In her autobiographical *Il mondo di Camilla* (Camilla's world), which was published later in 1980, the author retrospectively furnishes many of the provocative statements from the period. These accounts demonstrate her journalistic clarity and incisiveness, as well as a desire to preserve the lessons of history. The writer reminds her readers that from the beginning Pinelli's mother inquired why officials continued illegally to detain her son and that Allegra, a police superintendent, implicated the highest levels of government in his response, "Madame, we are highly pressured from Rome" (*M,* 223). After the prisoner's wife learned from journalists that her husband had fallen from the fourth floor of headquarters, she immediately telephoned Calabrese, another high-ranking official, to inquire why legal sources had failed to notify her. His answer revealed a lack of professional responsibility and sensitivity. "You know, we had a lot to do" (*M,* 223). The *Unità* reporter Aldo Palumbo, present in the courtyard of police headquarters at the moment of Pinelli's fall, described exactly what happened: "He hears something heavy falling in three phases: three dull thuds, one against the first eaves, another against the second, and in the end the crash on the ground. Certainly not the curved trajectory caused by the determined leap of one who throws himself from a height" (*M,* 223). The honesty of Palumbo's observations inculpates investigative authorities in the prisoner's death. "But what on earth are they doing up there? Why are they throwing a big box out of the window?" (*M*, 223). When Cederna questioned the cab driver Rolandi, who testified against the anarchist Valpreda in support of official proceedings, she learned that Guida, chief of police, had promised a lucrative reward: "Bravo, you won't have to work as a cab driver any more; you'll be taken care of" (*M*, 223). The same cab driver finally admitted in the presence of Assistant District Attorney Vittorio Occorsio that irregularities had occurred. "Ah, yes, in Milan they showed me a picture and they told me that was the man I had to recognize" (*M*, 223).

The excerpts from *Il mondo di Camilla* not only condemn the legal establishment of Milan but also suggest that people should have realized the truth and acknowledged it. At the same time, however, when few individuals managed to perceive the cobweb of corruption and lies, the writer courageously took a stand and opposed the public consensus. After the press initiated a deceitful, sensational campaign the day after Pinelli's death, she felt a moral responsibility to uncover the truth. Newspapers faithfully reported the police version of what had happened while Valpreda made the headlines as a "human beast," an "inhuman monster," and an "individual moved by a visceral and fascistic hatred for every form of democracy" (*M*, 224). Cederna's book on Pinelli exposed the extent to which the judiciary was subjected to political pressure and totally rehabilitated the accused anarchist, demonstrating that he was the victim of a cruel, state-sponsored conspiracy. In particular, she proved that magistrates habitually postponed trials in order to conceal the unethical practices of high officials.

Sparare a vista (1975), which also denounces the violent social repression of the 1970s and develops the same themes that appear in Cederna's book on Pinelli and Valpreda, represents an additional statement against the unpunished abuse of power. The writer describes police violence and exposes the indirect control corrupt officials have over the press, the dismissal of honest judges, and the cover-up of murders. Nevertheless, her faith in democracy and its values motivated her to write the most polemical of her politically oriented works, *Giovanni Leone: La carriera di un presidente*. Part One, "Chi è" (Who is he?), provides a portrait of Leone, tells how his image began to tarnish, indicates the lies in his speeches, and labels him an undignified blunderer. In addition, these chapters summarize the reasons for his rise to power: the influential connections of his upper middle-class family; his membership in traditional Catholic organizations; his tendency to avoid taking sides in controversies; his system of political control based on self-interest and favoritism; and finally his extolling of national values. Part Two, "La grande famiglia" (The great family), reveals the conniving use the president and his family made of authority for personal gain and lists many of their regular visitors who allegedly participated in frauds and bribery. The last three sections, "Speculazioni e scandali" (Gambles and scandals), "Il presidente" (The president), and "Gli ultimi scandali" (The final scandals), survey the long series of Leone's illegal activities.

The book appeared in April 1978 and became an instant best-seller in Italy. In tone and content, it condemns Leone's practice as a lawyer, professor, politician, and financial opportunist and caused such an indignant outcry in Italy that on 15 June of the same year President Leone resigned from office, seven months before the expiration of his term. Although the Italian leader was already under investigation, Cederna's public accusation provided the coup de grace that negated any possibility of political recovery. Her book essentially represents a devastating indictment of Leone, as well as of the entire governing class that supported him for decades. Chapter after chapter cites specific instances of corruption involving Leone himself, his friends, relatives, and business acquaintances; the entire text stands as an unflattering portrait of a debased politician who built his early career as a law professor at the University of Naples and his local political activities on behalf of the Christian Democrats into a vast, highly profitable superstructure of political and business alliances, which enriched him and his supporters at the expense of the state. Cederna documented the president's involvement in real estate speculations, zoning and building violations, political and legal services performed for underworld figures, and possible participation in the Lockheed payoffs in Italy. The impact of the book pointed to what many people felt in the country: Leone represented everything undesirable in contemporary Italy; Leone and his generation perpetuated a system based on patronage and the acceptance of *la bustarella,* the envelope full of money passed under the table; these perpetuators of an unjust social system were responsible for the terrorism plaguing the nation. The tragedy and irony of the situation was that few politicians remained unscathed by the revelations.

President Leone's three sons initiated a libel suit against Cederna but later withdrew their litigation. Three lawyers whom the writer had accused of extortion—one was the president's brother—brought her to court for libel. The public prosecutor sought a two-year jail term, the removal and destruction of the book, and substantial reparation. The judgment, which ruled only in favor of damage, was appealed by the public prosecutor, and a third trial was held. After much controversy, the original judgment was affirmed. Some felt that Cederna had distorted the truth, others that the informants on whom she had relied abandoned her in court. In any event, as Lucia Conti Bertini observed, Cederna offers her readers a lesson in courage.[11]

A less stressful atmosphere followed this period of political upheaval and, although Cederna never returned to the carefree spirit of the 1950s and 1960s, her writings became noticeably less vehement. In 1979 she wrote an introduction to *Milano in guerra* (Milan at war), a photographic history of the city from 1943 to 1945. In 1980, the autobiographical *Il mondo di Camilla* was published and appeared in the form of an interview. Cederna describes it as a journalist's book that, page by page, presents a spectrum of Italian history: "That continuous wave motion that has always characterized my work runs through this book: my incurable basic light-heartedness, my obstinate capacity to become indignant, to see certain events with a smile and a little humor and others with disdain, while sometimes, despite this disdain, noticing the ironic, histrionic, comic side" (*M,* 12). The work's wavelike structure moves from the present to the past and alternates happiness, sadness, seriousness, and humor. The writer and journalist in Cederna seem to take turns communicating and then to review the whole scenario together. *Il mondo di Camilla* examines all the exciting events of Cederna's life, displays some of the most remarkable personalities of the last thirty years, and finally reveals the soul of modern Italy.

In like manner, *Casa nostra: Viaggio nei misteri d'Italia* (Our home: A trip through the mysteries of Italy) (1983) further reveals the inner spirit of Cederna's homeland through a series of unusual descriptions of Italian cities and towns. The introductory stories are intriguing and humorous. She portrays Turin as the city of black magic and Reggio Emilia as a paradoxical municipality with a Communist government and a flagrant attitude of consumerism. Amusing commentaries soon give way to indignation, however, as attention focuses on organized crime in Naples or the scandal of Avellino, a town with an extraordinary number of people receiving disability payments from the government. Other chapters describe the heroin traffic and daily violence in the streets of Palermo. *Casa nostra* resembles a tour of contemporary Italy, a country still entrapped by the Mafia, bribery, and corruption, but also a land that has the ability to achieve genuine progress and justice for its people. *Vicino e distante* (Near and far away) (1984) continues the earlier descriptions of Italy through an accumulation of impressions of the past and present. A poignant vignette details how the exploited children of Naples united and found the courage to stand against organized crime.

Cederna's most recent volume, *De gustibus* (1986), consists of all the articles published by the writer between 1979 and 1986. Once again, she deals with trends, issues, and events but particularly highlights the language of advertising and fashion, commenting specifically on Americanisms and their general use by the Italian public. "Made in Italy" is a passage on style written as a mixture of the two languages. This perceptive rendition includes such expressions as *il nuovo look* (the new look), *respirare un feeling* (to breathe a feeling), *lo stile casuale* (casual style), *effetto hand-made* (hand-made effect), *la giacca con i taschini a patches per un look country* (the jacket with patched pockets for a country look), and *"fa" country la flanella* (flannel gives a country look) (*G*, 55–56). A few pages define what the writer refers to as *lessico pervertito* ("perverted sayings") and list such unbelievable neologisms found in the press as *si beve, si snacka* (people drink and snack) and *Managerialità* (manageriality). In addition, Cederna quizzes readers on misused clichés: "Who is seriously ill? 'Tourism.' What disease do parliamentarians suffer from? 'Disaffection.' Who risks having a paralysis? Any kind of public service and transportation, the political system, trade unions, and, even worse, the country's 'governability'" (*G*, 22–24). Cederna devotes much of her attention to changes in language and analyzes the reasons for the rise and fall of new idioms. When she writes about a trendy adjective, she examines how the press uses it and what it really means. When, on the other hand, certain words decline in usage, she carefully lists their replacements. *Non male* (not bad) substitutes for *bello* (beautiful) or *bellissimo* (very beautiful).[12] She criticizes journalists and writers who, misusing words, act "as if an invisible laziness or a collective infectious disease had suddenly struck them" (*G*, 22).

As a journalist, Cederna asserts her belief in an informative and instructive press. The integrity of her convictions teaches her to recognize problems, to report them, and to seek just solutions. Nevertheless, her great strengths remain an unshakable, positive outlook on life, an unfailing sense of humor, and the capacity to transform indifference into a firm commitment. In the concluding pages of *Il mondo di Camilla,* she identifies with Voltaire's comment on frivolity. "If nature had not made us a little bit frivolous, we would be very unhappy; most people do not hang themselves precisely because they are frivolous." Indeed, Cederna succeeds in incorporating the many and varied dimensions of her nation's life into her writings. This ability to portray Italian cultural and social history vividly, humorously, and truthfully in her reporting not only imbues her work with both literary and journalistic qualities but also serves to highlight creatively the heartbeat of contemporary Italy.

NOTES

1. Camilla Cederna, *La voce dei padroni* (Milan: Longanesi, 1962), p. 139. Future references to this book will be indicated as *Voce,* with the page number in parentheses following the text. All translations are my own throughout this essay. None of Cederna's works have been translated into English.

2. Camilla Cederna, *Signore e signori* (Milan: Longanesi, 1966), p. 561. Future references to this book will be indicated as *S & S,* with the page number in parentheses following the text.

3. Camilla Cederna, *Vicino e distante* (Milan: Mondadori, 1984), p. 58.

4. Camilla Cederna, *Giovanni Leone: La carriera di un presidente* (Milan: Feltrinelli, 1978), pp. 171–74.

5. Ibid., p. 70.

6. Camilla Cederna, *Il lato debole: Diario italiano* (Milan: Bompiani, 1977), *vol. 1, 1956–1962,* p. xi.

7. Cederna, *Vicino e distante,* p. 58.

8. Camilla Cederna, *Il lato debole, vol. 2, 1963–1968,* p. v.

9. Camilla Cederna, *Il mondo di Camilla* (Milan: Feltrinelli, 1980), p. 93. Future references to this book will be indicated as *M,* with the page number in parentheses following the text.

10. Camilla Cederna, *De gustibus* (Milan: Mondadori, 1986), p. 11. Future references to this book will be indicated as *G* with the page number in parentheses following the text.

11. Lucia Conti Bertini, "Il meglio di Camilla," *Il Ponte* 38, no. 4 (1982): 415–16.

12. Cederna, *Il lato debole, vol. 2, 1963–68,* p. 72.

From Margins to Mainstream: Some Perspectives on Women and Literature in Italy in the 1980s

CAROL M. LAZZARO-WEIS

The last twenty years have borne witness to significant changes in attitudes toward Italian women writers of fiction. Works of the long-ignored yet often commercially successful "signore della scrittura" have recently become the subject of critical interest and are beginning to find their way into anthologies of modern literature. Furthermore, a cursory look at lists of recently published books or a walk through bookstores anywhere in Italy reveals that more books by women are being published than ever before. This explosion of quantity and variety attests to the major impact of these writers on contemporary audiences. However, recent arguments of feminist critics against forming a separate literary category for women's writing reflect a growing fear that such an action would further ghettoize women's literature and make it a marginal, powerless, and easily avoided space. Biancamaria Frabotta expresses these reservations about Anna Nozzoli's originative study *Tabù e coscienza: La condizione femminile nella letteratura italiana del Novecento* (Taboo and awareness: The condition of women in twentieth-century literature).[1] Marginality, an important theme for both feminists and avant-grade writers in the 1970s, now appears as undesirable as the prospect of incorporation into a patriarchal mainstream appeared to radical writers of the 1960s.[2] To complicate matters further, this exclusion from the mainstream may be a paradoxical result of one of the major victories of the seventies—the establishment of feminist publishing houses whose increased activity has resulted in a decrease of acceptance of women's manuscripts by the larger, established publishing concerns.[3]

Several of the successes of the women's movement in the 1970s have produced ambiguous results. In her recent book *Liberazione della Donna: Feminism in Italy,* Lucia Chiavola Birnbaum reports that, despite victories on the juridical front, many neofeminists fear that the inclusion of some of their themes in the platform of conservative parties may indicate that the movement is being "coopted" or redefined according to hidden patriarchal standards.[4] According to feminist critic and writer Adele Cambria, this capitulation has already taken place on the literary scene. In a recent essay provocatively entitled "Il neo-femminismo in letteratura. Dove sono le ammazzoni?" (Neofeminism in literature: Where are the Amazons?), Cambria claims that with the exception of Elena Belotti's recent *Fiore dell'ibisco* (The hibiscus flower) (1985), feminism has made no inroads on women's fiction, which continues to be conciliatory, dependent, and regressive.[5] After qualifying her statement somewhat and mentioning a few positive themes in recent feminist literature, Cambria asks pointedly: "Is it the women in Italy who are not writing books capable of expressing the changes, transition, and movement produced in this country in the last two decades, or are the editors blocking them?" (145).

Maria Letizia Cravetta had already addressed the facility with which a male patriarchy absorbs feminist discourses and diverts women's writing from its specific subversiveness in one of the first publications of the feminist publisher Edizioni delle donne, a short, ironic *roman à clé, Tutti sanno* (Everyone knows) (1976). *Tutti sanno* begins with a series of letters between fictitious French and Italian editors, Emile Noget and Alfredo Gasperotti, who begin a journal, *Edipo Fiorito* (The Flourishing Oedipus). Although the organizers announce they will introduce new semiotic and subversive writings to the public, especially those of women, their real intent is to neutralize feminist writing. Their introductory exchange of letters frames an interpolated tale of Donata, an Italian feminist who had studied in Paris in 1968 and who, after a series of failed relationships with men and writing, withdraws to the provinces to teach and live with her geraniums and cats. In the end, Donata realizes that her decision to leave the French capital represented an attempt to avoid writing and to shield herself from illusions, disappointments, and suffering; she, therefore, vows to return to the battle of the pen. This traditionally written interpolated tale is, in reality, part of a thesis written by a woman to illustrate a certain Professor de Verleau's theories as they appear in his pioneering work *Histoire des considérations sur l'articulation critique du désespoir* (The history of considerations on the critical articulation of despair). When Noget writes to his collaborator Gasperotti, he insists on suppressing the scientific components of this work, arguing specifically that if the work were published as fiction, its feminist message would be easier to interpret in a more modern, yet still patriarchal and conciliatory key.

The question of the revolutionary nature of women's fiction remains inseparable from the still unresolved debates that began in the 1970s over what constitutes "feminine writing." Cambria's accusation that the theorizing of the past two decades concerning women's fiction and culture has produced few noticeable results is more understandable if one recalls the low place women's fiction held in the theories of such French feminist theoreticians as Hélène Cixous, Julie Kristeva, Luce Irigaray, and Monique Wittig. For the most part, the works of these critics have inspired Italian literary theory more than Anglo-Saxon critics.[6] In her introduction to Elisabetta Rasy's *Lingua della nutrice* (The language of the maternal provider), the influential semiotician and psychoanalyst Julie Kristeva calls Rasy's text an example of her type of feminist writing, a revolutionary theoretical prose that destroys traditional gender divisions and sensitizes women to the task of reformulating a new logic of love: "Are women only the agents of radical refusal, eternal witches when they are not docile followers of the doctrines of new masters of power or antipower? Or can they contribute to constructing a new legitimacy that includes their pleasure, an ethic guaranteed not by constraint but by a logic, a poly-logic of love?"[7]

Since Kristeva largely ignores women's fiction, Rosalind Jones describes her as "contemptuous" of the whole endeavor.[8] In *Les chinoises* (*About Chinese Women*) (1974), Kristeva argues that women writers are less able to attack the "Symbolic" (the social order), since their psychocultural self-images depend on a vicarious relationship to it. Jones reports that Kristeva dismisses women novelists for having narrow thematic concerns, the main one being the reinventing of family histories through which they construct a reassuring identity for themselves. In Kristeva's view, women writers stylistically fail to carry out the systematic dissection of language found in a writer like James Joyce; even the more experimental texts lack a concern for musical forms in composition. Women, Kristeva argues, cannot afford to lose their psychic and cultural identity by returning to unconscious bonds with their mothers, a return she claims has led to paranoid and separatist politics.[9] Her pessimism receives reinforcement from Nozzoli's observation that even feminist publishing houses, as if in imitation of mainstream publishers, favor either translations of known foreign authors or theoretical essays over the publication of fictional works by Italian women writers.[10] Caught between a patriarchal publishing market that threatens to neutralize them and definitions of feminine discourse that exclude them, women writers face bleak prospects indeed.

Kristeva is not alone in arguing that traditional novels condemn women to recounting images of their failures. Such American feminist critics as

Nancy Miller and Myra Jehlen also see the novel as an essentially patriarchal discourse that condemns women to viewing themselves as inferior beings.[11] French feminists Kristeva, Cixous, and Irigaray discount traditional women's prose because their theories focus on the development of a language that would not only displace binary opposition justifying masculine supremacy but would also liberate the feminine unconscious and reveal the linguistic repression of woman's desire.[12] Italian neofeminists never completely shared the belief that revolution through language alone could succeed. Many experimental writers, however, introduced and explored the theoretical premises of French feminism, which call for a discourse that would dismantle patriarchal strategies of oppression, destroy traditional gender identities, and eliminate restrictive cultural attitudes. Anna Nozzoli indicates the transforming influence of these themes on genres and suggests a "relationship in the making" between more traditional narrative fiction and feminist reflections on writing.[13] These intersections that have indeed produced changes in women's writing while avoiding compromise of its subversive role will be the focus of this essay.

The experimental and theoretical writings of Italian women reveal tactics of subjugation of the female on the psychological and social level through the dissection of certain themes—the male narcissistic death wish, regression, dependency, and belonging. The inclusion of these themes in recent women's histories, or *Bildungsromans,* makes this form a vehicle for feminist goals. Although Italian feminists avoid speaking of discovering a women's tradition, recent reprintings of previously published works indicate the formation of a consensus on the objective and strategies of women's literature. This new productivity represents a move away from theories of language based on revolutionary motives, and, in some cases, accepts an emerging philosophical trend in Italy called "il pensiero debole" (weak thought). According to Giovanna Borrodori, this outlook addresses an impasse in postmodern theories. Their insistence on language's loss of referential power and the total deconstruction of all subjectivity posed problems for Italian feminists and stood in direct opposition to their desire to portray female subjectivity and effect concrete social changes. "Weak thought" posits the idea of a subject reworking relationships with a past defined as an error of humanistic, logocentric thought.[14] The critic and writer Aldo Gargagni derives from this concept the notion of a "voce femminile" (feminine voice), which he defines as a marginal and critical viewpoint that exposes the violence and exclusions of traditional History.[15] In recent fictional works, some women writers consciously exercise this voice to incorporate feminist ideas on subjugation, dependency, and belonging into a new mainstream history that their works help to recuperate as part of the feminine experience and struggle with oppression.

Julie Kristeva's and Monique Wittig's theories of a genderless marginal space from which to subvert power and break down traditional male/female identities have always been more accepted by Italian feminist writers and critics than those hypotheses that proclaim a specific identity determined by the female body.[16] In "Miti, forme e modelli della narrativa nuova" (Myths, forms, and models of the new narrative) (1978), the writer, journalist, and critic Silvia Castelli lists marginality, alienation, failed revolt, and literary narcissisms as the major themes of all writers in the 1970s. During that period, writers in general experienced a psychological separation from their readers and lost their position as authoritative, speaking subjects. As a result, they became spectators vocalizing from "river banks and only capable of portraying the moment in which the world had killed them as writers."[17] Castelli discusses women's texts under the separate rubric "la gabbia e l'ombra" (the cage and the shadow), where *gabbia* refers to oppressive social norms that women must overthrow. Again, however, *ombra* is a space for both men and women. In fact, Castelli argues, male writers who had voluntarily inhabited this space during the Fascist period originally caused the phenomenon that she calls "feminization of the text."

Castelli does distinguish between masculine narcissism, characterized by a desire for death, and its feminine counterpart, a desire for self-understanding through mirror-introspection. The present crisis of identity in the patriarchy, however, forces the former into the space of the latter where both sexes work toward annulling differences.[18] Castelli's own experimental novel, *Pitonessa* (The female python) (1978), written in unpunctuated sentences and arbitrary paragraphs, exemplifies a body language identified by Frabotta as similar to that of Monique Wittig in *Le corps lesbien (The Lesbian Body)* (1973). According to Wittig's use of the term, *lesbian* indicates a genderless, political, and social class rather than sexual preference.[19] The mysterious "bambine" or "esse," who constantly disrupt women's stories about their husband's love of photography or inquiries about the fate of a husband in Africa, represents the free zone in which children grow up outside socialized, rigid, sexual differences.

Walter Pedullà remarks that *Pitonessa* challenges the great myth of equality that permeated much avant-garde literature in the 1960s.[20] Indeed, by the second half of the 1970s, feminists could no longer ignore that hierarchies still existed in the genderless political and writing spaces they advocated. Rosalind Jones links Kristeva's arguments for a postpolitical women's era, a "third generation" dedicated to the dissolution of personal and sexual identity through writing, to an increasing disillusionment with political parties and the waning of the belief that there could be a political solution to women's oppression.[21] In the early 1970s, such feminist writers as Armanda Guiducci and Dacia Maraini published confessions of various types of women to demonstrate that the abject states of females had a cultural base in capitalism.[22] Disillusionment with the Soviet Union's political actions after 1967 helped European feminists to come to the realization that patriarchal structures also provided a foundation for Marxist/socialist ideologies. Dacia Maraini's latest novel, *Il treno per Helsinki* (The train for Helsinki) (1984), recounts this discovery, first on an ideological level through the narrator's trip to an international Communist conference in Helsinki and second on a personal note through her love affair with Miele, a liberal socialist and modern Don Juan who uses women for his personal and political ends. Lucia Chiavola Birnbaum speaks of a feminist crisis in Italy after 1976. Cultural feminists argued that national change could only occur after attitudes and mentalities were modified; on the other hand, "historical" feminists still called for effecting change through political institutions.[23] In "Corteo di notte," Elisabetta Rasy describes this erosion in the belief of political solutions to the female question and the nascent idea of a revolution as a significant shift from the "Movimento femminista" (feminist movement) to a "Movimento delle donne" (a women's movement).[24]

Rasy's definition of language resembles Kristeva's concept of semiotics—an organization of signs and symptoms used not to communicate but to break down theories and ideologies. Kristeva's theory emphasizes the investigation of psychic repression rather than social or sexual oppression. Rasy's call in "Corteo di notte," to valorize certain feminine repressed states and to accord them a positive meaning as part of the semiotic, political battle, provoked a negative reaction from Biancamaria Frabotta on the grounds that such a strategy risked promoting nostalgia for archetypal feminine traits and directed attention away from facing and solving the many real problems caused by a rapidly changing society.[25] Frabotta's protests reveal an essential difference between many French feminists and their Italian counterparts. The former tend to explore repression in language whereas the latter hope that language will expose oppression of women based on sexual difference and then produce changes in society.[26] Significantly, however, Rasy's first novel, *La prima estasi* (The first ecstasy)

(1985), is not the glorification of regression but the story of a successful perversion. The writer gives a psychoanalytical portrait of Saint Teresa of Lisieux, whose refusal to leave the presymbolic infant phase results in the disastrous death wish predicted by Kristeva for women who attempt a retreat to early childhood stages.

The narcissistic desire to end one's life has enjoyed a prominent place in Italian feminist writing since the late 1970s. Experimental writers influenced by French theorists polemically contrasted the masculine death wish, mentioned by Castelli, with a more positive, feminine attitude. This theme derives from the reaction of French critics to poststructuralist and deconstructionist definitions of women as an absent, mysterious space.[27] In an essay often quoted by Italian feminists, Hélène Cixous defines women's writings as a place to express a desire that affirms life and eradicates (metaphoric) death: "It is man who teaches women (because man is always the master) to be aware of absence, aware of death."[28] In Ginevra Bompiani's *Specie del sonno* (A kind of sleep) (1975), Eros explains to Psyche that death lurks behind everything he seeks, behind men, women, his work, and his search for a daughter in his own image. The female protagonist, Sophie, of Bompiani's ironical *Mondanità* (Worldliness) (1980) is abandoned by her husband in an Istanbul mosque during their vacation, when he realizes she represents the primeval woman who denies death, transcendence, and meaning: "Because you are the woman who offers to death the sacrifice of presence . . . I want to find my death, not my life. You robbed me of it [death, thus meaning] the first time being my wife; a second time being the mother of my child; the third time being yourself." Sophie goes to live with her eccentric cousin Isadore in his dilapidated family chateau in France. Other inhabitants living in the "regno delle madri" (kingdom of mothers), as Sophie describes it, include Madame de Miral and her daughter Virginia, who is writing a dissertation on an Englishwoman writer. When Sophie sends her son out into the world, she implores him to search for love rather than death. In the end, Sophie disappears after a near encounter with her husband and son in Paris but not before she states clearly her belief in a void rather than in any transcendant meaning of death. "She was convinced that everything would continue this way without end, in an eternal and mythical repetition, to which she resigned herself."[29]

Cixous links the male death wish, which continues in modern philosophical theories of language, to bourgeois concepts of possession, acquisition, and consummation-consumption.[30] In Maria Schiavo's *Macellum: Storia violentata e romanzata di donne e di mercato* (*Macellum: A violent fictionalized version of women and the marketplace*) (1979), a series of essays which show how language masks the basic oppression of women, as well as their status as objects to be possessed and consumed, females again refuse to represent death and meaning for men. Schiavo does not claim her work to be a documentary account of the persecution of women. Instead she structures a series of encounters with historical and literary figures and searches for linguistic relationships between women's subservience and patriarchal theories on such topics as the male preoccupation with death, incest taboo, the oedipal myth, and castration. One recurring figure who facilitates these explorations is Don Juan. Schiavo depicts him as the man who glorifies death as transcendence, idealizes women, and makes them his reflection in order to deny their presence. Schiavo quotes Don Juan's comments on the abandoned Cordelia in *Diary of a Seducer*. "Cordelia loves me and hates me. What does a young girl fear? The spirit. Why? Because the spiritual represents the negation of her entire feminine existence."[31] When Don Juan abandons Cordelia, she cannot return to the marketplace because she has no existence outside of the rapport of ownership ("*appartenenza*") and dependency. Yet she exercises some power on the linguistic level. When Mary Magdalene comes to resuscitate her, she flatly declines. By refusing the spiritual afterlife, Cordelia affirms her independent existence. Schiavo had previously quoted Lucretius to argue that the afterlife was a concept created in order to strengthen notions of dependency and belonging.

Rosa Rossi's latest book, *L'ultimo capitolo* (The last chapter) (1984), also participates in this polemic on the male death wish.[32] The male protagonist is an archeologist who retreats to his summer home after his wife's death; he hopes that his nocturnal writings will ward off depression and stifle his strong desire to commit suicide. The book's title refers to the last chapter of Luke's gospel, when angels ask the women searching for Christ's body why they seek the living among the dead. In his writings, the narrator also searches for someone alive among the deceased, namely his wife whose image he had constructed as a specular reflection of his own desire. The archeologist only recovers from his inability to name things, including his spouse, when he realizes that he cannot fix his wife's identity even in death; he must face the uncontrollable "forza del nulla" (the force of nothingness) with human fear and respect.

Rosa Rossi's narrative, like Rasy's *Prima estasi*, indicates a return to the more communicative, representational trend in Italian feminist writings. In both texts, language is not used to liberate regressive, unconscious desire but rather to represent the experience of psychic regression. Therefore, critics who had disagreed on language issues in the 1970s now seem philosophically closer to each other. Armanda Guiducci's cultural history of women as bought commodities, *Donna e serva* (Women and servants) (1983), provides a more historically based inquiry into the subject of female oppression than Schiavo's *Macellum*. Guiducci specifically argues against the psychoanalytic analysis of dependency and belonging, which, she argues, must be examined in a cultural context. "It is not the inflexibility of language that causes the inflexibility of reasoning."[33] Familiar feminist psychoanalytical themes, however, inevitably appear in Guiducci's first novel, *A testa in giù* (Decapitation) (1984), the story of a woman's experience of psychic oppression in the name of love. The narrator relives her experience of masculine possessiveness as a way toward decapitation and assimilation of the male death wish: "Igor mi de-testava" (Igor de-tested-capitated me) (146). The narrator comes to the realization that her husband's gaze alone grants her an identity. "I always saw myself through his eyes, I am also the image of love that he gave me" (151). Like Rossi, Guiducci suggests that men's insistence on loving their specular image represents a form of regressive thinking, which women must learn to recognize and combat in order to escape childlike subservient roles in social relationships.

More recent feminist writings unite in denouncing both regression and oppression and endeavor to represent how both operations result from patriarchal strategies that need to be revealed and replaced. Despite their respective differences, the narratives of Guiducci, Schiavo, Bompiani, Maraini, and Rossi also continue to deconstruct the traditional logic of love and to work toward its redefinition. After Cordelia refuses resuscitation in *Macellum,* Schiavo asks the two basic questions that motivate her archaeological digs into the feminine unconscious. "Is love possible," since it is always founded on some type of exploitation, and "Is it possible to eliminate exploitation?" (123). Analyses of dependency, belonging, and exploitation necessarily abound in the writings of women, since these are the structures that have both traditionally defined love and prevented it. Furthermore, any meaningful understanding of the social or psychic relationship of women to the oppressive segment of society must also take into account how they have absorbed and helped to sustain those values that oppress them. Dacia Maraini explains how the oppressed assimilate the very ideals that seriously hamper them. Since women have internalized men's desire for them to be fragile, dependent, masochistic, voluble, and incapable, they tend to repress their own need for autonomy and independence.[34] Whether fiction should deconstruct these relationships through language or represent these structures realistically is a question not completely resolved. Traditional representational fiction, however, still constitutes a significant presence in Italy and continues to contribute to the dissemination of feminist ideas and to further analyses of the concepts of dependency and belonging.

The depression and weariness of a subordinate state of affairs have indeed often informed women's writings. Maria Messina's *Casa paterna* and its sequel *La casa del vincolo*, first published in 1921 and recently redistributed by Leonardo Sciascia's publishing house, Sellerio, illustrate how traditional male/female relationships in Sicily create physical and psychic dependencies in women. The autonomy and sexuality of Messina's female characters are denied in marital structures—a condition that causes them to remain perennial adolescents capable of seeing themselves only as flawed mirror images of men. Book jackets refer to Messina's books as "feminist," since they increase the reader's awareness of the oppressive situation of Sicilian women before World War II. Sellerio's reissue of Lucia Luisa Adorno's *Ultima provincia* (1983), first published in 1962, and the recent publication of Maria Luisa Aguirre D'Amico's *Come si può* (1986) fill in more of the historical gap by recounting the problems of educated Leftist women attempting to work and fulfill themselves in the 1950s before the watershed date of 1968. Adorno's autobiography, written in a comic, realistic mode reminiscent of the Sicilian writer Vittorio Brancati, is the story of her marriage to the obedient son of a conservative Sicilian prefect. D'Amico, Luigi Pirandello's granddaughter, offers a more sobering work, an account of her return to postwar Italy from Chile, where her family had fled in exile; she elaborates the difficulties she encountered in attempting to give her life meaning through involvement in politics and writing.

Feminist theoreticians who view these works and other earlier examples of women's fictional prose as inherently conservative base their judgment on one of two main assumptions: either they presume, like Myra Jehlen and Nancy Miller, that the novel's formal and linguistic conventions are encoded by men, and thus must serve to suppress women's writing; or they argue, like Jane Gallop, that the recognition of experience in language, or the representation of it, is essentially conservative because one can only recognize and thus recount what one already knows.[35] More traditional novels, especially when written in a realistic vein, tend to represent the distance that still separates theoretical advances in knowledge or demands for change from actual transformations in societal and cultural attitudes.

Frabotta points to these discrepancies when she states that, in Italy, women's sexuality and writing are still "antithetical poles," which only patience and discretion can bring together.[36]

According to the American critic Joanna Frye, this diametrical opposition in women's traditional prose narratives results from the fact that cultural ideology surrounds and encodes the actions of real women just as novelistic plots do; societal norms that still define them according to archaic and patriarchal expectations continue to separate love from work and sexuality from autonomy/writing. Frye, however, correctly indicates that the novel is not a closed form as many critics have assumed. Its capacity for self-criticism and incorporating evolving kinds of discourses and developing perceptions enables it to portray both change and stasis. While representing the problems of progressive emancipation, the impact such change makes, and the regressive resistance engendered, women's fictional prose can also portray female protagonists in the process of acting, writing, and transforming the cultural ideologies that seek to confine them. Finally, those critics who maintain that the depiction of experience remains innately conservative ignore the role the novel has always had in forming a new reading public, more aware of past mistakes and future possibilities. The constant return to representation in women's fiction not only enacts a criticism of patriarchal values inherent in the act of writing itself but also reflects a feminist desire to share experience, develop a recognition of commonality in women's lives, and combat a sense of personal isolation.[37] Elena Belotti is of the same mind when she refutes Cambria's attack on women's narrative prose and calls the novel an effective means of recording progressive modifications in values, as well as an instrument for propagandizing innovations and "making them part of the culture."[38]

Belotti's much acclaimed work *Il fiore dell'ibisco* affords a good example of this culturalizing and popularizing procedure. The encounter between a free-lance writer and Daniele, a boy whose governess the writer had been twenty years before, lends itself to the inclusion of such sensitive themes as nonbiological maternity and the development of sexual affection between an older woman and a younger man. The text, however, is primarily an anatomy, a compendium of many feminist and psychoanalytical theories of the past thirty years.[39] A digression on Daniele's mother and grandmother illustrates how and why suppressed and degraded women are unable to identify with one another. Chapters discussing the young protagonist's entry into the symbolic order, his discovery of his penis, and his attempt to seduce his governess recapitulate and popularize Freudian and Lacanian psychoanalytic theories of the male specular gaze. Belotti also documents the superficiality of much change. Daniele shows his former governess that he knows how to cook, and he proclaims himself a Leftist despite his rich bourgeois background. By expropriating certain "feminine" traits, Daniele feels he incarnates an androgynous vision that denies all differences between males and females who need to band together to fight political oppression. Yet, the discussions between the two reveal that he still places himself at the center of the universe, believing that women should, or more precisely, must, mirror his desires. Although the discussion of these theories results in a certain rapprochement between the former governess and her visitor, who act out their repressed sexual fantasies in a playful bath scene, the physical encounter that results is a disaster. Reality returns when Daniele admits their lovemaking was meant to avenge what he bitterly calls his girlfriend's "feminist" behavior. She had exploited him to become pregnant and then refused his marriage proposal. Significantly, however, the narrator does not regard the ruined liaison as a personal failure. Her marginal position as governess in an upper-class household had trained her to view things with a certain protective irony. She, in turn, destroys Daniele's cherished childhood illusion that she had once belonged to him alone by revealing that she had left her position to get an abortion. The battle of the sexes continues and, in the end, a saddened but not destroyed narrator contemplates and writes about the real changes produced by the cultural upheaval of the sixties and seventies.

Several recent women's histories, or what could be called female *Bildungsroman,* also portray protagonists trying to integrate changes into lives still defined according to outmoded traditions and conventions. Such is the case in Fabrizia Ramondino's *Althénopis* (1981), Marisa DiMaggio's *C'era una volta un re . . .* (Once upon a time there was a king . . .) (1985), and Daria Martelli's *Chi perde la sua vita* (He who loses his life) (1981).[40] *Althénopis* is the story of a young girl's childhood in a bourgeois family in Naples; *C'era una volta un re . . .* recounts a girlhood experience in a typical Sicilian village; *Chi perde la sua vita* relates another bourgeois childhood in Tuscany. *Althénopis* begins during World War II, when a family takes refuge in Santa Maria del Mare, and continues into the late seventies; the other narratives cover approximately the same time span but start after the war. Far from creating secure identities for women, these novels help to destroy a classically defined feminine identity and clearly illustrate the impossibility or the undesirability of regressing back to it. Although childhood unfolds in a somewhat idealized, imaginative, and genderless space of freedom, during this time of growth, the female narrators assimilate the rules for an untenable and outmoded feminine identity. In spite of their respective differences with *La prima estasi, L'ultimo capitolo, Il treno per Helsinki*, and *A testa in giù*, these three novels denounce the nostalgic regressive thinking of women, as well as of men, and show to what extent women's absorption of patriarchal values makes them complicit in their own oppression.

The portrayal of how undesirable it is to regress to any previous idealized feminine identity receives additional force from the deconstruction of the mother-daughter nexus through which many patriarchal values are transmitted and internalized. The longest chapter in the first part of *Althénopis* concerns degraded matriarchies that mimic male expectations and that consequently perpetuate the subservient status of women. The female community in *Althénopis* admits only married *signore* and refuses to recognize their unmarried counterparts, especially if they are educated. Like the narrator's mother, those who remain single spend their lives as sickly individuals until they can no longer make fruitful use of their talent. Women who receive formal instruction arouse even less interest. The reaction of female family members to their grandmother reputed to be one of five Italian women in the last century to have achieved a university degree is to remark that her pretentiousness was probably inherited by her daughters who, as a result, could not find husbands. The narrator points out that it is impossible to become anything in the matriarchy; the highest and only achievable honor consists of birth into this state. Men are also excluded from this perverted power structure, unless they have failed in some aspect and thus pay for entry into this oppressed form of existence.

Although the child-narrator does not identify with the matriarchy, its power is revealed in the brief third part entitled "Bestelle Dein Haus" (Prepare your house). The German citation, taken from Bach's Cantata op.106, is followed by a quotation from Brahm's Requiem announcing the final transformation to take place at the Last Judgment. In *Althénopis*, this metamorphosis occurs when the narrator returns home after her schooling to take her place beside her mother. At that point she becomes objectified; she represents the "Daughter who can only speak to her Mother in signs, not language" (233). The fact that the narrator speaks in the first person as a child and in the third person as an adult further reinforces her loss of individuality. The daughter also witnesses the mother's grateful regression to a state of childlike sexuality. She gleefully expresses giggling—"I am a baby"—when reprimanded for touching her genitals. There is not yet a mature female identity outside of the family that can be represented.[41]

Whereas Ramondino's *Althénopis* recounts events in a true-to-life mode, the atmosphere of DiMaggio's *C'era una volta* is more akin to the magic realism of Garcia Marquez, where fantastic events and learned mythical and literary allusions alternate with more naturalistic analyses. In the first chapter, the recently deceased Mamma Lucia sits under the altar and watches herself being replaced, but not forgotten, since only in death does a woman recuperate her reputation as a saintly person. While growing up in a small Sicilian village, the passive child Marianna and Mamma Lucia both witness a series of stock events: forced marriages, a love affair between a young pastor and a cousin, the priest's transfer and subsequent death from a broken heart, religious recitals, how the myth of America destroys traditions, and more. Change penetrates every aspect of this town whose inhabitants struggle to reinterpret all vicissitudes according to traditional structures. DiMaggio's parodic modern version of the Demeter/Kore myth relates the mother Cosima's search for her working daughter, who spends the night with her supervisor. The rules learned during childhood are meant to keep in place "the surreptitious and soporific status quo maintained in effect by truths as moldy as stale bread, by apocryphal gospels, eternal maxims, and glorious mysteries."[42] Like the narrator in *Althénopis,* Marianna also leaves town to begin her studies at the university. Her return later arouses in her overwhelming feelings of nostalgia for the sense of security she believes those villagers experience who never question dominant social and symbolic norms. Since the novel comically unmasks these structures, however, the protagonist cannot turn back. Like the prodigal daughter, she is condemned to roam forever, eventually disappearing like Sophie in Bompiani's *Mondanità,* who also could not return to a customary past and found no new identity to assume.

Martelli's *Chi perde la sua vita* is the story of the revenge of two degraded mothers. Martelli's narrator believed it possible to avoid degradation by receiving an education and imitating patriarchal values that taught her to suppress and detest characteristics of the weak, despicable "femmina."[43] Since this image is itself a construction of the patriarchy, the narrator's refutation of it becomes a reflection of her mother's asexuality and inability to relate to life. The same is true for Lucio, an artistic character who introduces the narrator to literature and with whom she falls in love, only to discover later his homosexuality. While inculcating in him a nostalgia for the traditions and folklore of the countryside from which she came, Lucio's mother had also made him incapable of dealing with the adult social order. Her possessive love, which had made him totally dependent upon her, prepared him not for eternal maternal life, but for death.

Chi perde la sua vita, like the narratives of Belotti, Ramondino, and DiMaggio, recounts the story of a failed encounter and demonstrates the difficulty of portraying autonomous female identities. By exposing certain oppressive psychic and cultural structures that hamper the development of mature relationships between the sexes, however, these writers participate in the feminist project of progressive liberation from these same paradigms.[44] They also aid in the creation of a new interpretive community capable of developing their own attitudes toward themselves.

Not surprisingly, many themes of dependency and regression receive mock treatment in comic narratives. Emma Rossi's delightful *Pensione Paradiso (già Porospenia)* (Paradise pension, formerly Porospenia) (1984) is a compendium of stock female attitudes toward men.[45] The brief chapters expose how many feminine stereotypes such as the weak prostitute, strong practical women, scholars, and actresses both participate in and are excluded from the system. Gaia de Beaumont's *Bella* (The beauty) (1985) takes a critical but light look at a fat woman's problems in society.[46] Journalist Barbara Alberti's *Buonanotte Angelo* (Goodnight Angelo) (1986) recounts the story of how a woman rediscovers maternal love when her obese and detestable son who spends his days watching television and stuffing himself with junk food is kidnapped and her drama becomes a television success. These books, especially those of Alberti, which are published by a mainstream press, attest to the widespread currency of many feminist themes that women—no longer in a traditionally defined and dominated position—are now writing about.

Assessing the changes in attitudes that women's literature may have brought about is a difficult, in fact impossible, task at this time. However, the reissue of older works indicates the formation of a consensus regarding what a literary tradition about women should represent. In her introduction to the reedition of Paola Masino's *Nascita e morte della massaia* (The birth and death of a housewife) (1982), Silvia Giacomoni highlights the main topics therein as the relationship between giving, having, commanding, and serving. These themes, originally expressed in 1938, become current again in light of contemporary writings that also emphasize these same motifs.[47] The reprinting of two volumes of essays by Anna Maria Ortese also attests to the identification of the critique of oppression and exclusion from society's mainstream as a central objective of women's writings.[48] *Il treno russo* (The Russian train) (1982), first published in the magazine *L'Europeo* in 1954, was written at the beginning of the postwar rapprochement with the Soviet Union and describes Ortese's trip to Russia and her attempts to find common ground with a foreign nation. The writer's traditional humanism surfaces in the final pages where she argues for the necessity of a belief in the universality of a basically good human nature. Another series of early essays (1958) by Ortese, published under the title *Silenzio a Milano* (Silence in Milan) (1984), represents society's oppressed and marginal members, whether they be in the Milan train station at night, in homes for juvenile delinquents and unwanted children, or in housing developments constructed for the homeless. Today, despite the more traditional aspects of Ortese, her works are read as part of a women's tradition expressing disillusionment with the political Left and its belief in theoretical solutions; at the same time, they protest the continuing suppression of the weak and their exclusion from mainstream History.

Two recent collections of short stories provide examples of the emerging critical voice spoken of by Gargagni, a voice informed and enriched by the insights gained from themes common to experimental and traditional forms of writing. Both Marisa Volpi's *Maestro della betulla* (The birch tree painter) (1986) and Marta Morazzoni's *Ragazza col turbante* (The girl with the turban) (1986) include the familiar themes of degradation, male specular vision, regression, and dependency. Volpi's first story, "Caminito," tells the tale of a student's relationship with her mentor, an English professor named Villalba. The rapport is tinged with sexual innuendoes, and the narrator speaks of Villalba as a father who is necessary to give form to her life and work. Volpi's account is comparable to Anna Banti's recent autobiography *Un grido lacerante* (1982). Banti, who had married her mentor, art historian Roberto Longhi, describes how she experienced feelings of inadequacy and dependency in the relationship, in spite of her own success. Whereas Banti expresses her long-repressed rage over her subservient status as a mere "donna di lettere" (woman of letters), Volpi presents her feelings of inadequacy and dependency as those that inform her specific gaze. Employing this perspective, she rewrites history and envisions the previously marginalized "feminine." The title story, "Il maestro della betulla," accordingly portrays a male outsider, Gaspard Dughet, the forgotten brother-in-law of the classical Poussin, who had consistently condemned his relative's art as excessive, disorderly, and, therefore, feminine. Volpi openly admits that her own emotional experiences facilitate the conceptualization of Dughet's exclusion, oppression, and revolt.

At first glance women seem absent from Morazzoni's collection of five short stories. No female authorial voice interrupts the narrative, as it does in *Il maestro della betulla*. The only woman protagonist appears as the subject of Vermeer's portrait *Girl with a Turban*, which a well-known

Dutch art dealer sells to a rich Dane around 1658. The two male characters remain conspicuously oblivious to women in real life, although they adore the female image in the painting, because it is one upon which they can freely project their theories and emotions. Three other stories concern the degradation and oppression of historical figures in their private lives: a conversation between Mozart and his wife in his final hours; the story of the majorduomo of Carl V whose vendetta is to burn the memoirs the emperor had entrusted to him; and DaPonte's humiliation at the hands of the court musician Salieri. The last story, which is the only nonhistorical text, recounts the silent revenge of Karl Kollner, the protagonist who refuses to die after a totally incapacitating stroke and who consequently remains an embarrassment to his family. These narratives portray victims refusing to succumb easily to their fate. Morazzoni studies the revolt and vengeance of the small who, like the silent female on the cover and in the title story, now return to tell history as "her-story."

The viewpoint found in *Il treno russo, Silenzio a Milano, Il maestro della betulla,* and *La ragazza col turbante* allows women writers to move away from the traditional sphere of personal fictional writing, which represents the divided self in everyday reality, and from the overtly metanarrative nature of much theoretical, experimental discourse. Furthermore, the concept of a "feminine voice" shifts the debate concerning the function of women's literature away from recent controversies concerning language and form. This questioning voice seems to return women's writing to the marginal, genderless, critical space that Castelli describes as the rightful place for all subversive writings. The main difference, however, is that it is specifically formed and informed by themes, motifs, and analyses from all varieties of recent women's writing. While unmasking hierarchical thinking and advocating changes in oppressive practices, the fiction of Ortese, Volpi, and Morazzoni continues to reflect upon the female experience, which is now defined as the struggle with subjugation on all levels.

In addition to a feminist analysis of unjust abuses of power in a critically representational mode, Morazzoni's and Volpi's historical fictions continue to write the story of women's experience in a patriarchal mainstream that they hope to transform. This is not to say that historical prose will or should dominate women's literary efforts in the future. If any emerging women's tradition is to avoid becoming the one-sided and oppressive voice it seeks to question and displace, it will need the continued input of themes and ideas derived from all forms of writing that continue to analyze in various ways the innovations and permutations caused by the feminist cultural revolu-

tion in progress. In this process, women's literature must constantly redefine its relationship to both the mainstream and the margins, since works
by women now contribute to the creation of both spaces.

NOTES

1. Biancamaria Frabotta, *La letteratura al femminile* (Literature in the feminine) (Bari: De
Donato, 1981), pp. 5–6. See also Elisabetta Rasy's critique of Elaine Showalter's work, *A
Literature of Their Own* (Princeton: Princeton University Press, 1977). Showalter concludes
that the genre that best expresses women's writing is the Gothic novel. Rasy finds this idea
fascinating but too personal and uses it as an example of the dangers of treating women's
writing as a separate category (Rasy, *Le donne e la letteratura* [Women and literature] [Rome:
Riuniti, 1984], pp. 32–34). Because most of the texts in this article have not been translated, all
translations from the Italian are mine.

2. See Walter Pedullà who states that feminism, the major political and cultural movement of
the seventies, was born from an ideology of marginality ("La realtà romanzesca dell'emarginazione" [Fictional realism in marginal literature], in *La letteratura emarginata* [Marginal
literature], ed. Walter Pedullà [Rome: Lerici, 1978]), esp. pp. 76–86.

3. See Anna Nozzoli, "La donna e il romanzo negli anni ottanta" (Woman and the novel in
the eighties), in *Empoli: Rivista di vita cittadina: Proceedings of the Conference on "La donna nella
letteratura italiana del '900,* ed. Sergio Gensini (Empoli: Il Comune di Empoli, 1983), pp. 45–57.

4. Lucia Chiavola Birnbaum, *Liberazione della Donna: Feminism in Italy* (Middletown,
Conn.: Wesleyan University Press, 1986), p. 204.

5. Adele Cambria, "Il neo-femminismo in letteratura: Dove sono le ammazzoni?" in *Firmato
donna: Una donna un secolo* (Signed woman: A woman a century), ed. Sandra Petrignani
(Rome: Il Ventaglio, 1986), p. 141. Further references to this edition will appear in parentheses
following the quotation.

6. Frabotta proposes that Italian authors have received, until recently, more inspiration from
these French critics than from their Anglo-Saxon counterparts (*La letteratura al femminile,*
p. 11). The reprinting in 1981 of Kate Millett's *Sexual Politics (La politica del sesso)* by Rizzoli and
the translation of Ellen Moers's *Literary Women: The Great Writers (Grandi scrittrici, grandi
letterate* (Milan: Edizioni di Communità, 1979) are two examples of interest in American
feminist criticism.

7. Julie Kristeva, "Premessa," to Elisabetta Rasy, *La lingua della nutrice* (Rome: Edizioni
delle donne, 1978), pp. 9–10. Kristeva again indicates Italy is a key participant in her new
dimension of feminism in an essay published a year later, "Le temps des femmes," in *Cahiers de
recherche des sciences de textes et de documents,* no. 5 (1979), trans. Alice Jardine and Henry Blake
as "Women's Time," *Signs* 7 (1981): 20.

8. Rosalind Jones, "Julie Kristeva on Femininity: The Limits of a Semiotic Politics,"
Feminist Review 18 (1984): 63.

9. Ibid., pp. 64–65.

10. Nozzoli, "La donna e il romanzo," pp. 47–48.

11. Nancy Miller concludes *The Heroine's Texts: Readings in the French and English Novel,
1722–1782* (New York: Columbia University Press, 1980) by saying that until we experience
great cultural change, women may have to stop reading novels (158). Myra Jehlen, in "Archimedes and the Paradox of Feminist Criticism," *Signs* 6, no. 4 (1981), argues that since the novel
has its base in the social structures of patriarchal society, it can be of little use to the feminist
need for change (600).

12. Furthermore, since many of their writings until now have searched for traces of the "feminine" in patriarchal language, their theoretical essays deal almost exclusively with male authors, especially James Joyce, some surrealists, and Mallarmé. Two exceptions are French writer Marguerite Duras and the Brazilian Clarice Lispector. In a recent article "The Pain of Sorrow," *PMLA* 20, no. 2 (1987): 138–52, Kristeva discusses both authors as part of "a literature of maladies."

13. Nozzoli, "La donna e il romanzo," p. 54.

14. Giovanna Borrodori, "'Weak Thought' and the 'Aesthetics of Quotationism': The Italian Shift from Deconstruction," *University of Wisconsin-Milwaukee Center for Twentieth Century Studies,* Working Paper no. 6 (1988): 1–12.

15. Aldo Gargagni, "La voce femminile," *Alfabeta* 64 (1984): p. 16.

16. In *Letteratura al femminile,* pp. 135–38, Frabotta criticizes the many maternal metaphors found in Cixous's writing and argues against Irigaray's notion that women cannot represent themselves in the symbolic order from which they have been traditionally excluded. This critique does not suggest that these writers have no influence at all in Italy, as we shall see. Italian feminists, however, remain skeptical of theories that derive from a lack or an absence. Thus, Kristeva's theory of marginality defined as a position that needs to redefine itself constantly in relationship to the changing mainstream and Wittig's experiments with gender-less literature originally found more followers. For a brief but pithy discussion of Kristeva's theory of marginality, see Toril Moi, *Sexual/Textual Politics* (New York: Methuen, 1985), pp. 163–67.

17. Silvia Castelli, "Miti, forme e modelli della narrativa nuova," in Pedullà, *La letteratura emarginata,* p. 122.

18. Ibid., pp. 125, 133.

19. Frabotta, *Letteratura al femminile,* pp. 137–38.

20. Pedullà, "La realtà romanzesca dell'emarginazione," p. 79.

21. Jones, "Julie Kristeva on Femininity," pp. 66–68.

22. The confessional novels of Maraini's picaresque thief Teresa in *Memorie di una ladra* (Memoirs of a thief) (Rome: Bompiani, 1974) and Guiducci's housewife and prostitute in *Due donne da buttare (Two disposable women)* (Milan: Rizzoli, 1976) were written as part of a campaign to dispel the myth that women could fulfill themselves outside the marketplace that determined their worth(lessness). See also Birnbaum's discussion in *Liberazione della Donna,* esp. pp. 149–53.

23. Birnbaum, *Liberazione della Donna,* pp. 105–7. Birnbaum comments: "Sources for this concept may be closer to ultimate beliefs than to social analysis: individual conversion must precede social transformation." This echoes many critics who find Kristeva's semiotic politics too individualistic and anarchistic. See Moi, *Sexual/Textual Politics,* pp. 170–79.

24. Elisabetta Rasy, "Corteo di notte," in *Lingua della nutrice,* p. 17. This essay had appeared in French as "Cortège de nuit" in the Winter 1977 issue of *Tel Quel* on feminism, edited by Kristeva.

25. Frabotta, *Letteratura al femminile,* p. 148.

26. Frabotta's criticism of Kristeva's theory of marginality reflects the same preoccupation: "The only commitment possible then is one of individual dissidence through theoretical and ethic considerations worked out in isolation and in exile" (Ibid., p. 153).

27. This is not to say that all French feminist writing only examines repression in language. For a more detailed account of postmodern theories of language and feminism, see Alice Jardine, *Gynesis: Configurations of Women and Modernity* (Ithaca, N.Y.: Cornell University Press, 1985).

28. Hélène Cixous, "Le sexe ou la tête," *Cahiers du Grif,* no. 13 (1976): 5–15, trans. Annette

Kuhn as "Castration or Decapitation," *Signs* 7, no. 1 (1981): 36–55. This idea had appeared in Cixous's writings previous to that date as well.

29. Ginevra Bompiani, *Mondanità* (Milan: La Tartaruga, 1980), pp. 13–14, 101. For a more detailed account of *Mondanità* as a *Bildungsroman,* see Carol M. Lazzaro-Weis, "The Female *Bildungsroman:* Calling It into Question," *NWSA* 2, no. 1 (1989), forthcoming.

30. Cixous, "Castration or Decapitation," pp. 46–50.

31. Maria Schiavo, "Diario di un seduttore," *Macellum: Storia violentata e romanzata di donne di mercato* (Milan: La Tartaruga, 1979), p. 27. Further citations to *Macellum* will be given parenthetically in the text. For a more detailed discussion of Macellum and Maraini's *Treno per Helsinki,* see Carol M. Lazzaro-Weis, "The Subject's Seduction: The Experience of Don Juan in Italian Feminist Fiction," *Annali d'italianistica* (1989), forthcoming.

32. Rosa Rossi, *L'ultimo capitolo* (Rome: Lucarini, 1984). Besides writing several fictional works, Rossi has also written a theoretical treatise on the relationship of women to language, *Le parole delle donne* (Rome: Riuniti, 1978).

33. Armanda Guiducci, *Donna e serva* (Milan: Rizzoli, 1983), p. 61. Guiducci's other novel is *A testa in giù* (Milan: Rizzoli, 1984). Further citations to *A testa in giù* will be given parenthetically in the text.

34. Dacia Maraini, "Quale cultura per la donna," in *Donna, cultura e tradizione,* ed. Pia Bruzzichelli and Maria Luisa Algini (Milan: Mazzotta, 1976), pp. 64–65.

35. Jane Gallop, "Quand nos lèvres s'écrivent: Irigaray's Body Politic," *Romanic Review* 84, no. 1 (1983): 83. Gallop's theories are very influenced by French theoreticians whose distrust of forms of traditional representation she echoes.

36. Frabotta, *Letteratura al femminile,* p. 148.

37. Joanna Frye, *Living Stories, Telling Lives* (Ann Arbor: University of Michigan Press, 1986), pp. 1–12, 192–94.

38. Elena Belotti, "Giovane Scrittore, Sì, Giovane Scrittrice, No," in Petrignani, *Firmato donna. Una Donna un secolo,* p. 151.

39. I am following here Northrop Frye's definition of an anatomy as a work that gives a comprehensive survey of an intellectual attitude. See *Anatomy of Criticism* (Princeton: Princeton University Press, 1957), pp. 311–12.

40. Fabrizia Ramondino's *Althénopis* (Turin: Einaudi, 1981) is praised by many critics for its beautiful prose style and the work has been translated into more than twelve languages. The English translation, *Althénopis* is by Michael Sullivan (Manchester: Carcanet, 1988). Marisa DiMaggio's *C'era una volta un re . . .* (Rome: Il Ventaglio, 1985) received the Premio Donna Città di Roma award and the Premio Viareggio in 1985. Daria Martelli received the Premio letterario Noi Donne in 1983 for *Chi perde la sua vita* (Rome: Transmedia, 1981). *Althénopis* is analyzed in detail in Lazzaro-Weis, "The Female *Bildungsroman.*"

41. In Ramondino's more recently published collection of tales, *Storie di patio* (Turin: Einaudi, 1984), the child's narrating viewpoint is again privileged.

42. DiMaggio, *C'era una volta un re,* p. 49.

43. In one chapter, the narrator relates how she learned to downgrade the "feminine": in a high school exposé she must repeat the judgment of nineteenth-century critic DeSanctis on the art of the 1700s, which he classifies as "corrupt, feminine and vulgar." It was Parini, DeSanctis continues, who brought "virility" to art in Italy (*Chi perde la sua vita,* pp. 119–20).

44. Anna Nozzoli defines in this way the goal of feminine writing in her analysis of Francesca SanVitale's novel *Madre e figlia* (1981), the story of two women entrapped in a traditional symbiotic relationship. See "La donna e il romanzo," p. 53.

45. Emma Rossi, *Pensione paradiso (già Porospenia)* (Ancona: Il Lavoro Editoriale, 1984). The symbolism of the name Porospenia is explained through a translation from Plato that concludes the narrative. Poros, or Craftiness in Greek, and Penia, Poverty, are the parents of

Eros, conceived the same day as Aphrodite and thus destined to become her permanent companion. For this reason, explains Plato, love is not only delicate and beautiful but has many contradictory faces.

46. Gaia de Beaumont, *Bella* (Milan: Frassinelli, 1985). De Beaumont's previous *Venditore d'inchiostro* (The ink seller) (Milan: Frassinelli, 1983), the story of an elderly and eccentric French painter's idealized love for a young girl to whom he writes anonymous love letters, mocks many male projections and various love myths.

47. Paola Masino, *Nascita e morte della massaia* (Milan: La Tartaruga, 1982), p. 8. This work was slated for publication in 1938 after certain chapters parodying the Fascist regime were censured. It was never published, however, due to the Allied bombing of the editorial house where it had been accepted. Paola Masino claims to have written this book in response to the question of her former lover, writer Massimo Bontempelli, who wanted to know how a nice girl like her had become a cleanliness fanatic. Masino, a prolific writer and librettist, edited Bontempelli's works in 1960 after his death.

48. Ortese was born in Rome in 1914. Among her many successful books are *Il mare non bagna Napoli* (The sea does not wash Naples), which won the Premio Viareggio in 1953, and *Iguana* (1965). These and other novels by Ortese have been translated into several languages. The translator Henry Martin is currently preparing two volumes of selected stories by Ortese to be published in translation by McPherson and Company.

Bibliography

GENERAL

Bakhtin, M. M. *The Dialogic Imagination*. Austin: University of Texas Press, 1981.

Barrett, Michele. *Women's Oppression Today: Problems in Marxist Feminist Analysis*. London: Villiers Publications, 1980.

Barthes, Roland. "Introduction à l'analyse structurale des récits." *Communications* 8 (1966). Translated by Lionel Duisit as "An Introduction to the Structural Analysis of Narrative." *New Literary History* 6 (1974–75): 237–72.

————. *S/Z*. Translated by Richard Miller. New York: Hill and Wang, 1974.

————. *Le Texte et l'image*. Paris: Edition Paris Musées, 1986.

Benveniste, Emile. *Problèmes de linguistique générale*. Translated by M. E. Meek as *Problems of General Linguistics*. Coral Gables: University of Miami Press, 1971.

Bianchini, Angela. *Voce donna*. Milan: Bompiani, 1979.

Birnbaum, Lucia Chiavola. *Liberazione della Donna: Feminism in Italy*. Middletown, Conn.: Wesleyan University Press, 1986.

Blelloch, Paola. *Quel mondo dei guanti e delle stoffe*. Verona: Essedue Edizioni, 1987.

Borrodori, Giovanna. "'Weak Thought' and the 'Aesthetics of Quotationism': The Italian Shift from Deconstruction." *University of Wisconsin-Milwaukee Center for Twentieth Century Studies*. Working Paper no. 6 (1988): 1–12.

Caesar, Michael, and Hainsworth, Peter, eds. *Writers and Society in Contemporary Italy*. Warwickshire: Berg, 1986.

Carrano, Patrizia. *Le signore grandi firme*. Rimini: Guaraldi, 1978. This work contains interviews with ten journalists: Natalia Aspesi, Camilla Cederna, Oriana Fallaci, Brunella Gasperini, Miriam Mafai, Anna Maria Mori, Gabriella Poli, Carla Ravaioli, Lidia Ravera, and Lietta Tornabuoni.

Castelli, Silvia. "Miti, forme, e modelli della narrativa nuova." In *La letteratura emarginata,* edited by Walter Pedullà, pp. 113–203. Rome: Lerici, 1978.

Cecchi, Emilio, and Natalino Sapegno, eds. *Storia della letteratura italiana: Il Novecento*. Vol. 9. Milan: Garzanti, 1969.

————. *Storia della letteratura italiana del Novecento*. Milan: Mondadori, 1972.

Chapman, Charlotte Gower. *Milocca: A Sicilian Village*. Cambridge, Mass.: Schenkman, 1971.

Chesler, Phyllis. *Women and Madness*. New York: Avon, 1973.

Cixous, Hélène. "Le sexe ou la tête." *Cahiers du Grif,* no. 13 (1976): 5–15. Translated by Annette Kuhn as "Castration or Decapitation." *Signs* 7, no. 1 (1981): 36–55.

Colaiacomo, Paola, et al. *Come nello specchio: Saggi sulla figurazione del femminile.* Turin: La Rosa, 1981.

Comerci, Mariella. *I profili della luna.* Rome: Bulzoni, 1982.

Contini, Gianfranco. *Letteratura dell'Italia unita: 1861–1968.* Florence: Sansoni, 1968.

———. *La letteratura italiana Otto-Novecento.* Florence: Sansoni, 1974. Pp. 352–61.

Cornelison, Ann. *Women of the Shadows.* New York: Vintage Books, 1977.

Costa-Zalessow, Natalia, ed. *Scrittrici italiane dal XIII al XX secolo.* Ravenna: Longo Editore, 1982.

De Man, Paul. "Autobiography as De-facement." *MLN* 94 (1979): 920–23.

De Sanctis, Francesco. *History of Italian Literature.* Translated by Joan Redfern. New York: Barnes and Noble, 1968.

"Donne e letteratura." *Nuova DWF Donnawomanfemme,* no. 5 (1977): 3–152.

Durham, Carolyn A. "Patterns of Influence: Simone de Beauvoir and Marie Cardinal." *The French Review* 60, no. 3 (1987): 341–48.

Eakin, Paul John. *Fictions in Autobiography: Studies in the Art of Self-Invention.* Princeton: Princeton University Press, 1985.

Engels, Frederick. *The Origins of the Family, Private Property and the State.* 1884. New York: International Publishers, 1942.

Esslin, M. "Approaches to Reality." *The New Theater of Europe.* Vol. 4. New York: Dell, 1970.

Fernandez, Dominique. *Le roman italien et la crise de la conscience moderne.* Paris: Bernard Grasset, 1958. Translated as *Il romanzo italiano e la crisi della coscienza moderna.* Milan: Lerici, 1960.

Forti, Marco. *Prosatori e narratori nel Novecento italiano.* Milan: Mursia, 1984.

Frabotta, Biancamaria. *La letteratura al femminile.* Bari: De Donato, 1981.

———, ed. *Femminismo e lotta di classe.* Rome: Savelli, 1975.

Freud, Sigmund. *The Complete Psychological Works of Sigmund Freud.* Translated and edited by James Strachey. London: The Hogarth Press & Institute of Psychoanalysis. Vol. 22: "Femininity," pp. 112–35; Vol. 21: "Female Sexuality," pp. 225–43.

———. *On Dreams.* New York: Norton, 1952.

Frye, Joanna. *Living Stories, Telling Lives.* Ann Arbor: University of Michigan Press, 1986.

Frye, Northrop. *Anatomy of Criticism.* Princeton: Princeton University Press, 1957.

Gallop, Jane. "Quand nos lèvres s'écrivent: Irigaray's Body Politic." *Romanic Review* 84, no. 1 (1983): 77–83.

Gargagni, Aldo. "La voce femminile." *Alfabeta* 64 (1984): 16.

Gastaldi, Mario, and Carmen Scano, eds. *Dizionario delle scrittrici italiane contemporanee.* Milan: Gastaldi, 1957.

Gatt-Rutter, John. *Writers and Politics in Modern Italy.* New York: Holmes and Meier, 1978.

Getto, Giovanni, and Gianni Solari. *Il Novecento: Cultura, letteratura, società.* Milan: Minerva Italica, 1980.

Gubar, Susan. "'The Blank Page' and the Issues of Female Creativity." In *Writing and Sexual Difference,* edited by Elizabeth Abel, pp. 73–94. Chicago: University of Chicago Press, 1982.

Heilbrun, Carolyn G. *Reinventing Womanhood.* New York: W. W. Norton, 1979.

Iser, Wolfgang. *The Implied Reader: Patterns of Communication in Prose Fiction from Bunyan to Beckett.* Baltimore: Johns Hopkins University Press, 1974.

Jardine, Alice. *Gynesis: Configurations of Women and Modernity.* Cornell: Cornell University Press, 1985.

Jehlen, Myra. "Archimedes and the Paradox of Feminist Criticism." *Signs* 6, no. 4 (1981): 575–601.

Jones, Ann Rosalind. "Inscribing Femininity: French Theories of the Feminine." In *Making a Difference: Feminist Literary Criticism,* edited by Gayle Green and Coppélia Kahn, pp. 80–112. New York: Methuen, 1985.

———. "Julie Kristeva on Femininity: The Limits of a Semiotic Poetics." *Feminist Review* 18 (1984): 56–73.

———. "Writing the Body: Toward an Understanding of *L'Ecriture Féminine.*" *Feminist Studies* 7 (1981): 2, 247–63.

Krichmar, Albert, ed. *Women's Movement in the Seventies: An International English-Language Bibliography.* Metuchen, N.J.: Scarecrow Press, 1977.

Kristeva, Julie. *Les chinoises.* Paris: Editions des femmes, 1974.

———. "The Pain of Sorrow." *PMLA* 20, no. 2 (1987): 138–52.

———. "Premessa" to Elisabetta Rasy, *La lingua della nutrice.* Rome: Edizioni delle donne, 1978.

———. "Le temps des femmes." *Cahiers de recherche des sciences de textes et de documents,* no. 5 (1979): 5–19. Translated by Alice Jardine and Henry Blake as "Women's Time." *Signs* 7 (1981): 13–35.

Lacan, Jacques. "Subversion du sujet et dialectique du désir dans l'inconscient Freudien." *Ecrits.* Translated by Alan Sheridan as "The Mirror Stage as Formative Function of the I." *Ecrits.* London: Tavistock, 1977, pp. 1–7.

Lauretis, Teresa de. "Feminist Studies/Critical Studies: Issues, Terms, and Contexts." *Feminist Studies/Critical Studies,* edited by Teresa de Lauretis. Bloomington: Indiana University Press, 1986.

Lawton, Benjamin R. Review of *The Modern Italian Novel from Pea to Moravia,* by Sergio Pacifici, and of *Writers and Politics in Modern Italy,* by John Gatt-Rutter. *Modern Fiction Studies* 25 (1979/80): 701–3.

MacKinnon, Catherine. "Feminism, Marxism, Method, and the State: An Agenda for Theory." *Signs* 7, no. 3 (1983): 515–44.

Mehlman, Jeffrey. *A Structural Study of Autobiography.* Ithaca: Cornell University Press, 1974.

Mercier, Michel. *Le roman féminin.* Vendôme: Presses Universitaires de France, 1976. Translated as *Il romanzo al femminile.* Milan: Il Saggiatore, 1979.

Mill, John Stuart. *The Subjection of Women.* 1869. Cambridge: M.I.T. Press, 1970.

Miller, Nancy. *The Heroine's Text: Readings in the French and English Novel, 1722–1782.* New York: Columbia University Press, 1980.

Millett, Kate. *Sexual Politics.* New York: Doubleday, 1970. Translated as *La politica del sesso.* Milan: Rizzoli, 1981.

Moeurs, Ellen. *Literary Women: The Great Writers.* New York: Doubleday, 1976. Translated as *Grandi scrittrici, grandi letterate.* Milan: La Communità, 1979.

Moi, Torril. *Sexual/Textual Politics.* New York: Methuen, 1985.

Montefoschi, Silvia. "Ruolo materno e identità personale." *Nuova DWF Donnawomanfemme,* nos. 6–7 (1978): 143–74.

Morino, Alba, ed. *Diario di una donna* by Sibilla Aleramo. Milan: Feltrinelli, 1978.

Murphy, James E. "The New Journalism: A Critical Perspective." In *Journalism Monographs,* no. 34 (1974): 1–38, edited by Bruce H. Westley.

Nabokov, Vladimir. *Speak Memory: An Autobiography Revisited.* New York: Putnam, 1966.

Nozzoli, Anna. "La donna e il romanzo negli anni ottanta." In *Empoli: Rivista di vita cittadina: Proceedings of the Conference on "La donna nella letteratura italiana del '900,"* edited by Sergio Gensini, pp. 45–57. Empoli: Il Comune di Empoli, 1983.

———. "Sul romanzo femminista degli anni settanta." *Nuova DWF Donnawomanfemme,* no. 5 (1977): 55–74.

———. *Tabù e coscienza: La condizione femminile nella letteratura italiana del Novecento.* Florence: La Nuova Italia, 1978. This work contains essays on writers from the early part of this century, novelists associated with futurism, and feminist writers of the 1970s, as well as specific analyses of Gianna Manzini, Anna Banti, Fausta Cialente, and Elsa Morante.

Olney, James. "Autobiography and the Cultural Moment: A Thematic, Historic and Bibliographical Introduction." In *Autobiography: Essays Theoretical and Critical,* edited by James Olney. Princeton: Princeton University Press, 1980.

Pacifici, Sergio. *A Guide to Contemporary Italian Literature: From Futurism to Neorealism.* Carbondale: Southern Illinois University Press, 1962.

———. *The Modern Italian Novel from Capuana to Tozzi.* Carbondale: Southern Illinois University Press, 1973.

———. *The Modern Italian Novel from Manzoni to Svevo.* Carbondale: Southern Illinois University Press, 1967.

———. *The Modern Italian Novel from Pea to Moravia.* Carbondale: Southern Illinois University Press, 1979.

———, ed. *From "Verismo" to Experimentalism: Essays on the Modern Italian Novel.* Bloomington: Indiana University Press, 1969.

Pampaloni, Geno. "La nuova letteratura." In *Storia della letteratura italiana: Il Novecento,* edited by Emilio Cecchi and Natalino Sapegno, 9: 749–879. Milan: Garzanti, 1969.

Paolini, Pier Francesco, ed. "Italian Writing Today." *The Literary Review* 28, no. 2 (1985): 181–328.

Parca, Gabriella. *I Sultani.* 1965. Milan: Rizzoli, 1977.

Pedullà, Walter. "La realtà romanzesca dell'emarginazione." In *La letteratura emarginata,* edited by Walter Pedullà, pp. 10–111. Rome: Lerici, 1978.

Peritore, G. A., ed. *Letteratura italiana: I contemporanei.* Vol. 3. Milan: Marzorati, 1970.

Persani, M. A., and N. De Giovanni. *Femminile a confronto.* Rome: Lacarta, 1984.

Petrignani, Sandra. *Le signore della scrittura.* Milan: La Tartaruga, 1984. This work contains interviews with Lalla Romano, Paola Masino, Alba De Cèspedes, Maria Bellonci, Laudomia Bonanni, Annamaria Ortese, Fausta Cialente, Livia De Stefani, Anna Banti, and Elsa Morante.

———, ed. *Firmato donna. Una donna un secolo.* Rome: Il Ventaglio, 1986. This collection contains such essays as Elena Belotti's "Giovane Scrittore, Sì, Giovane Scrittrice, No" and Adele Cambria's "Neo-feminismo in letteratura. Dove sono le ammazzoni?" which study the relationship between women writers and key problems in this century. In addition, it deals with authors from earlier periods of history: Gaspara Stampa, Angelica Tarabotti, Elisabetta Caminer, and Caterina Percoti.

Piccioni, Leone. *La narrativa italiana tra romanzo e racconti.* Milan: Mondadori, 1959.

Pratt, Annis. *Archetypal Patterns in Women's Fiction.* Bloomington: Indiana University Press, 1981.

Proust, Marcel. *By Way of St. Beuve.* Translated by Sylvia Townsend Warner. London: Hogarth Press, 1984.

———. *On Art and Literature.* Translated by Sylvia Townsend Warner. New York: Meridian Books, 1958.

Resnick, Margery, and Isabelle de Courtivron. *Women Writers in Translation: An Annotated Bibliography, 1945–1982.* New York: Garland Publishing, 1984.

Ruffili, Paolo. "La scrittura al femminile." *Il lettore di provincia* 49–50 (1982): 82–87.

Showalter, Elaine. "Feminist Criticism in the Wilderness." In *Writing and Sexual Difference,* edited by Elizabeth Abel, pp. 9–36. Chicago: University of Chicago Press, 1982.

———. *A Literature of Their Own.* Princeton: Princeton University Press, 1977.

Spagnoletti, Rosalba, ed. *I Movimenti femministi in Italia.* Rome: Savelli, 1971.

Squarotti, Giorgio Barberi. *Poesia e narrativa del secondo Novecento.* Milan: Mursia, 1978.

"Sulla scrittura. Percorsi critici sui testi letterari del XVI Secolo." *Nuova DWF Donnawomanfemme,* no. 25/26 (1985): 5–104.

Testaferri, Ada, ed. *Donna: Women in Italian Culture.* University of Toronto Italian Studies, 7. Ottawa: Dovehouse, 1989.

"L'Una e l'altro: Rappresentazione e autorappresentazione del femminile." Supplement to *Nuova DWF Donnawomanfemme* 16 (1981).

Warner, Marina. *Alone of All Her Sex: The Myth and the Cult of the Virgin Mary.* New York: Knopf, 1976.

Whitfield, John H. *A Short History of Italian Literature.* Baltimore: Penguin Books, 1960.

Wilkins, Ernest Hatch. *A History of Italian Literature.* Cambridge: Harvard University Press, 1974.

Wittig, Monique. *Le corps lesbien.* Paris: Editions des Femmes, 1973.

———. "The Straight Mind." *Feminist Issues* 1, no. 1 (1980): 103–10.

Wolfe, Tom. "The New Journalism." *Bulletin of the American Society of Newspaper Editors,* September 1970, pp. 17–23.

———. "Why They Aren't Writing the Great American Novel Anymore." *Esquire,* December 1972, pp. 152–59.

Woolf, Virginia. *To the Lighthouse.* 1927. New York: Harcourt, Brace and World, 1955.
———. *A Room of One's Own.* 1928. Harmondsworth: Penguin Books, 1972.
Zaccaria, Paola. "Italy: A Mortifying Thirst for Living." In *Sisterhood Is Global: The International Women's Movement Anthology,* edited by Robin Morgan, pp. 365–75. New York: Doubleday/Anchor Press, 1984.

BIBLIOGRAPHIES FOR INDIVIDUAL WRITERS

ANNA BANTI

Only *Artemisia* has been translated into English.

Banti, Anna. *Allarme sul lago.* Milan: Mondadori, 1954.
———. *Artemisia.* 1947. Milan: Mondadori, 1974. Translated by Shirley D'Ardia Carracciolo as *Artemisia.* Omaha: University of Nebraska Press, 1988.
———. *Il bastardo.* Florence: Sansoni, 1953.
———. *La camicia bruciata.* Milan: Mondadori, 1973.
———. *Campi Elisi.* Milan: Mondadori, 1963.
———. *La casa piccola.* Milan: Mondadori, 1961.
———. *Il coraggio delle donne.* 1940. Milan: La Tartaruga, 1983.
———. *Corte Savella.* Milan: Mondadori, 1960.
———. *Da un paese vicino.* Milan: Mondadori, 1975.
———. *Discorsi sulle arti e sui mestieri.* Florence: Sansoni, 1981.
———. *Le donne muoiono.* Milan: Mondadori, 1951.
———. *Due storie.* Milan: Mondadori, 1969.
———. *Fra Angelico.* Milan: Garzanti, 1953.
———. *Giovanni da San Giovanni: Pittore della contraddizione.* Florence: Sansoni, 1977.
———. *Un grido lacerante.* Milan: Rizzoli, 1981.
———. *Itinerario di Paolina.* Rome: Augustea, 1937.
———. *Je vous écris d'un pays lointain.* Milan: Mondadori, 1971.
———. *Lorenzo Lotto.* Florence: Sansoni, 1953.
———. *Matilde Serao.* Turin: UTET, 1965.
———. *La monaca di Sciangai.* 1957. Milan: Mondadori, 1963.
———. *Le monache cantano.* Rome: Tumminelli, 1943.
———. *Le mosche d'oro.* Milan: Mondadori, 1962.
———. *Noi credevamo.* Milan: Mondadori, 1967.
———. *Opinioni.* Milan: Il Saggiatore, 1961.
———. *Quando anche le donne si misero a dipingere.* Milan: La Tartaruga, 1982.
———. *Rivelazione di Lorenzo Lotto.* Florence: Sansoni, 1981.
Biagini, Enza. *Anna Banti.* Milan: Mursia, 1978.
Bissell, Ward. "Artemisia Gentileschi—A New Documented Chronology." *Art Bulletin* 50, no. 2 (1968): 153–68.
Bolletino d'arte (1916), pp. 46–55.
Bottari, Giovanni Gaetano, and Stefan Ticozzi. *Raccolta di lettere sulla pittura, scultura ed architettura scritta da' più celebri personaggi dai secoli XV, XVI,*

XVII. 1822. Hildesheim and New York: Georg Olms Verlag, 1976. Vol. 1, pp. 349–55.

Criño, Anna Maria. "More Letters from Orazio and Artemisia Gentileschi." *The Burlington Magazine* 102 (1960): 264–65. In Italian.

Garrard, Mary D. "Artemisia and Susannah." In *Feminism and Art History: Questioning the Litany,* edited by Norma Broude and Mary D. Garrard, pp. 147–73. New York: Harper and Row, 1982.

———. "Artemisia Gentileschi: The Artist's Autograph in Letters and Paintings." In *The Female Autograph,* edited by Donna C. Stanton and Jeanine Parisier Plottel, pp. 91–106. New York: New York Literary Forum, 1984.

———. *Artemisia Gentileschi: The Image of the Female Hero in Italian Baroque Art.* Princeton: Princeton University Press, 1989.

———. "Artemisia Gentileschi's Self-Portrait as the Allegory of Painting." *Art Bulletin* 62, no. 1 (1980): 97–112.

Greer, Germaine. "The Magnificent Exception." In *The Obstacle Race: The Fortunes of Women Painters and Their Work,* pp. 189–208. London: Picador, 1981.

Harris, Ann Sutherland, and Linda Nochlin. "Artemisia Gentileschi." In *Women Artists: 1550–1950,* pp. 118–25. New York: Knopf, 1981.

Levey, Michael. "Notes on the Royal Collection—II: Artemisia Gentileschi's 'Self-Portrait' at Hampton Court." *The Burlington Magazine* 104 (1962): 79–80.

Livi, Grazia. Introduzione to *Il coraggio delle donne,* pp. 7–12. Milan: La Tartaruga, 1983.

Longhi, Roberto. "Gentileschi padre e figlia." *L'Arte* 19 (1916): 245–314. Reprinted in *Scritti Giovanili: 1912–1922,* vol. 1, pp. 219–83. *Opere Complete di Roberto Longhi.* Florence: Sansoni, 1961.

Menzio, Eva, ed. *Artemisia Gentileschi/Agostino Tassi: Atti di un processo per stupro.* Milan: Editioni delle Donne, 1981.

Parker, Rozsika, and Griselda Pollock. *Old Mistresses: Women, Art and Ideology.* London and Henley: Routledge and Kegan Paul, 1981. See esp. pp. 14–27.

Wittkower, Rudolf, and Margot Wittkower. "Agostino Tassi—The Seducer of Artemisia Gentileschi." In *Born Under Saturn,* pp. 162–65. London: Weidenfeld and Nicholson, 1963.

CAMILLA CEDERNA

None of Camilla Cederna's work has been translated into English.

Arbasino, Alberto. "Letter from Italy." *Vogue,* 1 March 1972, pp. 56–58.

Cederna, Camilla. *Casa nostra: Viaggio nei misteri d'Italia.* Milan: Mondadori, 1983.

———. *De gustibus.* Milan: Mondadori, 1986.

———. *Fellini 8½.* Bologna: Cappelli, 1963.

———. *Giovanni Leone: La carriera di un presidente.* Milan: Feltrinelli, 1978.

———. *Il lato debole: Diario italiano 1956–1976.* 3 vols. Milan: Bompiani, 1977.

———. *Maria Callas.* Milan: Longanesi, 1968.

———. *Milano in guerra.* Milan: Feltrinelli, 1979.

———. *Il mondo di Camilla.* Milan: Feltrinelli, 1980.

226   Bibliography

———. *Noi siamo le signore*. Milan: Longanesi, 1958.

———. *Nostro Italia del miracolo*. Milan: Mondadori, 1980.

———. *Le pervestite*. Genoa: Immordino, 1968.

———. *Pinelli: Una finestra sulla strage*. Milan: Feltrinelli, 1971.

———. *Signore e signori*. Milan: Longanesi, 1963.

———. *Sparare a vista: Come la polizia del regime DC mantiene l'ordine pubblico*. Milan: Feltrinelli, 1975.

———. *Vicino e distante*. Milan: Mondadori, 1984.

———. *La voce dei padroni*. Milan: Longanesi, 1962.

Conti Bertini, Lucia. "Il meglio di Camilla." *Il Ponte* 38, no. 4 (1982): 415–16.

Ronconi, Enzo, ed. "Camilla Cederna." *Dizionario della letteratura italiana contemporanea*. 2 vols. Florence: Vallecchi, 1973. 1: 215.

FAUSTA CIALENTE

Only *Ballata levantina* has been translated into English.

Cecchi, Emilio. Prefazione to *Cortile a Cleopatra* by Fausta Cialente. Milan: Feltrinelli, 1962.

Cialente, Fausta. *Ballata levantina*. Milan: Feltrinelli, 1961. Translated by Isabelle Quigly as *The Levantines*. Boston: Houghton Mifflin, 1963.

———. *Cortile a Cleopatra*. 1936. Florence: Sansoni, 1953.

———. *Interno con figure*. Rome: Riuniti, 1976.

———. *Un inverno freddissimo*. Milan: Feltrinelli, 1966.

———. *Natalia*. 1929. Milan: Mondadori, 1982.

———. *Pamela o la bell'estate*. Milan: Feltrinelli, 1962.

———. *Le quattro ragazze Wieselberger*. Milan: Mondadori, 1976.

———. *Il vento sulla sabbia*. Milan: Mondadori, 1972.

———, trans. *Piccole donne* by Louisa M. Alcott (*Little Women*). Florence: Marzocco, , 1976.

———, trans. *Le piccole donne crescono*, by Louisa M. Alcott (*Little Women*). Florence: Marzocco, 1977.

Clementelli, Elena. "Fausta Cialente." *I Contemporanei*. Milan: Marzorati, 1974. 4:354–63.

ORIANA FALLACI

All of Oriana Fallaci's major works have been translated into English.

Arico, Santo L. "Breaking the Ice: An In-Depth Look at Oriana Fallaci's Interview Techniques." *Journalism Quarterly* 63, no. 3 (1886): 587–93.

———. "Oriana Fallaci's Discovery of Truth in *Niente e così sia*." *European Studies Journal* 3, no. 2 (1986): 11–23.

Fallaci, Oriana. *Gli antipatici*. Milan: Rizzoli, 1963. Translated by Pamela Swinglehurst as *The Egotists*. Chicago: H. Regnery, 1968.

———. *Intervista con la storia*. Milan: Rizzoli, 1974. Translated by John Shepley as *Interview with History*. New York: Liveright, 1976.

————. *Lettera a un bambino mai nato*. Milan: Rizzoli, 1975. Translated by John Shepley as *Letter to an Unborn Child*. New York: Simon and Schuster, 1976.

————. *Niente e così sia*. Milan: Rizzoli, 1969. Translated by Isabelle Quigly as *Nothing and Amen*. New York: Doubleday, 1972.

————. *Penelope alla guerra*. Milan: Rizzoli, 1961. Translated by Pamela Swinglehurst as *Penelope at War*. London: Joseph, 1966.

————. *Quel giorno sulla luna*. Milan: Rizzoli, 1970.

————. *Se il sole muore*. Milan: Rizzoli, 1965. Translated by Pamela Swinglehurst, as *If the Sun Dies*. New York: Atheneum House, 1966.

————. *Il sesso inutile*. Milan: Rizzoli, 1961. Translated by Pamela Swinglehurst as *The Useless Sex*. New York: Horizon Press, 1964.

————. *Un uomo*. Milan: Rizzoli, 1979. Translated by William Weaver as *A Man*. New York: Simon and Schuster, 1980.

Picchione, Luciana Marchionne. Review of *Un uomo* by Oriana Fallaci. *Canadian Journal of Italian Studies* 4 (1979): 327–28.

NATALIA GINZBURG

With the exception of *Vita immaginaria* and all of her plays, Natalia Ginzburg's major works have been translated into English.

Amadori, M. G. "Natalia Ginzburg ultima crepuscolare." *La Fiera Letteraria* 28 (Jan. 1962): 55–60.

Balcini, R. "Questo mondo non mi piace." Interview with Natalia Ginzburg. *Panorama,* 3 May 1973, pp. 20–24.

Baldacci, L. "Con la Ginzburg alla ricerca delle parole perdute." *Epoca,* 28 April 1963, pp. 45–48.

Bergin, T. "A Light for Fools." *Saturday Review,* 21 September 1963, pp. 15–18.

Brophy, B. "Voices in the Evening." *New Statesmen,* 2 August 1963, pp. 31–35.

Bullock, A. "Uomini o topi? Vincitorie vinti nei *Cinque romanzi brevi* di Natalia Ginzburg." *Italica* 60, no. 1 (1983): 38–54.

Calvino, I. "Natalia Ginzburg e la possibilità del romanzo borghese." *L'Europa Letteraria* 31 (June–Aug. 1961): 12–20.

Castelli, F. "Natalia Ginzburg di fronte a Dio." *Civiltà Cattolica,* 18 September 1971, pp. 10–13.

Citati, P. "*Tutti i nostri ieri* di Natalia Ginzburg." *Belfagor* 46 (May 1953): 40–42.

Ginzburg, Natalia. *Borghesia*. Turin: Einaudi, 1977. Translated by Beryl Stockman as *Borghesia*. Manchester: Carcanet, 1988.

————. *Caro Michele*. 1973. Turin: Einaudi, 1985. Translated by Sheila Cudahy as *No Way*. New York: Harcourt Brace Jovanovich, 1974.

————. *Cinque romanzi brevi*. Turin: Einaudi, 1964.

————. *La città e la casa*. Turin: Einaudi, 1985. Translated by Dick Davis as *The City and the House*. New York: Seaver Books, 1986.

————. *È Stato Così*. Turin: Einaudi, 1947. Translated by Frances Frenaye as *The Dry Heart*. Garden City: Doubleday, 1949.

———. *Famiglia*. Turin: Einaudi, 1977. Translated by Beryl Stockman as *Family*. Manchester: Carcanet, 1988.

———. *La famiglia Manzoni*. Turin: Einaudi, 1983. Translated by Marie Evans as *The Manzoni Family*. New York: Seaver Books, 1987.

———. *Lessico famigliare*. Turin: Einaudi, 1963. Translated by D. M. Low as *Family Sayings*. 1967. Revised edition. Manchester: Carcanet, 1984.

———. *Mai devi domandarmi*. Milan: Garzanti, 1970. Translated by Isabel Quigly as *Never Must You Ask Me*. London: Joseph, 1973.

———. *Paese di mare ed altre commedie* (plays). Milan: Garzanti, 1973.

———. *Le piccole virtù*. Turin: Einaudi, 1962. Translated by Dick Davis as *The Little Virtues*. New York: Seaver Books, 1986.

———. *Sagittario*. Turin: Einaudi, 1957. Translated by Avril Bardoni as *Sagittarius*. New York: Seaver Books, 1987.

———. *La strada che va in città*. Turin: Einaudi, 1942. Translated by Frances Frenaye as *The Road to the City*. Garden City: Doubleday, 1949.

———. *Ti ho sposato per allegria ed altre commedie* (plays). Turin: Einaudi, 1967.

———. *Tutti i nostri ieri*. Turin: Einaudi, 1952. Translated by Angus Davidson as *All Our Yesterdays*. 1956. Manchester: Carcanet, 1985.

———. *Valentino*. Turin: Einaudi, 1951. Translated by Avril Bardoni as *Valentino*. New York: Seaver Books, 1987.

———. *Vita immaginaria*. Turin: Einaudi, 1974.

———. *Le voci della sera*. Turin: Einaudi, 1961. Translated by D. M. Low as *Voices in the Evening*. New York: Dutton, 1963.

Low, D. M. Preface to *Family Sayings*. London: Hogarth Press, 1967.

Mitgang, H. "Family Sayings." *New York Times,* 30 April 1967, p. 10.

Picchione, Luciana Marchionne. *Natalia Ginzburg*. 1967. Florence: Il Castoro, La Nuova Italia, 1978.

Soave Bowe, C. "The Narrative Strategy of Natalia Ginzburg," *Modern Language Review* 68 (1973): 42–47.

ARMANDA GUIDUCCI

None of Armanda Guiducci's work has been translated into English.

Guiducci, Armanda. *A colpi di silenzio*. Milan: Rizzoli, 1982.

———. *All'ombra di Kali*. Milan: Rizzoli, 1979.

———. *A testa in giù*. Milan: Rizzoli, 1984.

———. *Dallo zdanovismo allo strutturalismo*. Milan: Feltrinelli, 1967.

———. *La domenica della rivoluzione*. Milan: Lerici, 1961.

———. *Donna e serva*. Milan: Rizzoli, 1983.

———. *La donna non è gente*. Milan: Rizzoli, 1977.

———. *Due donne da buttare*. 1976. Milan: Rizzoli, 1980.

———. *La mela e il serpente*. Milan: Rizzoli, 1974.

———. *Il mito Pavese*. Florence: Vallecchi, 1967.

———. *Pavese*. Milan: Mursia, 1972.

———. *Poesie per un uomo*. Milan: Mondadori, 1965.

GINA LAGORIO

None of Gina Lagorio's work has been translated into English.

Bo, Carlo. "Attesa, festa e dolore." *Corriere d'Informazione,* 17 April 1977, p. 12.
Felici, Lucio. "Gina Lagorio." *Otto/Novecento* 2 (March–April 1980): 121–47.
Fenoglio, Beppe. *Opere.* 5 vols. Turin: Einaudi, 1978.
Folliero, Silvana. Review of *Approssimato per difetto. Il Ponte* 2–3 (Feb.–March 1973): 413–19.
Lagoria, Gina. *Angelo Barile e la poesia dell'intima transparenza.* Capua: L'airone, 1973.
———. *Approssimato per difetto.* 1971. Milan: Garzanti, 1981.
———. *Attila re degli Unni:* Florence: Sansoni, 1964.
———. *Beppe Fenoglio.* Florence: La Nuova Italia, 1975.
———. *Un ciclone chiamato Titti.* Bologna: Cappelli, 1969.
———. "Il coraggio delle donne." In *Penelope senza tela,* edited by Franco Moelia. Ravenna: Longo, 1984.
———. *Cultura e letteratura ligure del '900.* Genoa: Sabatelli, 1972.
———. "Fenoglio: L'epopea della terra di destino." *Rivista milanese di economia* 13 (Jan.–March 1985): 41–60.
———. *Freddo al cuore.* Milan: Mondadori, 1989.
———. *Fuori scena.* Milan: Garzanti, 1979.
———. *Golfo del paradiso.* Milan: Garzanti, 1987.
———. *Introduzione a Roland Barthes.* Florence: Sansoni, 1986.
———. *Le novelle di Simonetta.* Milan: Ceschina, 1960.
———. *L'opera in versi e in prosa.* Milan: Garzanti, 1985.
———. *Poesia italiana del Novecento.* Milan: Garzanti, 1980.
———. *Il polline.* Milan: Mondadori, 1966.
———. *Qualcosa nell'ana.* Milan: Garzanti, 1975.
———. *Russia oltre l'Urss.* Rome: Riuniti, 1989.
———. *Sbarbaro: Un modo spoglio di esistere.* Milan: Garzanti, 1981.
———. *Sbarbaro controcorrente.* Parma: Guanda, 1973.
———. *La spiaggia del lupo.* Milan: Garzanti, 1977.
———. *Sui racconti di Sbarbaro.* Parma: Guanda, 1973.
———. "Testimonianza di Gina Lagorio." *Proceedings of the Conference on "Piemonte e la letteratura nel '900,"* pp. 673–74. San Salvatore Monferrato: Assessorato alla cultura del comune di San Salvatore Monferrato, 1979.
———. *Tosca dei gatti.* Milan: Garzanti, 1983.
———, ed. *La malora e altri racconti,* by Beppe Fenoglio. Turin: Einaudi, 1968.
———, ed *Una questione privata,* by Beppe Fenoglio. Milan: Garzanti, 1982.
Livi, Grazia. Introduction to Anna Banti's *Corraggio delle donne.* Milan: La Tartaruga, 1983.
Mida, Massimo. "Le buone intenzioni non servono." *Paese Sera,* 19 September 1972, p. 3.
Mollia, Franco. "La condizione de Penelope." In *Penelope senza tela,* edited by Franco Mollia. Ravenna: Longo, 1984.

———. "Gina Lagorio senza padrini." *Il lettore di provincia* 31–32 (March 1978): 112–14.

Mungai, Antonio. "Una donna gatto ci spiega il mestiere di scrivere." *Corriere Medico,* 9 December 1983, p. 10.

Pavese, Cesare. *The Moon and the Bonfire.* Translated by Louise Sinclaire. Harmondsworth: Penguin, 1963.

Pietralunga, Mark. "Color viole delle Langhe." *Astrologo* 14–15 (Dec. 1987): 27–28.

Prisco, Michele. "Elena, attrice fuori scena." *Oggi,* 11 January 1980, p. 46.

GIANNA MANZINI

None of Gianna Manzini's work has been translated into English.

Cecchi, Emilio. "Gianna Manzini." *Storia della letteratura italiana: Il Novecento,* edited by Emilio Cecchi and Natalino Sapegno. 9 vols. Milan: Garzanti, 1969. 9: 683–87.

De Benedetti, Giacomo. "La Manzini, l'anima e la danza." In *Intermezzo,* edited by Giacomo De Benedetti, pp. 126–45. Milan: Mondadori, 1963.

Fava-Guzzetta, Lia. *Gianna Manzini.* Florence: La Nuova Italia, 1974.

Forti, Marco, ed. *Gianna Manzini: Tra letteratura e vita.* Milan: Mondadori, 1983. This is the proceedings of a conference on Gianna Manzini held at Pistoia-Florence in 1983: Piero Bigongiari, "Lo spostamento linguistico di Gianna Manzini"; Domenico De Robertis, "La voce della Manzini"; Geno Pampaloni, "Per Gianna Manzini"; Giorgio Petrocchi, "Il dialogo della Manzini"; Ferruccio Ulivi, "La confessione infinita di Gianna Manzini"; Clelia Martignoni, "Introduzione alla Mostra bio-bibliografica"; Margherita Ghilardi, "Io, l'argomento e la novella"; Francesca Sanvitale, "Tempo innamorato: L'esordio"; Giorgio Luti, "Struttura e tempo narrativo nei *Racconti* di Gianna Manzini"; Leone Piccioni, "L'arte della Manzini e *Lettera all'editore*"; Clelia Martignoni, "*Forte come un leone*"; Anna Nozzoli, "I ritratti della Manzini"; Lia Fava Guzzetta, "Gianna Manzini e la forma-romanzo"; Giacinto Spagnoletti, "L'ultima Manzini: da *Ritratto in piedi a Sulla soglia*"; Marco Forti, "Commenti conclusivi."

Luti, Giorgio. "La ronda romana e il ritorno all'ordine." *Letteratura italiana: Il Novecento.* 10 vols. Milan: Garganti, 1979. 5: 3891–97.

Manzini, Gianna. *Album di ritratti.* Milan: Mondadori, 1964.

———. *Allegro con disperazione.* Milan: Mondadori, 1965.

———. *Un'altra cosa.* Milan: Mondadori, 1961.

———. *Animali sacri e profani.* Rome: G. Casini, 1953.

———. *Arca di Noè.* Milan: Mondadori, 1960.

———. *Boscovivo.* Milan: Treves, 1932.

———. *Cara prigione.* Milan: Mondadori, 1958.

———. *Carta d'identità.* Rome: Nuove Edizioni Italiane, 1945.

———. *Il cielo addosso.* Milan: Mondadori, 1950.

———. "Domenico Theotokopoulos detto El Greco." Introduction to *L'opera completa del Greco.* Milan: Rizzoli, 1969.

———. *Un filo di brezza.* Milan: Panorama, 1936.

————. *Foglietti*. Milan: All'insegna del Pesce d'oro, 1954.

————. *Forte come un leone*. Rome: Documento, 1944.

————. *Ho visto il tuo cuore*. Milan: Mondadori, 1950.

————. *Incontro con falco*. Milan: Corbaccio, 1929.

————. *Lettera all'editore*. Florence: Sansoni, 1945; Milan: Mondadori, 1946.

————. *Ritratti e pretesti*. Milan: Il Saggiatore, 1960.

————. *Ritratto in piedi*. Milan: Mondadori, 1971.

————. *Rive remote*. Milan: Mondadori, 1940.

————. *La sparviera*. Milan: Mondadori, 1956.

————. *Sulla soglia*. Milan: Mondadori, 1973.

————. *Tempo innamorato*. 1928. Milan: Mondadori, 1973.

————. *Il valzer del diavolo*. Milan: Mondadori, 1947.

————. *Venti racconti*. Milan: Mondadori, 1941.

Nozzoli, Anna. "Gianna Manzini: Metafora e realtà del personaggio femminile." *Tabù e coscienza: La condizione femminile nella letteratura italiana del Novecento*, pp. 65–84. Florence: La Nuova Italia, 1978.

"Omaggio a Gianna Manzini" (Homage to Gianna Manzini) in the 6 May 1956 issue of *La Fiera Letteraria*. This issue was dedicated to Manzini and it contains articles by Anceschi, Bigongiari, Bo, Camerino, Cecchi, Debenedetti, De Robertis, Luzi, Pagliaro, Palazzeschi, Ulivi, Ungaretti, and others.

Panareo, Enzo. *Gianna Manzini*. Milan: Mursia, 1977.

Sobrero, Ornella. "Gianna Manzini." *Letteratura italiana: Il Novecento*. 10 vols. Milan: Garzanti, 1979. 6: 5469–95.

Ulivi, Ferruccio. "G. Manzini fra prosa e racconto." *Letteratura italiana*. See Sobrero. 6: 5495–5501.

————. "Narrativa emozionale di G. Manzini." *Letteratura italiana*. See Sobrero. 8: 7515–26.

————. "'La prosa d'arte' nel Novecento." *Letteratura italiana*. See Sobrero. 5: 3922–38.

DACIA MARAINI

All of Maraini's novels have been translated into English except *Il treno per Helsinski*.

Maraini, Dacia. *Crudeltà all'aria aperta* (poems). Milan: Feltrinelli, 1966.

————. *Donna in guerra*. Turin: Einaudi, 1975. Translated by Mara Benetti and Elisabeth Spottiswood as *Women at War*. Brighlingsea, Essex: Lighthouse Books, 1984, now published by Italia Press: New York, 1989.

————. *L'età del malessere*. Turin: Einaudi: 1963. Translated by Frances Frenaye as *The Age of Malaise*. New York: Grove Press, 1963.

————. *Memorie di una ladra*. Rome: Bompiani, 1974. Translated by Nina Rootes as *Memoirs of a Female Thief*. Levittown, N.Y.: Transatlantic Arts, 1974.

————. "Quale cultura per la donna." In *Donna, cultura e tradizione*, edited by Pia Bruzzichelli and Maria Luisa Algini, pp. 60–66. Milan: Mazzotta, 1976.

————. *Il treno per Helsinki*. Turin: Einaudi, 1984.

————. *La vacanza*. Milan: Bompiani, 1962. Translated by Stuart Hood as *The Holiday*. London: Weidenfeld, 1966.

232   Bibliography

Pallotta, Augustus. "Dacia Maraini: From Alienation to Feminism." *World Literature Today* 58, no. 3 (1984): 359–62.

ELSA MORANTE

All of Elsa Morante's major work has been translated into English except *Alibi, Il mondo salvato dai ragazzini, Il gioco segreto, Lo scialle andaluso,* and *Le bellissime avventure di Caterì dalla trecciolina.*

Caesar, Michael. "Elsa Morante." In *Writers and Society in Contemporary Italy,* edited by M. Caesar and P. Hainsworth, pp. 211–33. Warwickshire: Berg, 1986.
Capozzi, Rocco. "'Sheherazade' and Other 'Alibis': Elsa Morante's Victims of Love." *Rivista di Studi Italiani* 5–6 (forthcoming).
De Benedetti, Giacomo. "L'isola di Arturo." In *Saggi (1922–1966),* edited by Franco Contorbia, pp. 379–96. Milan: Mondadori, 1982.
De Stefani, Luigina. "Elsa Morante." *Belfagor* 26 (1971): 290–308.
Garboli, Cesare. *La stanza separata.* Milan: Mondadori, 1969.
Janmart, Anne. "Lettres féminines en Italie: Natalia Ginzburg et Elsa Morante." *Revue Générale* 8–9 (1982): 53–63.
Morante, Elsa. *Alibi* (poems). Milan: Longanesi, 1958.
———. *Aracoeli: Romanzo.* Turin: Einaudi, 1982. Translated by William Weaver as *Aracoeli.* New York: Random House, 1984.
———. *Le bellissime avventure di Caterì dalla trecciolina.* Turin: Einaudi, 1941.
———. *Il gioco segreto* (stories). Milan: Garzanti, 1941.
———. *L'isola di Arturo: Romanzo.* Turin: Einaudi, 1957. Translated by Isabelle Quigly as *Arturo's Island.* London: Collins, 1959.
———. *Menzogna e sortilegio.* Turin: Einaudi, 1948. Translated by Adrienne Foulke as *House of Liars.* New York: Harcourt Brace, 1951.
———. *Il mondo salvato dai ragazzini.* Turin: Einaudi, 1968.
———. "Nove domande sul romanzo." *Nuovi Argomenti* 38–39 (1959): 17–38.
———. "Otto domande sull'erotismo in letteratura." *Nuovi Argomenti* 51–51 (1961): 46–49.
———. "Pro o contro la bomba atomica." *L'Europa Letteraria* 4 (1965): 31–42.
———. "Qualcuno bussa alla porta." *I Diritti della Scuola,* from 25 September 1935 to August 1936.
———. *Lo scialle andaluso* (stories). Turin: Einaudi, 1963.
———. *La storia.* Turin: Einaudi, 1974. Translated by William Weaver as *History: A Novel.* New York: Knopf, 1977.
Morante, Marcello. *Maledetta benedetta.* Milan: Garzanti, 1986.
Pasolini, Pier Paolo. Review of *Il mondo salvato dai ragazzini* by Elsa Morante. *Paragone,* October 1968, pp. 120–26; April 1969, pp. 136–42.
Pupino, Angelo. *Struttura e stile della narrativa di Elsa Morante.* Ravenna: Longo, 1968.
Ragni, Eugenio. "Elsa Morante." In *Letteratura italiana contemporanea,* edited by Gaetano Mariani and Mario Petrucciani, pp. 767–81. Rome: Lucarini, 1980.
Ravanello, Donatella. *Scrittura e follia nei romanzi di Elsa Morante.* Venice: Marsilio, 1980.

Schifano, J. N. "Parla Elsa Morante: Barbara e divina." *L'Espresso,* 2 December 1984, pp. 122–33.

Sgorlon, Carlo. *Invito alla lettura di Elsa Morante.* Milan: Mursia, 1972.

Venturi, Gianni. *Elsa Morante.* Florence: La Nuova Italia, 1977.

LALLA ROMANO

None of Lalla Romano's work has been translated into English.

Antonielli, S. "Il mio progetto intellettuale: Intervista a L. Romano." *Fondazione Corrente,* 16 December 1980.

Catalucci, A. *Invito alla lettura di Lalla Romano.* Milan: Mursia, 1980.

Cucchi, M. "Le foto gialle della memoria." *L'Unità,* 16 October 1986.

Faggi, V. "Lalla Romano, una vita con sentimento." *Il Secolo XIX,* 23 July 1987.

Giuliani, A. "Ritratto dell'autrice da cucciola." *Reppublica* 2 (December 1986).

Lamarra, A. M. "Cerco un lessico per la memoria." *L'Unità,* 5 June 1980.

Martinelli, G. "Cerco una via verso la cima: intervista a Lalla Romano." *Il Gazzettino,* 3 December 1982.

Paganin, P. "Lalla Romano: sapore di storia." *L'Unità,* 24 June 1987.

Righetti, D. "Lalla Romano racconta i suoi 80 anni." *Il Giorno* 8 (November 1980).

Romano, Lalla. *L'autunno* (poems). Milan: La Meridiana, 1955.

———. *Diario di Grecia.* Turin: Einaudi, 1961.

———. *Fiore* (poems). Turin: Frassinelli, 1941.

———. *Giovane è il tempo* (poems). Turin: Einaudi, 1974.

———. *Una giovinezza inventata.* Turin: Einaudi, 1979.

———. *Inseparabile.* Turin: Einaudi, 1981.

———. *Lettura di un'immagine.* Turin: Einaudi, 1975.

———. *Maria.* Turin: Einaudi, 1953.

———. *Le metamorfosi.* Turin: Einaudi, 1951.

———. *Nei mari estremi.* Milan: Mondadori, 1987.

———. *L'ospite.* Turin: Einaudi, 1973.

———. *Le parole tra noi leggere.* Turin: Einaudi, 1969.

———. *La penombra che abbiamo attraversato.* Turin: Einaudi, 1964.

———. *Pralève.* Turin: Einaudi, 1978.

———. *Romanzo di figure.* Turin: Einaudi, 1986.

———. *Lo stregone.* Milan: Rizzoli, 1967.

———. *Un sogno nord.* Turin: Einaudi, 1989.

———. *Tetto murato.* Turin: Einaudi, 1957.

———. *La treccia di Tatiana.* Turin: Einaudi, 1986.

———. *L'uomo che parlava solo.* Turin: Einaudi, 1961.

———. *La villeggiante.* Turin: Einaudi, 1975.

———, trans. *Diario (1822–1863),* by Eugene Delacroix (*Journal [1822–1863]*). Turin: Chianatore, 1945.

———, trans. *L'educazione sentimentale,* by Gustave Flaubert (*L'éducation sentimentale*). Turin: Einaudi, 1984.

———, trans. Leon Morin, prete, by Béatrix Beck (*Léon Morin, prêtre*). Turin: Einaudi, 1954.

———, trans. *Tre racconti,* by Gustave Flaubert (*Trois contes*). Turin: Einaudi, 1944.
Sgorlon, C. "Enigma tra le pareti." *Il Giornale,* 4 October 1981.

FRANCESCA SANVITALE

None of Francesca Sanvitale's work has been translated into English.

Forti, Marco. "Francesca Sanvitale o la perenne crudeltà della favola." *Lunario Nuovo* 4, no. 18–19 (1982): 30–38.
Sanvitale, Francesca. *Il cuore borghese.* Florence: Vallechi, 1972.
———. "Invito alla lettura." Introduction to *Le idee di una donna e Confessioni letterarie/Neera.* Florence: Vallechi, 1977.
———. *Madre e figlia.* Turin: Einaudi, 1980.
———. *Mettendo a fuoco.* Rome: Gremese Editore, 1988.
———. "Ognuno di noi è pieno di storie da raccontare" (interview). *Uomini e Libri* 16, no. 36 (1980): 36.
———. *La realtà e un dono.* Milan: Mondadori, 1987.
———. *L'uomo del parco: Romanzo.* Milan: Mondadori, 1984.

WORKS BY OTHER WOMEN WRITERS IN ITALY

Adorno, Lucia Luisa. *L'ultima provincia.* 1962. Palermo: Sellerio, 1983.
Alberti, Barbara. *Buonanotte Angelo.* Milan: Mondadori, 1986.
Aleramo, Sibilla. *Una donna.* 1906. Milan: Feltrinelli, 1985. Translated by Rosalind Delmar as *A Woman.* Los Angeles: University of California Press, 1980.
Belonci, Maria. *Delitto di stato.* Milan: Mondadori, 1981.
———. *Lucrezia Borgia, la sua vita e i suoi tempi.* Milan: Mondadori, 1939. Translated by Bernard Wall and Barbara Wall as *The Life and Times of Lucrezia Borgia.* New York: Grosset and Dunlap, 1953.
———. *Marco Polo.* Milan: Rizzoli, 1984. Translated by Teresa Waugh as *The Travels of Marco Polo.* New York: Facts on File, 1984.
———. *Rinascimento privato: Romanzo.* Milan: Mondadori, 1985.
———. *Segreti dei Gonzaga: Ritratto di famiglia.* Milan: Mondadori, 1947. Translated by Stuart Hood as *A Prince of Mantua: The Life and Times of Vincenzo Gonzaga.* New York: Harcourt Brace, 1956.
———. *Tu vipera gentile.* Milan: Mondadori, 1972.
Belotti, Elena. *Il fiore dell'ibisco.* Milan: Rizzoli, 1985.
Bompiani, Ginevra. *Mondanità.* Milan: La Tartaruga, 1980.
———. *Le specie del sonno.* Milan: F. M. Ricci, 1975.
Castelli, Silvia. *Pitonessa.* Turin: Einaudi, 1978.
Cerati, Carla. *La condizione sentimentale.* Padua: Marsilia, 1977.
———. *Un matrimonio perfetto.* Padua: Marsilio, 1975.
Céspedes, Alba de. *La bambolona.* Milan: Mondadori, 1967.
———. *Chansons des filles de mai, poèmes.* Paris: Editions du Seuil, 1948.
———. *Dalla parte di lei, romanzo.* Milan: Mondadori, 1949.
———. *Fuga, racconti.* Milan: Mondadori, 1941.
———. *Invito a pranzo, racconti.* Milan: Mondadori, 1955.

————. *Nel buio della notte: Romanzo*. Milan: Mondadori, 1976.

————. *Nessuno torna indietro*. Milan: Mondadori, 1938.

————. *Opere*. Milan: Mondadori, 1963.

————. *Prima e dopo*. Milan: Mondadori, 1955.

————. *Quaderno proibito*. Milan: Mondadori, 1952. Translated by Isabel Quigly as *The Secret*. New York: Simon and Schuster, 1957.

————. *Sans autre lieu que la nuit*. Paris: Editions du Seuil, 1973.

Cravetta, Maria Letizia. *Tutti sanno*. Rome: Edizioni delle donne, 1976.

D'Amico, Maria Luisa Aguirre. *Come si può*. Palermo: Sellerio, 1986.

De Beaumont, Gaia. *Bella*. Milan: Frassinelli, 1985.

————. *Un venditore d'inchiostro*. Milan: Frassinelli, 1983.

DiMaggio, Marisa. *C'era una volta un re.* . . . Rome: Il Ventaglio, 1985.

Duranti, Francesca. *La casa sul lago della luna*. Milan: Rizzoli, 1987.

————. *Effetti personali*. Milan: Rizzoli, 1988.

————. *Lieto fine*. Milan: Rizzoli, 1987.

Ferri, Giuliana. *Un quarta di donna*. Padua: Marsilio, 1973.

Fiumi, Luisella. *Come donna zero*. Milan: Mondadori, 1974.

Grasso, Laura. *Madre amore donna*. Florence: Guaraldi, 1977.

Jarre, Marina. *Una donna diversa*. Milan: Garzanti, 1974.

————. *Un leggero accento straniero*. Turin: Einaudi, 1972.

————. *Monumento al parallelo*. Rome: Samonà e Savelli, 1968.

————. *Negli occhi di una ragazza*. Turin: Einaudi, 1971.

————. *La principessa della luna vecchia*. Turin: Einaudi, 1977.

————. *Viaggio a Ninive*. Turin: Einaudi, 1975.

Loy, Rosetta. *Le strade di polvere*. Turin: Einaudi, 1987.

Magrini, Gabriella. *Lunga giovinezza*. Milan: Mondadori, 1976.

Martelli, Daria. *Chi perde la sua vita*. Rome: Transmedia, 1981.

Masino, Paola. *Nascita e morte della massaia*. 1938. Milan: La Tartaruga, 1982.

Messina, Maria. *La casa del vincolo*. 1921. Palermo: Sellerio, 1982.

————. *Casa paterna*. 1921. Palermo: Sellerio, 1981.

Morazzoni, Marta. *La ragazza col turbante*. Milan: Longanesi, 1986.

Ortese, Anna Maria. *Iguana*. Florence: Vallecchi, 1965. Translated by Henry Martin as *The Iguana*. Kingston, N.Y.: McPherson and Co., 1987.

————. *Il mare non bagna Napoli*. 1953. Milan: Rizzoli, 1972.

————. *Poveri e semplici*. Milan: Rizzoli, 1974.

————. *Silenzio a Milano*. Milan: La Tartaruga, 1984.

————. *Il treno russo*. Catania: Pellicanolibri, 1982.

Rame, Franca. *Non parlarmi degli archi, parlami delle tue galere*. Dovera: F. R. Edizioni, 1984.

Ramondino, Fabrizia. *Althénopsis*. Turin: Einaudi, 1981. Translated by Michael Sullivan as *Alethénopsis*. Manchester: Carcanet, 1988.

————. *Storie di patio*. Turin: Einaudi, 1984.

Rasy, Elisabetta. *Le donne e la letteratura*. Rome: Editori Riuniti, 1984.

————. *La lingua della nutrice*. Rome: Edizioni delle donne, 1978.

————. *La prima estasi*. Milan: Mondadori, 1985.

Rossi, Emma. *Pensione Paradiso (già Porospenia)*. Ancona: Il Lavoro Editoriale, 1984.

Rossi, Rosa. *Le parole delle donne*. Rome: Riuniti, 1978.

———. *L'ultimo capitolo*. Rome: Lucarini, 1984.

Saraceno, Chiara. *Dalla parte della donna*. Bari: DeDonato, 1971.

Schiavo, Maria. *Marcellum: Storia violentata e romanzata di donne e di mercato*. Milan: a Tartaruga, 1979.

Stefani, Livia de. *Gli affatturati*. Milan: Mondadori, 1955.

———. *Passione di Rosa*. Milan: Mondadori, 1958. Translated by Carla Barford and Sheila Hodges as *Rosa*. London: Eyre and Spottiswoode, 1963.

———. *La signora Cariddi*. Milan: Rizzoli, 1971.

———. *La vigna di uve nere*. Milan: Mondadori, 1953.

Viganò, Renata. *L'Agnese va a morire*. Turin: Einaudi, 1972.

———. *Matrimonio in brigata*. Milan: Vangelista, 1976.

Volpi, Marisa. *Il maestro della betulla*. Florence: Valecchi, 1986.

Wertmuller, Lina. *La testa d'Alvise*. Translated as *The Head of Alvise*. New York: Morrow, 1982.

Notes on Contributors

SANTO L. ARICÒ is associate professor of French and Italian at the University of Mississippi. His publications include articles on Oriana Fallaci, Juliette Adam, Jean-Jacques Rousseau, and modern language pedagogy. He is completing a book on Rousseau's art of persuasion in *La Nouvelle Héloise*.

FIORA A. BASSANESE is associate professor at the University of Massachusetts, Boston, and is chair of the Italian department. She has done research on women writers of the Italian Renaissance, modern prose fiction in Italy, and the literature of Trieste. She is the author of *Gaspara Stampa* (1982).

GIOVANNA BELLESIA received her Ph.D. from the University of North Carolina at Chapel Hill. She currently teaches Italian at Smith College. Her research interests center on the translations of Elio Vittorini, Cesare Pavese, and Eugenio Montale.

PAOLA BLELLOCH is assistant professor of French and Italian at Trenton State College. Her publications focus on French and Italian women writers. She is the author of *Quel mondo dei guanti e delle stoffe. . . . Profili di scrittrici italiane del '900* (1987).

FLAVIA BRIZIO is assistant professor of Italian at the University of Tennessee in Knoxville. She is presently completing a study on the stylistic components of Lalla Romano's novels.

ROCCO CAPOZZI is professor of Italian at the University of Toronto. He has published articles on Carlo Bernari, Paolo Volponi, Giuliano Gramigna, Umberto Eco, Elsa Morante, and Italo Calvino. He is also the author of *Carlo Bernari tra fantasia e realta* (1984).

DEBORAH HELLER received her Ph.D. from Harvard University. She is associate professor of humanities at York University. She is the author of a variety of articles that deal mainly with George Eliot, Ibsen, and Wordsworth.

CAROL M. LAZZARO-WEIS is assistant professor of French and Italian at Southern University in Baton Rouge. She recently held a research grant from the Council of Southern Universities to study contemporary Italian women writers and is now preparing a book on this subject. She has also published articles on the Abbé Prévost and Leonardo Sciascia.

CORINNA DEL GRECO LOBNER teaches comparative literature and Italian at the University of Tulsa. She has published in such journals as the *James Joyce Quarterly, Italica, Irish University Review, Rivista di Studi Italiani,* and *Parola.* She is the author of *James Joyce's Italian Connection: The Poetics of the Word* (1989).

GIOVANNA MICELI-JEFFRIES is assistant professor of Italian at the University of Wisconsin and has written articles on Elio Vittorini, Ungaretti, Italo Svevo, and Sibilla Aleramo. She is the author of *Lo scrittore, il lavoro e la letteratura: La rappresentazione del lavoro nella narrativa di Italo Svevo* (1988).

MARK F. PIETRALUNGA teaches Italian at Florida State University. His book *Beppe Fenoglio and English Literature: A Study of the Writer as Translator* (1986) analyzes the relationship between the author's translations and creative writings.

PAOLA MALPEZZI PRICE is assistant professor of French and Italian at Colorado State University. Her current research interests are poetry by women of the Renaissance, contemporary literature, and feminist criticism.

ANTHONY J. TAMBURRI teaches Italian at Purdue University. He has written articles on Aldo Palazzeschi, Italo Calvino, and Guido Gozzano. He is also author of the monograph *Of Saltimbanchi and Incendiari: Aldo Palazzeschi and Avant-Gardism in Italy* (1988) and coeditor of the anthology *From the Margin to the Center: Writings in Italian Americana* (1988).